Reading, Writing, and Digitizing

Reading, Writing, and Digitizing: Understanding Literacy in the Electronic Age

By

Alice S. Horning

CAMBRIDGE SCHOLARS PUBLISHING

Reading, Writing, Digitizing:
Understanding Literacy in the Electronic Age,
by Alice S. Horning

This book first published 2012

Cambridge Scholars Publishing

12 Back Chapman Street, Newcastle upon Tyne, NE6 2XX, UK

British Library Cataloguing in Publication Data
A catalogue record for this book is available from the British Library

ISBN (10): 1-4438-4038-6, ISBN (13): 978-1-4438-4038-5

To Deb and Amy: I've watched you go from *Hop on Pop* and *Frog and Toad*, to *Harry Potter*, to book clubs of your own, to recommending and buying books for me. From summer book bets to graduate school, your development from novice to expert readers and writers has been a source of intense personal as well as professional pleasure and parental pride.

TABLE OF CONTENTS

Acknowledgments

A number of people have provided a variety of different kinds of help with this book over the course of a number of years. My chief debts are two: first, Paul Munsell read the original version of this book in many drafts, providing careful commentary and pushing me to think of many "maybes" in my efforts to define and describe what is happening to human literacy. Second, Lynn Troyka has read the semi-final version of the book, prodding me to expand my thinking, to get out from behind my sources, to abandon my preference for convoluted sentences and to make the book as lively as our conversations about it have been. I am deeply grateful to both for their scholarship, their wisdom, their expert teaching and guidance. My adventures in reading began when my sister Linda, long fed up with my continuous pestering to be read to, taught me to read around age four. Neither of us remembers how she did it, but the *Alice and Jerry* books, perhaps because they had my name, had something to do with it. Subsequently, she bought me my very own copy of my lifelong favorite book, *Johnny Tremain*, and has always been a role model of an expert meta-reader and writer. In addition, a number of colleagues have read parts of the book and shared their expertise and insights: Erik Drake, Catherine Haar, Cynthia Haller, Claire Harrison, Patricia Hironymous, Clark Iverson, Kasia Kietlinska, and Robert Lamphear. Finally, I am grateful to Oakland University for providing a sabbatical leave in the winter of 2009, during which I was able to complete some of the research reported here and develop the ideas discussed in this book. Naturally, errors, infelicities, and omissions are mine alone. Thanks to everyone who helped along the way.

INTRODUCTION AND OVERVIEW

In the past few years, I've been invited to speak or lead workshops at several colleges and universities around the country, and I also present fairly often at conferences for faculty in higher education. I often begin my talks by reporting a common experience. I report that whenever I ask faculty in general conversation about the greatest single problem they face in the classroom today, in less than five minutes, the topic of reading comes up. Faculty members typically complain about what I have come to think of as the "don't, won't, can't" problem with students' reading. They report that students don't read assigned material, regardless of consequences and that students won't read it unless faculty use some inducement that will have a major impact on students' grades in the course; moreover, the faculty often observe that students *can't* read in the ways faculty expect, even if a carrot or stick is attached to the reading. When I report this experience, members of my audiences almost always start nodding in agreement.

The "don't, won't, can't" problem is pervasive and ubiquitous, despite the commonplace observation that students are doing more reading and writing now because of the Web and gizmos that allow widespread access to and use of it. Nevertheless, surveys of the students themselves and of employers who hire college graduates to work in a range of fields reflect the weak literacy skills students have; these studies will be discussed in more detail later in the book. It seems clear, in light of this set of reflections, that those working on literacy skill development at all levels need to understand the fundamental psycholinguistics of literacy and the best strategies for helping students move from novice toward expert status as readers and writers. I am confident that teachers in every discipline in higher education, as well as those working in community-based settings such as libraries, adult basic education, and English as a second language programs can benefit from understanding literacy in order to help their students/patrons/clients become expert meta-readers and writers. This phrase, meta-readers and writers, is a neologism I have created to reflect my argument that literacy experts understand and produce meaning in texts by working before, after, around and within them in specific ways. I am also confident that all students can and must become more effective meta-readers and writers if they are to succeed in personal, educational, and professional venues and also as members of a democratic society.

Reading, Writing and Digitizing offers a new theoretical proposal concerning expert and novice readers and writers based on the psycholinguistics of literacy. It is intended for five audiences of teachers and others who work with students or clients who want or need to develop expert literacy. A first audience is literacy scholars. The book brings together research from a variety of disciplines not usually juxtaposed in support of the theory, along with case study research providing a potential new direction for further studies. Composition specialists who administer writing programs (members of the Council of Writing Program Administrators (WPA) in the United States and others doing WPA work) comprise a second audience; in my experience, these professionals may lack substantial background in the psycholinguistics of literacy. Third, fellows of the National Writing Project at its various sites around the US may find this volume a helpful introduction to the psycholinguistics of reading and writing, and to the nature of novice versus expert literacy. The fourth group is comprised of those in composition pedagogy courses, preparing to teach writing at the college level, and/or those integrating writing into courses in a variety of disciplines (usually known as Writing Across the Curriculum or Writing in the Disciplines). Finally, anyone who works to support the development of stronger literacy skills (parents, librarians, community education instructors) can also benefit from the discussion. All of these groups of readers may find the additional background in psycholinguistics useful to enhance their understanding of the nature and importance of expert literacy.

This book has five specific goals. First, it presents a theory of meta-reading and writing that describes what literacy experts are able to do in their interactions with written text. They do what the word "meta" describes: go before and after, into and around, beyond and beside written text to understand and create meaning. Second, the case studies that begin the book reveal the differences between literacy novices and experts in terms of their awarenesses about texts and their skills; these will become more clear as the discussion unfolds. As a third goal, the book provides an analysis of the mental abilities people have and the features that texts contain that make literacy possible. A fourth goal is to examine how experts understand and produce texts in both traditional and digital venues in order to argue that, despite the claims of those who work with new media, reading and writing are the same psycholinguistic processes on paper or screens. Finally, the book ends with a set of focused strategies for instruction that will be useful to any reader working with people engaged in literacy development. Readers of this book will be better equipped to support the literacy development of others through their enhanced understanding of the psycholinguistics of reading and writing. They will be able to help novices move toward expertise through their understanding of the differences between literacy novices and experts.

This book is needed now more than ever, even though it appears that students and others are doing more reading and writing now because of the Internet where a deluge of information grows by the day. However, the vast majority of these students are literacy novices, lacking key skills urgently needed to function well in our increasingly complex and competitive contemporary society. Recent studies such as *To Read or Not to Read*, released in 2007 by the National Endowment for the Arts in the United States (NEA), suggest that there have been significant declines in the reading ability of all Americans, but especially teens and young adults, a problem that has "serious civic, social, cultural, and economic implications" (U.S. National Endowment for the Arts, 2007, p. 7).

Other studies in the United States by the American College Testing organization (2006), and by the federal government, support the NEA findings (U.S. Department of Education, 2006; 2007), as do findings of such international studies as the International Adult Literacy Survey (Murray, 1998) and the Adult Literacy and Life Skills survey (*Learning*, 2005). A study of critical thinking, reading and writing, published in 2011, suggests that students in colleges and universities in the United States may not improve these skills in their undergraduate work (Arum & Roksa, 2011). All of these studies have limitations of various kinds in methodology, in the lengths and types of texts, in the reliance on self-report data or timed tests. Still, teachers of literacy K-12, particularly in high schools, as well as college teachers of reading and writing are all too familiar with this problem. This book provides those working with literacy in schools, colleges, universities, libraries and community settings with a detailed framework for understanding expert contemporary literacy from a psycholinguistic perspective, and offers strategies for the development of the essential skills needed in our electronic age.

What makes the widespread decline in literacy according to these various tests and other measures all the more surprising and disappointing is that being a good reader is truly self-rewarding and provides so many wonderful experiences. Without conscious effort for the most part, good readers can handle an amazing array of different kinds of materials, reading at blinding speeds of several hundred words a minute. Achieving literacy is really a wonder: for most people its acquisition is simple and straightforward; once learned, it is never forgotten. Our literate capacity can be transferred to other languages, and even variations in writing systems slow down reading only a little. The acquisition of writing takes a bit more effort, but for mature writers, similar claims about speed and transfer can be made. Word processing by computer and text messaging by any accomplished "texter" can be done at speeds of a hundred words a minute or more. In some ways, literacy seems like a trick, which is defined by the dictionary as a sleight of hand or eye, using quick, clever movements that entertain us. Like magic, it seems that the more carefully we try to look, the more the exact nature of the trick eludes us.

But literacy is not magic. It can be understood, enhanced and made more universal than it presently is through an examination and understanding of the awarenesses and skills of expert readers and writers. And such an understanding is more crucial now than ever before, not only because there is clear evidence that literacy, in general, is in decline, but also because literacy is now the province of perhaps the most important technological development of our age: the Web. Literacy is evolving through its use on the Web as well as through social media of various kinds. Understanding this evolution, and what it means for traditional reading and writing, is crucial because of the ever-widening use of the Web. Moreover, for individuals to function well in a democratic society, to be able to work and play successfully, and to be able to access, use, and contribute to the cornucopia of information on the Web efficiently and effectively, superior literacy skills are simply essential.

The following brief overview shows that this book has several parts; readers may find this condensed review or the more detailed one following of use in choosing relevant sections to read. The first part of the book gives some basic background and the data set that provides the origins of the theory of expert meta-reading and writing, along with some discussion of the mental abilities and language features that form the base for literacy. Then the theory itself is presented in two chapters dealing with meta-readers' and writers' awarenesses and skills. Implications of the theory for digital reading and writing appear toward the end of the book, followed by a chapter that offers practical approaches to teaching novices as they move toward expert meta-reading and writing.

After this Introduction, then, the first section of the book begins with a chapter which presents definitions of and distinctions among key terms relevant to literacy. The second chapter offers the case studies of expert and novice readers, working with extended passages of non-fiction prose in both print and electronic forms; these case studies provide a base for the proposed theory and are where the theory got its start. I began collecting the case studies before I had the theory. The data in the cases led me to apply psycholinguistic principles and distinctive feature theory to construct my view of meta-reading and writing. Chapters 3 and 4 examine the mental capacities and distinctive features essential to expert literacy in detail. With this background in hand, the second section consists of Chapters 5 and 6, which provide the theory in two parts. Chapter 5 presents the proposal that expert readers and writers have specific awarenesses concerning written language. This chapter reviews schema theory and discusses the meaning of expertise as it has been studied in terms of literacy as well as in other fields. Chapter 6 provides the second part of the theory, an extended discussion of the skills expert readers and writers have when working with texts. These skills are essential to critical literacy in the electronic age and studies show that while novice readers can comprehend main ideas, they may lack some or all of these skills. A third portion, consisting of Chapters 7 and 8, takes up reading and writing respectively in both traditional print as well as electronic environments. Finally, Chapter 9 summarizes the theory of meta-reading and writing and provides three kinds of recommendations: for teachers themselves, for teaching and learning in all kinds of educational settings, and for classrooms in higher education specifically, where strategies for intensive and extensive work on reading and writing can help novices develop expert critical literacy skills as they become meta-readers and writers.

A More Detailed Look Ahead

Chapter 1 presents some key definitions and distinctions, beginning with the question of what, exactly, it means to be literate. This chapter takes up the matter of defining literacy and the many terms that go with it in current usage, such as critical literacy, digital literacy, Web literacy, functional literacy, and others. Personal literacy narratives such as those collected by Deborah Brandt (2001) provide some insights, especially across generations and into the electronic age, as does work with English language learners in Generation 1.5. The nature of academic expectations for literacy and how educators in school and community settings help students meet those expectations provide an essential perspective on contemporary literacy. The chapter's claims are supported with data from studies in the United States and from studies by the Organisation for Economic Cooperation and Development, UNESCO and other sources on literacy around the world, in school settings and elsewhere.

Chapter 2, Case Studies of Experts and Novices, presents case studies of experts and novices to demonstrate through extended discussion how the meta-reader and writer theory plays out when people work with texts.

The chapter includes studies of five adult expert readers, reading passages of non-fiction prose and writing brief summaries of them. The data also includes self-report background information on these readers' literacy autobiographies and their current reading practices. The expert readers all took the Reading portion of the ACT exam, to provide a baselinc mcasure comparable to that of the novices. The eight novice readers are all students with varying levels of reading skill and an array of backgrounds who completed the same tasks as the experts. While some of the novices volunteered for the study through their developmental reading classes at the college level, others are Honors College students. One of the novices is not a native speaker of English, so his case offers a look at the challenges involved in developing expertise in reading and writing in a language with a different writing system.

The mental capacities of expert readers are discussed in Chapter 3, which explores and illustrates the human thinking abilities that make expert literacy possible. The data from the case studies made me realize that my readers and writers were tapping these abilities in the tasks I set. There are seven major mental abilities essential to literacy: a group of five general cognitive abilities, including identification or recognition, categorization, discrimination, prediction, and limited short-term memory, and two major linguistic abilities, the use of syntax, and the use of psycholinguistic redundancy. This chapter describes these mental capacities and synthesizes the research studies that have explored the nature of cognitive and linguistic processing. The goal is to help readers of the book understand the psychological and linguistic abilities people bring to bear when reading and writing. Exercises and other hands-on kinds of experiences illustrate these mechanisms, modeled after those used by Kenneth Goodman (1996) and Stephen Kucer (2005) in books on reading and literacy. These experiences here and in the following chapter provide the psycholinguistic evidence for meta-readers' and writers' awarenesses as they work with texts.

Chapter 4, on the distinctive features used by experts, explains the aspects of written language used by experts. The theory of meta-readers and writers proposes that experts apply their mental capacities as described in Chapter 3 to distinctive features of language per se. The features fall into four categories: first, rudimentary visual features necessary to reading the alphabet or other writing system and the marks of punctuation that are involved in visual processing; second, the basic categories of words and their meanings; third, the intermediate analysis of the types of sentences and texts as well as different kinds of discourse arrays, such as charts, tables, graphs and so on; and finally, the most complex category where the conventional genres, rhetorical modes and forms of argumentation and schemata mark the peak of expert literacy. The basic mental abilities all play a role in experts' abilities with each category. Here again, paper and Internet exercises and examples show how the features are used by expert readers and writers.

At this point, in Chapter 5, readers of the book will have all of the basic background that led me to construct the theory of meta-reading and writing: key terms, case studies with novices and experts, an understanding of the mental abilities that make literacy possible, and the distinctive features of language that readers and writers use in literate activities. Using this background, this chapter and the next propose the theory in detail: experts are meta-readers and writers. This special term captures the idea that experts have an awareness of text structure, context and language as they interact with texts. These three different kinds of awareness overlap a bit; these categories as described sound more separate than they are in actual practice.

Meta-reading awareness includes, first of all, meta-textual awareness of the organization and structure of the text. This meta-textual awareness allows readers to see the organizational structure of the text or how the ideas are presented, developed and exemplified. Meta-readers also have a meta-contextual awareness of where the text comes from and how it fits into the larger scheme of things—topic, research, author, disciplinary issues, and related matters. These experts are able to see the text as part of an on-going conversation about key issues or ideas in a discipline, drawing on prior knowledge of the topic, the author's likely purpose and whatever else may bear on the text. Third, expert readers have a meta-linguistic awareness of language of the text. They have sufficient high level vocabulary to understand complex texts and get meaning. In particular, experts understand the implications of some words. Meta-linguistic awareness goes beyond individual words, though, to include various aspects of the language of the text, such as the sentence structures or patterns (parallel structure, for example), tone, register and other features of the language per se. Understanding these awarenesses of expert readers will help literacy teachers see the needs of novice readers and writers more clearly.

Beyond meta-reading awareness, experts have an array of essential skills that make it possible for them to read non-fiction prose efficiently and effectively. These skills, presented in Chapter 6, include analysis, synthesis, evaluation and application. In each area, the skills contribute to meta-readers' and writers' expertise with texts. Those working with novices can be more effective if they understand not only the awarenesses described in Chapter 5, but also the specific skills that experts use, explored in detail in this chapter. These skills are sketched here briefly as they are essential features of experts' meta-reading and writing.

Skills in analysis: To analyze means to be able to take something apart and see how it works. Expert meta-readers are able to analyze texts in part because they can read quickly, since one of the key findings of reading research is that readers who read too slowly lose track of the developing ideas of the text. They also read flexibly, drawing on their awarenesses of structure, context, and language. Experts often have had long experience with textbooks and other genres of non-fiction prose, and specific skills for dealing with the array of genres they read regularly.

Skills in synthesis: Experts can combine, compare, contrast or see the relationship of the text they are reading to other texts or sources of information to synthesize ideas and if needed, write about what they have learned or found in those texts. Expert readers know how to draw inferences and conclusions from a text. The writer's point may or may not be explicitly stated, but it is there to be drawn out by an expert reader. This skill relates to the "beyond" or "after" aspect of what makes experts *meta*-readers and writers. Expert readers can see the key points of more than one text, and mark those for their own purposes in writing or elsewhere, omitting details, examples, comparisons and other developmental techniques.

Skills in evaluation: Expert readers and writers build on these basic skills in order to conduct critical evaluations and apply what they glean from their reading. Their additional skills in evaluation entail reading for authority, currency, relevancy, accuracy, objectivity or bias, and appropriateness (Association for College and Research Libraries, 2008).

Skills in application: Finally, expert readers and writers have skills in application—knowing where and how to use information from reading in writing, speaking or just understanding. They can take whole ideas or arguments or lines of reasoning and use them in their own lives or work. They might use what they have read to answer a question or solve a problem, or they might integrate their reading of the work of others into their own writing. In short, meta-readers and writers can not only get ideas from extended non-fiction prose texts, synthesize different readings on the same issue or topic, and evaluate the material, but also these experts can make use of whatever they have read for their own purposes. The chapter includes a detailed illustration from the work of a student in one of my courses, on her way to developing expertise in reading and writing. The example shows the student's growth in both awarenesses and skills; while she is hardly an expert, her progress across two assignments shows how both intensive and extensive work on reading can help novices on their way to expertise.

Chapter 7 considers reading in traditional and electronic environments. Expert literacy in the digital age builds on expert literacy as we have known it from centuries past, but goes beyond it in many ways, some of which are already clear. It will continue to draw on the mental capacities of experts, both cognitive and linguistic, along with the distinctive features of written language that make the feat of literacy possible at all. The case studies show us that experts use their mental capacities and distinctive features in combination with their awarenesses and skills as meta-readers and writers.

Meta-reading and writing are increasingly important in dealing with the Internet. There, the additional mental capacities of bricolage and juxtaposition are essential. Bricolage is a term drawn from art, referring to an ability to put together parts (Burbules, 1998, p. 107). Burbules defines bricolage as "*assembling* texts from pieces that can be represented in multiple relations to one another" (p. 107). The second mechanism needed to deal with the Internet in terms of both production and perception, is juxtaposition, the placing of items close to one another for comparison or contrast (Burbules, 1998, p. 107). In foregrounding the visual, a Web page asks readers to see elements and images as they are arrayed, next to each other for various specific purposes. Along with these mental capacities useful in a digital environment, the Web requires the additional distinctive features of image, sound, movement, and link which challenge human literate capacity, as they require hyperreading. In digital reading and writing, readers and writers must see, notice, and attend to how the various pieces of a Web page are related to each other by their position on the screen. Understanding these additional mental capacities and distinctive features that support experts' literacy reveals these abilities in an electronic context. Careful analysis of reading in the digital environment shows that while it makes use of bricolage and juxtaposition and while it works on the features of image, sound, movement and links, it is not fundamentally different than reading on paper. All the awarenesses and skills expert meta-readers use on paper are equally essential to reading in a digital environment. The chapter is illustrated with links to materials on the Internet to support the argument.

Chapter 8 takes up writing in traditional and electronic environments. Experts' reading abilities play a role in their writing, whether on paper or screen, because their reading creates for them what second language scholar Stephen Krashen (1983) calls the "din" of language. A more rigorous description of this process leads cognitive psychologists to call the same phenomenon "implicit learning" (Reber, 1967), as discussed in Chapter 5. Experts know what written language sounds like and looks like; for many novices, written language and especially academic writing is like a foreign language (see my early book *Teaching writing as a second language* (1987) for a full discussion of this claim). Meta-reading equips writers to prepare effective texts in any environment, traditional, digital, social media, large screen or small. This chapter brings together the discussion of meta-reading and writing.

The distinctive features of Web pages, including links, are examined in detail, with some examples. The goal of the illustrations is twofold. First, close examination of pages and links demonstrate the fundamental mental abilities described through this book, as well as experts' awarenesses and their skills. Careful analysis shows that the psycholinguistic processes involved in writing are the same on both pages and screens. Here, the process of Web page creation is explored as a new manifestation of expert literacy. A case study examines writing for the Web in the creation of a simple website.

The final chapter addresses the issue of what teachers might do with novices on Monday morning, presenting a sampling of strategies for helping novices become meta-readers and writers. The analysis of expert readers and writers discussed in the book is summarized in the opening part of this chapter. Knowing how meta-readers and writers work with texts, those who work with novices in any setting can benefit from the basic understanding of the psycholinguistics of reading and writing presented here. General approaches are offered for all kinds of teaching and learning situations, such as community education programs. However, Monday morning strategies for helping novice readers and writers in post-secondary classes across the curriculum are also needed. This chapter presents strategies for teaching intensive reading that can work with any kind of material, whether the texts being read are for courses across the curriculum or for personal interest or other reasons, and whether these texts appear on paper or on a screen.

Novice readers and writers can learn to go beyond reading the text for main ideas, to develop and apply the awarenesses and skills of experts for deeper analysis, synthesis, evaluation and application. An array of approaches to helping readers and writers build expert skills is provided. This final chapter also explores the use of extensive reading as a means of helping novice readers and writers build expertise. The work involves having novices read extended non-fiction prose texts in a particular subject area, to develop meta-textual, meta-contextual and meta-linguistic awareness. Extensive reading of pages and screens can help novices develop expert writing abilities because it helps create Krashen's "din" (1983) in their heads when they write. Expert meta-readers and writers have the ability to comprehend and create written language and make use of texts for a variety of purposes. This final chapter reviews the discussion of the nature of expertise in literacy and the awarenesses and skills on which it is based. This chapter suggests ways that teachers and learners can move from novice toward expert literacy in a variety of venues by building the awarenesses and skills of meta-reading and writing.

CHAPTER ONE

DEFINITIONS AND DISTINCTIONS

Introduction

Definitions of literacy are essential to opening the discussion but also a real challenge. Readers of this book who guide literacy learners through direct teaching, mentoring or other kinds of support want students to be successful; achieving that goal is difficult without an explicit definition. Some scholars argue that the definition of literacy has become complicated, less because of its primary meaning related to reading and writing, and more because of its use as a term to describe skill or expertise in any subject area or discipline such as "computer literacy" or "music literacy." Indeed, Open University literacy scholar David Vincent has suggested we use the phrase "literacy literacy" to capture the need for a tighter focus on reading and writing (2003). So a clear definition provides an essential basis for the rest of the discussion.

But defining literacy is not so easy. I've been studying literacy, one way or another, for about thirty years and really thought I knew something about it. I am a reasonably literate person: I read many different kinds of materials, have good comprehension and a large vocabulary, seldom have difficulty understanding a writer's point, can easily compare and contrast two articles on the same topic and have no difficulty assessing texts I read for accuracy, currency, authority and so forth. These skills are all parts of what many scholars define as critical literacy. Of course, I have all these skills in my native language. In the languages with which I have some familiarity, French, German and Hebrew, my literacy skills are much weaker. Although I can call words off the printed page accurately in all three languages, I would hardly describe myself as literate in any of them.

A few years ago, I had contact with Hebrew while traveling in Israel revealing just how complex and challenging literacy is, even at a minimal level like being able to read a menu. I know letter-sound relationships in Hebrew, have a limited vocabulary and marginal grammar knowledge. Confronted with signs, I'm stuck. For example, I learned the word for rest room (kind of essential), but then, on one occasion followed that sign to stand in front of two doors labeled with Hebrew words but lacking the international pictures for men and women. I could sound them out, but had no idea what the words meant. Sounding out the words, a slow and difficult, albeit possible process, still left me stuck for want of vocabulary. I was flummoxed by the language. Even reading a fast food menu was beyond me. It's a good thing the McDonald's menu had pictures, that the teenager behind the counter had a little English, and that the restaurant accepted credit cards. Otherwise, I would have been very hungry.

It would be fair to say I am a literacy novice in Hebrew, given these experiences. Reading a daily newspaper is completely out of reach; books are not remotely possible. And yet, I do know something and can follow a text being read out loud if it is printed in standard block print with the vowel markings included. It is hard to describe the sense of isolation and disorientation that results from this situation. However, my experiences with Hebrew have provided me with a different kind of understanding what it means to be literate. Even though I can call words off the printed page, and follow a text read aloud, the lack of real reading ability left me feeling cut off from the world around me. If I had to use Hebrew, I would not be successful in college, could not apply for a job, and it would be impossible for me to make an informed decision in an election. I want to argue that my limited experience with Hebrew shares some features with the experience of those who lack strong literacy skills in their native language.

While my situation with Hebrew is in only some ways like the situation of people who are speakers of a language they cannot read, it is in at least one way like the problem I want to address in this chapter. My status as someone who recognizes the letters and can render a text aloud in Hebrew is somewhat like that of American college students who can "read" English. Like them, though, I cannot get meaning from print at the level expected in college-level classes. That is, like me with Hebrew, American college students lack the kind of critical literacy ability described above. These students are upset if they are placed in a developmental reading course in college because they *can* read, if reading is defined as calling words off the page. But in fact, for the purposes of college work in reading and writing, with textbooks, Web resources, scholarly journals and other kinds of materials, they and many other college students are literacy novices. That is, I suggest, they lack the critical literacy skills needed for success in college and for their personal and professional lives beyond higher education.

I want to begin with a proposed definition of this academic critical literacy, and then examine an array of sources to see whether the basis for this definition is sound, as it provides the foundation for the rest of the discussion. So, here is the starting point:

> Academic critical literacy is best defined as the psycholinguistic processes of getting meaning from or putting meaning into print and/or sound, images, and movement, on a page or screen, used for the purposes of analysis, synthesis, evaluation and application; these processes develop through formal schooling and beyond it, at home and at work, in childhood and across the lifespan and are essential to human functioning in a democratic society.

The definition is meant to capture several key points. First, it implies the notion that literacy is not a single thing, but a set of processes and that people do not have it or lack it, but may develop it over the lifespan through schooling and outside of school. The definition is also meant to capture the fact that the nature of literacy is in a state of change as digital environments continue to grow and develop. However, as the rest of the book makes clear, the fundamental processes of reading and writing are the same in print as they are on a screen. This version of the definition of critical literacy is meant as a starting point for discussion.

The difficulty with this definition and all that will be discussed here is summarized well in the 2002 *Literacy in America* encyclopedia (Kazemek & Rigg, 2002, p. 313). These scholars point out that the US is becoming an increasingly "multilingual society and a multi-literate society" (p. 313). The multilingualism arises from immigration and population patterns that are bringing increasing numbers of speakers of other languages into the country; these people may or may not be literate in their native languages and may or may not learn English. The multi-literacy arises from the growth of "critical multiliteracies that involve the ability to use a wide range of print and nonprint texts in an ever-expanding and increasingly sophisticated world of information, entertainment and advertisement" (p. 313). Any definition of literacy is going to have to address these matters.

I'm interested in the meaning of the word literacy applied to college students for a number of reasons. First, among my colleagues who are college writing teachers, I often hear the claim that students are "illiterate," with varied meanings. In my own experience, I often see among the under-prepared students I work with significant struggles with written text. The inability to work with written text, both understanding and producing it, is a real problem. Moreover, a number of the definitions are quite unsatisfactory since they describe fairly rudimentary abilities with written text like being able to write one's name. Finally, literacy is not precisely all-or-nothing phenomenon that pertains only to students, but is a continuum of abilities that requires thorough and careful definition. And as a corollary point, these issues are also relevant for learners of English who speak other languages. Second language scholar Ilona Leki has noted that

> [i]n view of the place of English in the world today and the role it sometimes plays in both empowering and dramatically constraining the lives and futures of people from different L1 backgrounds, I feel an interrogation of the characteristics of L1 English literacy and its place among the other literacies in the world is a task that L1 English literates are morally and ethically obliged to undertake. (2004, p. 127)

My goal in this chapter and in the book as a whole is to take up Leki's challenge.

In order to do so, a detailed review of the proposed definitions of and approaches to literacy, as well as other related terms that have been suggested is essential. What is needed now is a full definition of these terms in the current print and electronic context of adult American society in school and out of school, and also in the context of adult learners of English as a second language. My proposed explicit definition of literacy and related terms like multi-literacy not only provide the basis for the theoretical proposal offered in this book, but also create the basis for practical recommendations for teaching and learning.

Definitions from the Dictionary: A Starting Point

So, ordinarily, if you want a definition, the first place to look is in the dictionary, either an unabridged, or to really pursue words back to their sources in English, the *Oxford English Dictionary*. After I had been working on this project for a while, I turned first to the unabridged dictionary and what I found there surprised me. I looked at both literacy and illiteracy and saw that the writers of my dictionary, the *Random House Unabridged* (Stein, 1966) did a nice job of tying literacy and illiteracy together in a clear and consistent way. Here are the definitions:

> Literacy: 1. the quality or state of being literate, esp. the ability to read and write. 2. possession of education. (Literacy, 1966, p. 836)
> Literate: adj… 1. able to read and write. 2. having an education; educated. 3. having or showing knowledge of literature, writing, etc.; literary; well-read. 4. characterized by skill, lucidity, polish, or the like. … n.:5. a person who can read and write. 6. a learned person. (Literate, 1966, p. 836)

> Illiteracy: 1. lack of ability to read and write. 2. state of being illiterate; lack of education. 3. a mistake in writing or speaking, felt to be characteristic of an illiterate person…. (Illiteracy, 1966, p. 710)
> Illiterate: 1. unable to read and write. 2. lacking education. 3. showing lack of culture, esp. in language and literature. 4. displaying a marked lack of knowledge in a particular field: *He is musically illiterate.* (Illiterate, 1966, p. 710)

These various definitions are surprising in two particular ways. First, they mention ability in reading and writing without detail or embellishment. It's not clear if reading and writing means being able to read or record one's name in a first or a second language, or call words off a printed page, or get meaning from print, or analyze, synthesize, evaluate and apply written material, or just what is meant by ability to read and write.

A second surprise, though, is that these definitions expand the notion of literacy to the way it is often used now, referring to education and knowledge in a particular area. So, the dictionary's example is "musically illiterate" but it could well be "computer illiterate" or some other similar phrase. The use of literacy in this sense of education and knowledge is widespread. It is what people often mean in conventional uses of the word literacy. They don't really mean reading and writing ability in any sense, but are instead referring to the kind of expertise, background and training that often arise from education; they may also use literacy to mean an ability to perform in a specific area, like with computers or technology or music and so on.

The other basic source to consult for definitions is the *Oxford English Dictionary*. Like my unabridged, the *OED* takes up both literacy and illiteracy as follows:

> Literacy: The quality or state of being literate; knowledge of letters; condition in respect to education, *esp.* ability to read and write. (Simpson & Weiner, 1989, Vol. 8, p. 1026)
> Illiteracy: a. The quality or condition of being illiterate; ignorance of letters, unlearnedness, absence of education; *esp.* inability to read and write. Also used more generally in sense: ignorance, lack of understanding (of any pursuit, activity, etc.). b. An error due to want of learning. (Simpson & Weiner, 1989, Vol. 9, p. 656)
> Illiterate: A. adj. 1. a. Of persons: Ignorant of letters or literature; without book-learning or education; unlettered, unlearned; …Also, more generally, characterized by ignorance or lack of learning or subtlety (in any sphere of activity). … b. Of things: Characterized by or showing ignorance of letters, or absence of learning or education; unlearned, unpolished. (Simpson & Weiner, 1989, Vol. 9, p. 656)

Like the unabridged, then, the *OED* presents two senses of literacy and illiteracy. One of these has to do with abilities in reading and writing, albeit unspecified, and the other, more general knowledge or understanding or ability in, as the *OED* says, "any sphere of activity." Often in current usage, these two meanings get conflated, but they need to be kept distinct if we are to understand them in terms of how people comprehend and use written language. For the purposes of exploring what people need to be able to do with reading and writing, I focus in this chapter exclusively on abilities to understand and produce written language.

About "illiteracy"

Before continuing with other approaches to the definition problem, a discussion of the use of the word "illiteracy" is in order. Readers might think that an investigation of illiteracy *per se* would be quite a straightforward topic. But one of the surprises is that it is NOT straightforward at all, partly because the word has various pejorative connotations. Conventional dictionary definitions like those discussed above make illiteracy seem simple: lack of ability to read and write, or more generally, lack of education. There are a number of other definitions beyond lack of ability to read and write that have been offered. To address this problem, Blake and Blake (2002, p. 8-11) review the history of the word 'literacy' from Greek times to the present. They come to the conclusion that literacy should be simply defined as the ability to read and write. Discussing the pejorative connotations of "illiteracy," Blake and Blake note that other terms like "nonliterate" or "preliterate" (2002, p. 8), drawn from classical studies, may be more neutral. However, they do not change the essential character of illiteracy, an inability to read and write, and they do not remove the pejorative connotations of the word.

The Blakes expand their definitions to include the phrase "functional literacy" by which they mean "an acceptable grasp of the skills of reading and writing for functioning in the society as a young adult" (Blake & Blake, 2002, p. 13). Functional literacy has been widely described and is often what is measured in surveys of literacy discussed later in this chapter. These surveys entail measurement of the performance by a sample population on a variety of literacy and numeracy tasks. One result of these surveys and other measures of literacy is a clear description of those who are functionally illiterate:

> They are able to read a recipe, follow a map, and work the keys of a McDonald's cash register. On the other hand, they have trouble filling out a job application, typing data into a computer, using standard punctuation

> in a paragraph, getting their checkbooks to balance, or taking a written test for a driver's license. (Blake & Blake, 2002, p. 2)

Thus, those who are functionally illiterate cannot, as I have suggested, perceive or produce meaning in written form whether on paper or on a screen and use that information as a basis for analysis, synthesis, evaluation, and application. The dictionary also offers a specific definition of the functional illiterate: "a person whose ability to read or write is inadequate for the needs of his job, the demands of a situation, or the like" (Functional illiterate, 1966, p. 574).

Because of the conflation of the definitions, the word "illiteracy" has come to have a strong pejorative implication. Its negative overtones do not arise from the simple lack of ability to read and write, but from the notion that illiterates are uneducated in some way or in many ways. Because of the negative implications of this term and because this book offers a theory of literacy intended to treat it as an array of abilities that can be developed and expanded through education and through experience beyond schooling, I choose not use this term in the rest of the book. The phrase "literacy novices" describes those who are developing literacy.

Definitions: Literacy in the brain

Reading scholar Stanislas Dehaene (2009) sheds some additional light on the defining characteristics of literacy in his report of a variety of brain imaging studies. These studies reveal the impact of literacy on the human brain in ways that suggest some defining characteristics. Dehaene points out that there are a number of reasons why the brains of people who can work with written language and those who can't might appear different on MRI scans and other tests. These differences might be the result of "social exclusion or of genetic or neurological disease, conditions which in and of themselves can cause profound changes in brain activity" (2009, p. 208).

However, when the brains of people who do not have these problems and who are otherwise similar in terms of their education, socio-economic status and other characteristics are compared, it is very clear that literacy changes the brain in marked ways. Studies reported by Dehaene show that there is much more activity among literate individuals in the anterior insula, a part of the brain close to Broca's area, essential to comprehension (2009, p. 209). The left hemisphere of the brain is overall more highly active in literate research participants. Moreover,

> ...literacy did not only alter brain activity during language listening tasks, but also affected the anatomy of the brain. The rear part of the corpus

> callosum, which links the parietal regions of both hemispheres, had thickened in the literate subjects. This macroscopic finding implies a massive increase in the exchange of information across the two hemispheres—perhaps explaining the remarkable increase in verbal memory span in literates. (Dehaene, 2009, p. 209)

This work suggests that a literate person can be defined or described as someone who has these specific brain changes or capabilities. Morevoer, there is much work going on to understand the brain's ability to change, from birth and across the lifespan that reflects its plasticity (Malabou, 2008); literacy is only one of many experiences that leads to brain development.

Definitions: College students

As noted in the Introduction, my colleagues often complain about students' reading problems in terms of a variety of concerns. First, they note that students generally do not choose reading as a leisure, school or work activity. Many or perhaps most typical undergraduate students are not aware of the amount of reading they do as the surf the World Wide Web. Moreover, they are generally uncritical if and when they do read, especially screens, so that simply locating information on a topic via a Google search provides them with the "research" needed to support an idea or create a paper. This concern is just one of those I often hear from college writing teachers. This view is held by these teachers despite the fact that students read and write many text messages, and often these messages are written like Hebrew, in the sense that vowels are commonly omitted. Interestingly, the absence of vowels does not seem to interfere with comprehension, a result of the psycholinguistic phenomenon of redundancy in language. This point has been made by both reading specialist Frank Smith (2004) and linguist Steven Pinker (Pinker, 1994, p. 181). Still, teachers commonly think that students lack literacy skills.

The second concern my colleagues have, though, is really about students' limited critical literacy. The issue is not so much that students can't read (i.e., call words off the printed page) or don't get meaning from print but rather that they are not critically literate. That is, they cannot summarize a text accurately, but more importantly, they cannot go beyond summary to analysis, synthesis, evaluation and application. They have no sense about appraising a piece of written text for authority, currency, relevancy, accuracy, objectivity and appropriateness. They cannot do these things with printed material like books and journals, and they cannot and do not do it with sources they find on the Internet.

In addition, they cannot even look critically at the kinds of materials they might find through search strategies: Wikipedia is just as good as a specialized encyclopedia in a subject area as far as many students are concerned. A thoughtful review of the authority and validity of Wikipedia as a source by historian Randall Stross (2006) raises the questions about authority, accuracy and related issues; students I gave this report to recently did understand why Wikipedia is not an appropriate choice as a scholarly source in research, but were greatly surprised by the article's points about the anonymity of Wiki authors, the lack of editorial supervision, and so on. And they were surprised despite the fact that they had already received detailed bibliographic instruction from a library faculty member; the instruction specifically addresses the criteria by which sources should be appraised. Critical literacy is elusive even in the face of direct instruction.

College reading as defined by the ACT exam

Another concern sometimes raised by my colleagues applies to college students generally, but looks specifically at students who are not fully prepared for college, based often on some standardized exam like the ACT. The ACT measures students' reading ability by testing their comprehension of short passages of text in a timed multiple choice format, producing a score from 1 to 36 on the reading portion of this college entrance examination, widely used in the United States for admissions and placement decisions by colleges and universities. At my institution, a fairly typical medium-sized state institution in the Carnegie Doctoral Research category, we currently recommend a developmental college reading course for students whose ACT Reading test score is at 19 or below. The ACT organization has looked at this issue in some detail, and there has recently been a National Survey of America's College Students (NSACS), done by the Pew Charitable Trusts (2006), using the same instrument as the national survey of the adult population to be discussed below. These measures all hinge on various definitions of literacy, whether they are stated explicitly or not.

The report on United States national data drawn from administration of the ACT test of high school students presents useful findings on some aspects of these students' reading (American, 2006). The ACT analysis shows quite precisely the kinds of abilities students lack as they enter college, as discussed in this report, which can be found at the ACT website: http://www.act.org/research/policymakers/reports/reading.html. The ACT exam has an entire section devoted to reading; its questions examine students' abilities, first, in literal and inferential comprehension, second, in understanding textual elements such as main ideas, supporting details, vocabulary, generalizations and related items, and finally, in dealing with differing degrees of text complexity that arise from items summarized by the initials RSVP. These initials capture these elements of text complexity: relationships, richness, structure, style, vocabulary and purpose (American, 2006, p. 13-16).

The study's findings, based on data from 563,000 students who took the ACT in 2003-2005, show that "students who can master the skills necessary to read and understand complex texts are more likely to be college ready than those who cannot" (American, 2006, p. 16). This research suggests that what it means to be literate goes well beyond literal and even inferential comprehension, and beyond the ability to recognize key text elements or deal with vocabulary; ACT's definition of literacy hinges on handling complex texts. Moreover, the ACT report notes that

> performance on complex texts is the clearest differentiator in reading between students who are likely to be ready for college and those who are not. And this is true for both genders, all racial/ethnic groups, and all family income levels. (American, 2006, p. 17)

The ability to read and understand complex texts is clearly a very useful measure, and is fully explicated in the report, and is pertinent to this discussion as well.

The report goes on to make explicit what ACT means when it refers to complex texts. Complexity specifically entails these elements:

> **Relationships**: Interactions among ideas or characters in the text are subtle, involved or deeply embedded.
> **Richness**: The text possesses a sizable amount of highly sophisticated information conveyed through data or literary devices.
> **Structure**: The text is organized in ways that are elaborate and sometimes unconventional.
> **Style**: The author's tone and use of language are often intricate.
> **Vocabulary**: The author's choice of words is demanding and highly context dependent.
> **Purpose**: The author's intent in writing the text is implicit and sometimes ambiguous. (American, 2006, p. 17)

The ability to deal with these elements is an ability that should develop throughout students' high school years in order for them to be ready to do college level reading successfully. The ACT report points out that reading bears on every subject in college. The research findings show that students who meet the ACT benchmark score of 21 are more likely to enroll in college and be successful, and not just in English, history, and other subjects where there is intensive reading, but also in science, math, and other areas as well (American, 2006, p. 11-12). The ACT's definition and test measure some, though certainly not all, crucial aspects of literacy.

The students I see in the Critical Thinking and Reading course at my university whose ACT Reading scores are in some cases much below ACT's benchmark of 21, reveal why they could fairly be described as literacy novices. As we work on basic textbook materials in class, it's clear that they have difficulty in every area of reading, including all of those captured by the RSVP description. They have a hard time figuring out topic and main idea in even short passages of text. They can't sort major and minor details presented by a writer to support an idea. They can't draw inferences, compare or contrast positions on an issue in two different passages on the same topic, or follow the logic of an argument. Their vocabulary is poor and they lack skills to deal with unknown words by getting meaning from context or using word analysis. Finally, they are unable to evaluate an author's claims using evidence from prior knowledge or other reading or class material. Like me reading Hebrew, they can follow a text read aloud from the printed page and know some but not many vocabulary words, probably many more than I do in Hebrew, but cannot really get meaning from print. Certainly for the purposes of doing inquiry projects or integrating outside sources in support of an argument on an issue, these students lack the necessary skills to perform well. But even students whose ACT reading scores are at or above 21 lack at least some of these skills also.

Furthermore, it seems likely that students' inability to read can help to explain the current epidemic of plagiarism. Naturally, some plagiarism can be described as simple theft: students buy papers written by others, lift portions of works found on line and paste them into texts without citation knowingly and deceitfully, use work provided to them by friends, and so on. But the more worrisome, common kind of plagiarism may well be a result of the students' inability to read. They do not get the full meaning from the texts they look at, don't see how to analyze and synthesize different positions on an issue, don't know how to compare two writers' views on a question. Careful study of these kinds of problems is being conducted in a series of research projects by composition scholars Sandra Jamieson and Rebecca Moore Howard (2011); close examination of students' use of sources in this research reflects their status as literacy novices. I have argued elsewhere that plagiarism is fundamentally a reading problem (Horning, 2010).

ACT has continued to work on reading and related issues since the 2006 report that focused exclusively on reading. In 2010, ACT released a report examining the relationship of ACT test scores to the newly adopted Common Core State Standards for K-12 education in the United States (ACT, 2010; Council of Chief State School Officers, 2010). These standards offer a detailed set of goals for K-12 education, providing specific abilities students should have to be successful in college and beyond. ACT's 2010 study analyzes more than 256,000 eleventh grade students' performance on the ACT to see how many students achieved ACT's "benchmark" scores that indicate likely success in college. In this study, only 38% of students achieved a benchmark score of 21 on the Reading section of the ACT (ACT, 2010). In addition, skills with complex, informational texts, with sophisticated vocabulary, and with content area texts, notably in science as well as other subjects, are also weak and need much more attention (ACT, 2010). These findings are consistent with those of earlier studies by ACT and other groups. Yet another report, released by ACT in 2011, makes clear that 28% of students failed to meet the benchmarks in all of the areas tested and only 52% met the benchmark in Reading.

While ACT is careful to note that the Common Core State Standards are newly-developed/adopted and have not yet had a long-standing and widespread impact on teaching and learning in K-12 schools, it should be clear that students have significant problems with reading. The validity of the ACT as a predictor of college success has been called into question in some research, such as in a study on the efficacy of various tests, Bettinger, Evans and Pope (2011). Even so, the numbers of students taking the ACT and their weak performance are both indicative of their difficulties with short passages on paper. Bettinger et al. examined the predictive validity of the ACT's various subsections and found that only English and Math have good predictive validity for positive college outcomes. However, the test has been taken by a large number of students and there is some relationship between scores on the Reading section and students' performance in college, so it is a useful measure to consider when examining students' reading problems, keeping in mind its limitations.

If the definition of literacy includes the ACT's measurement of the ability to read and make use of complex texts as defined here, entering college students appear to be literacy novices. If they do not achieve the benchmark score of 21, their ability to handle complex texts is limited as is their success in college. ACT's definition of success (a 2.0 GPA and returning for a second year of college) also warrants evaluation. Any higher standard, such as a 2.5 GPA or a 3.0 would increase the numbers of students who are literacy novices. This definition of literacy, then, helps to explain why college faculty members frequently complain about students' reading and literacy.

College students' reading at graduation

Most of those complaining college teachers would probably like to think that going to college improves students' literacy, moving them along on a course from novice to expert status. However, a second recent study, conducted by the Pew Charitable Trusts on college students' literacy levels at graduation suggests otherwise (2006). The Pew survey, called the National Survey of America's College Students (NSACS), tested a sample of college students nearing the end of their academic work. The definitions of literacy (to be discussed in more detail in the following section) and the instrument used in this survey are the same as those used in the National Assessment of Adult Literacy, also discussed below. The survey "collected data from a sample of 1827 graduating students at 80 randomly selected 2-year and 4-year colleges and universities (68 public and 12 private) from across the United States" (Pew, 2006). Full results, which appear on the Pew website, show that while college students generally have higher literacy levels than the population at large, they are still not as skilled in prose, document and quantitative literacy as they could be or should be (Pew, 2006, p. 20-21).

In particular, fewer than half of college students and much fewer than half of the population attain scores at the "proficient" level on any of the three dimensions of literacy according to both the Pew and the national assessments (Pew, 2006, p. 19). Moreover, the Pew study was designed to help colleges and universities but also looks at the preparedness for the workforce, so it "helps educators and employers develop a better picture of the skills of the emerging labor force" (Pew, 2006, p. 1). Literacy is not only essential to performance in college, but also to performance on the job, so there is a lot of interest in it for economic and employment reasons as well as educational reasons. And the picture resulting from these studies is that students graduating from college are not nearing the levels of literacy expertise they will need.

Many colleges, universities and community colleges have a population of students whose test scores indicate a need for developmental work in reading, but even those that don't, including even the best colleges and universities in the country, have students whose reading skills are not where they should be, and writing skills that are also not strong, partly as a by-product of their reading. This description pertains not only to those entering but also those graduating from college. Among faculty, there is a widespread feeling that many students lack the literacy skills necessary for success in college and for full participation in a democratic society, that is, they lack the critical literacy defined earlier in this chapter; these studies provide evidence to support this impression. Additional national and international studies show that many college graduates are novices in their mastery of the skills defining literacy, along with citizens in general in the United States and in many countries around the world.

Definitions: National and international surveys

The lack of literacy is a big problem everywhere as reflected in national and international definitions and tests of literacy. Most of the national and international studies of adult literacy that have been conducted in the last fifteen years or so draw on the basic work done first in the National Adult Literacy Survey (hereafter NALS) in the United States, published in 1993 by the National Center for Education Statistics (Kirsch et al., 1993). The survey was conducted to provide information on household literacy in the United States by surveying a large sample of the population in response to a request from the U.S. Congress. NALS followed two other earlier surveys that used similar methodologies, asking people to respond to a series of tasks to measure their prose, document and quantitative literacy skills. NALS was the first large-scale study of adult literacy in America, undertaken as a joint project of the U.S. Department of Education's National Center for Education Statistics and its Division of Adult Education and Literacy with the assistance of the Educational Testing Service (Kirsch et al., 1993, p. xi).

Since NALS is the springboard for other studies, a full description, provided in its first report, is helpful:

> During the first eight months of 1992, trained staff conducted household interviews with nearly 13,600 individuals aged 16 and older who had been randomly selected to represent the adult population in this country. In addition, approximately 1,000 adults were surveyed in each of 12 states that chose to participate in a special study designed to produce state-level results that are comparable to the national data. Finally, some 1,100 inmates from 80 federal and state prisons were interviewed to gather information on the skills of the prison population. Each individual was asked to spend about an hour responding to a series of diverse literacy tasks and providing information on his or her background, education, labor market experiences, and reading practices. (Kirsch, et al., 1993, p. xii)

The tasks given in the survey provide a measure of literacy on each of the three dimensions, prose, document, and quantitative literacy, on a scale consisting of five levels.

The levels of literacy and the tasks required of those who participated in the survey are also carefully described in the various reports on this project; they provide a clear definition of literacy. The survey set five levels of adult literacy and tested Americans' abilities directly with tasks designed to measure skills at each level, using both prose sources and documents of various kinds. The tasks call for reading of a variety of different materials like newspaper columns, government publications, and instruction manuals for consumer products; participants are expected to draw out information and inferences from charts, graphs, tables and similar materials. The materials used were all printed on paper, fairly short and in English. The focus here is on the measurement of prose and document literacy, though quantitative literacy was also tested in the survey, including specifically the ability to extract numerical information and do calculations or make inferences based on it.

In the initial NALS report (Kirsch, et al., 1993), prose literacy is defined this way:

> The ability to understand and use information contained in various kinds of textual material is an important aspect of literacy. Most prose materials administered in this assessment were expository—that is, they inform, define, or describe—since these constitute much of the prose that adults read. ...The prose materials were drawn from newspapers, magazines, books, brochures, and pamphlets...
>
> Each prose selection was accompanied by one or more questions or directives which asked the reader to perform specific tasks. These tasks represent three major aspects of information-processing: locating, integrating and generating. Locating tasks require the reader to find information in the text based on conditions or features specified in the question or directive. ...Integrating tasks ask the reader to compare or contrast two or more pieces of information from the text. ...In the generating tasks, readers must produce a written response by making text-based inferences or drawing on their own background knowledge. (Kirsch, et al., 1993, p. 73-74)

Those participating in the survey worked on 41 tasks at different levels of difficulty, using different kinds of texts.

Document literacy, a second component of literacy, is defined this way in the 1993 NALS report:

> Another important aspect of being literate in modern society is having the knowledge and skills needed to process information from documents. We often encounter tables, schedules, charts, graphs, maps and forms in everyday life, both at home and at work. …The ability to locate and use information from documents is therefore essential.
>
> Success in processing documents appears to depend at least in part on the ability to locate information in complex arrays and to use this information in appropriate ways. Procedural knowledge may be needed to transfer information from one source or document to another, as is necessary in completing the applications or order forms.
>
> …Questions and directives associated with these tasks are basically of four types: *locating, cycling, integrating,* and *generating*. Locating tasks require the readers to match one or more features of information stated in the question to either identical or synonymous information given in the document. Cycling tasks require the reader to locate and match one or more features, but differ in that they require the reader to engage in a series of feature matches to satisfy conditions given in the question. The integrating tasks typically require the reader to compare and contrast information in adjacent parts of the document. In the generating tasks, readers must produce a written response by processing information found in the document and also making text-based inferences or drawing on their own background knowledge. (Kirsch, et al., 1993, p. 84)

To measure document literacy, participants were offered 81 tasks at different levels of difficulty using different kinds of documents. The last two types of tasks should ring bells for writing teachers. Integrating and generating tasks relate clearly to the skills need for inquiry-based work of all kinds including research papers, Power Point presentations, website construction and so on.

The findings of the NALS project give a solid overall picture of the status of literacy in America as of the early 1990s. Approximately 20 percent of the adult population performed at the two highest levels of literacy on all three dimensions (Kirsch, et al., 1993, p. xv). This outcome suggests that the vast majority of citizens cannot perform at the highest levels of literacy needed to function in contemporary society, that is, they are literacy novices. So those college students described earlier as literacy novices are not alone. It seems likely that easily half or more of the students currently taking the Critical Thinking and Reading course at my institution would not perform at the highest levels of literacy defined by the survey, and that perhaps half of all the students at my institution would score similarly. The NALS survey did not address the college student population specifically, but the recent Pew study shows that, as noted above, college students do a little better than the population at large, but not even half of either group attains scores at the "Proficient" level.

The findings of the 2003 National Assessment of Adult Literacy (hereafter NAAL) show little change from the NALS findings in 1993 (U.S. Dept. of Education, 2006). While there was some improvement in overall average scores in quantitative literacy, and some improvement in prose and document literacy for some minority groups, there was virtually no change in the status of literacy in the population as a whole over these 10 years (U.S. Dept. of Education, 2006, p. 1-4). It is fair to say that the overall situation has not changed; too many Americans are not scoring at the Proficient level on these carefully done national surveys of the population.

The definition of literacy that emerges from the NALS survey, NAAL, and the Pew study focuses on four key capacities that highly literate individuals should have in dealing with prose and documents, as described previously: locating, cycling, integrating and generating. Thus, literacy expertise defined by the US government means people must be able to locate (find by matching), cycle (match at multiple points), integrate (compare and contrast at multiple points), and generate (write based on info processing, inferences and background knowledge). Few college reading or writing teachers would find much to argue with here. Most would say, I think, that these elements capture the essence of expertise in critical literacy.

But it is not a goal we are achieving effectively in the population at large or among college students. It may well be the single biggest reason for the appalling college drop out rate of about 50% (Tinto, 1993, p. 1; U.S. Department of Education, National Center for Education Statistics, 2005). It is also not a goal that colleges and universities can achieve on their own. There must be support for it from the public schools at all levels. And for now, there is no such support, despite No Child Left Behind, despite work on assessment of student abilities at various levels and despite various government programs at both the state and national levels.

Some of the problem is actually in the state-mandated testing programs that do not move students toward the goal of prose and document literacy. Some of the problem is that even in some of the best school districts in the country, students seldom receive ANY direct instruction in reading after fifth or sixth grade; the instruction they do get may focus on literary analysis, which does not promote the skills in critical literacy that require locating, cycling, integrating and generating described above, and for which only extensive reading of non-fiction prose will do. The new Common Core State Standards may help, as they specifically recommend much more work with reading extended nonfiction prose, but it is too soon to assess the impact of this document.

If we compare the broad-based, government-sponsored survey reported in NALS and its follow-up findings internationally in the International Adult Literacy Survey (hereafter IALS) (Murray, et al., 1998), it is clear that there is widespread difficulty with literacy beyond the US. The IALS had to address a number of challenges in trying to measure literacy abilities across languages and cultures and the technical report details the key issues at some length. However, a number of steps were taken in the analysis of the data from the survey to address these problems.

The survey was carefully done under the auspices of the Organisation for Economic Cooperation and Development, a group of 34 countries chiefly from the first world, founded in 1961 to "promote policies that will improve the economic and social well-being of people around the world" according to its website (www.oecd.org). And the overall results of the IALS survey show that in many countries, a similar situation to that in the US can also be found; it's important to keep in mind that these reports do not look at developing countries anywhere in the world where education, computer access and other issues lead to even more limited literacy abilities. The more recent results of the 2003 NAAL survey confirm this claim that many adults remain literacy novices.

To explain fully the nature of literacy expertise, the leading scholars on the NALS, NAAL and IALS surveys created a theory of the underlying processes that are essential to literacy (Murray, et al., 1998, p. 144-45). This analysis by Kirsch and Mosenthal, two academic reading scholars who have published extensively on reading research, shows that there are two sets of variables that play a role in the difficulty of literacy tasks like those in the surveys: task characteristics and material characteristics (cited in Murray, et al., 1998, p. 145). For prose and document literacy, the task characteristics that play a key role in difficulty are the type of match the reader needs to make, the plausibility of distractors that may lead the reader to an incorrect answer, the type of information, whether abstract or concrete, and the structural complexity of the material, ranging from simple lists to multiple documents. For prose and document literacy, the material characteristics that account for difficulty include some readability measures like the number of syllables per hundred words, the number of sentences per hundred words, the number of labels or headings, the type of document and how much information the reader must get from the text. Of all these measures, just a few make a real difference according to the IALS report:

> for both prose and document literacy, the variables most highly related to task difficulty were type of match, plausibility of distractors, and type of information. Readability, as measured by number of syllables and number of sentences per hundred words of text, was less significant. (Murray, et al., 1998, p. 145)

In addition, the skills described here are similar for both prose and document literacy and for quantitative literacy as well, suggesting that there is a general set of literacy skills that are essential for all readers, regardless of their language or culture.

The International Adult Literacy Survey gives the following very general definition of literacy:

> For the purpose of this survey literacy has been interpreted as "Official Language Literacy" and defined as "the information processing skills (reading, writing and numeracy skills) necessary to use printed material commonly encountered at work, at home and in the community." (Murray, et al., 1998, p. 17)

So the national and international surveys set a definition that is skill-based. It does specify that to be literate, people must be able to both understand and produce written language. It also specifies that people must be able to use their skills in various environments. It is not as detailed in terms of dealing with complex texts as the ACT definition; however it does specify what people need to be able to DO with written language.

By merging the information from the national and international surveys, key features of a definition of expert literacy emerge. It seems clear that people need to be able to both understand written language and produce it in a variety of contexts and situations. They need to be able not only to read to get essential information or ideas, but also to go beyond basic content to appreciate the elements captured in the ACT's analysis of relationships, richness, structure, style, vocabulary and purpose (the RSVP mnemonic discussed above). And beyond all these essential aspects of comprehension, people need to be able to evaluate and use what they read to produce their own ideas and information in written form. Readers must be able to rely also on their own prior knowledge and inferences drawn from what they have read and to demonstrate these abilities now on both pages and screens. These ambitious goals are essential to full participation in a democratic society, and are increasingly critical in our ever "flatter," electronically interconnected world (Friedman, 2006, p. 339-40). These goals are the ones in my proposed definition of expert critical literacy.

International definitions

Yet another international definition comes from the United Nations Development Program, which is interested in literacy from a global perspective. It draws on a definition used by the United Nations' Educational, Scientific and Cultural Organization (UNESCO); the World Bank (2011), interested in literacy from an economic perspective, also relies on the UNESCO definition. The following definition is presented in the UNDP's Human Development Report for 2004, which includes discussion of adult literacy rates around the world: "The adult literacy rate is defined as the percentage of people ages 15 and above who can, with understanding, read and write a short, simple statement about their everyday life" (United Nations, 2004).

This report goes on to point out the difficulties in measuring literacy rates. The information is often drawn from national census data, relying on citizens' self-reports. Alternatively, countries around the world may use levels of education as the basis for literacy rates even though attendance and level of completion can be variable.

These comments on the problem of defining literacy provide very useful insights into its complex nature. Schooling implies literacy, but does not always produce the level of literacy needed to participate fully in contemporary society. On the other hand, schooling may be a viable measure in some places, since at least some of what constitutes literacy is cultural and requires consideration of the social context in which people develop literacy skills. The advantage of the measurements taken by the ACT reading test and the definitions used by NALS, NAAL and IALS is that they entail direct measures of test takers' or survey participants' actual performance on literacy tasks rather than on school measures or self-report data.

The United Nations declared 2003-2012 the International Literacy Decade. In conjunction with this declaration, it established the goal of increasing adult literacy around the world by 50% according to its website (United Nations, 2006). The UN's approach entails the use of survey instruments, but draws on the same essential definitions of levels of literacy and component skills used in NALS, NAAL and IALS. And in a 2005 report on the role of new technologies in the global efforts connected to the UN's Literacy Decade, respected International Literacy Institute authors Wagner and Kozma note that

> Individual participation in this [information-literate society and knowledge economy] … requires the skills needed to use technology as a means to access, disseminate and create new information and knowledge products

> for the benefit of the individual and society. But the use of these information resources also requires basic text literacy. (2005, p. 19)

Thus, international and technology-based definitions bring us back to the same essential definitions proposed and developed in surveys in the United States and other western nations. These definitions also make clear the essential need for "basic text literacy;" the definition of academic critical literacy focuses on basic text literacy for just this reason.

Broader definitions: Adult basic education, community literacy and libraries, ethnographic/social practice perspectives

College and university faculty, test developers, and UNESCO officials are not the only ones interested in literacy definitions or measures. For example, George Demetrion, director of basic literacy programming for the Literacy Volunteers of Greater Hartford, who has been working in the area of adult literacy since 1987, has reviewed the issues relevant to literacy from a community perspective. In *Conflicting Paradigms in Adult Literacy Education* (2005), he explores the political implications of various aspects of adult literacy, adult basic education and second language learning.

In this context, he claims that literacy is "a metaphor for knowledge that includes the skills of reading and writing, but is defined by the symbols and sign systems operative in a given sociocultural setting" (2005, p. 267). Reviewing the development of standards for adult literacy, Demetrion describes the widespread disagreement and difficulties over the definition and setting of standards for adult literacy programs (2005, p. 130). The problem of definition ties directly to the setting of standards and, as Demetrion points out, it is impossible to set standards without an agreed-upon definition of what constitutes literacy (2005, p. 133). Thus, the problem of definition is shared by community-based programs as well. The definition of academic critical literacy I have offered focuses specifically on reading and writing and integrates the sociocultural aspect of the definition Demetrion provides.

Another place that is an important center for literacy is, of course, the library. Cuban and Cuban, a librarian and educator respectively, have expanded the definition of literacy to include what they call "multiple literacies" which they define as follows:

> *Critical literacy*. Reading and writing as a politically charged activity that challenges social conventions and institutions, and proposes social and political changes...
> *Digital literacy*. Reading and writing through electronic formats; being able to critically analyze and integrate electronic information, including using data to experiment, creating databases, creating web pages, and desktop publishing.
> *Environmental literacy*. Engagement with "green" issues and sustainability of the environment, such as global warming, as well as questioning mainstream scientific knowledge.
> *Health literacy*. Being able to read and write a range of health messages; manage personal health and critically analyze health care; and address health barriers, as well as cultural, age, gender, and race issues with regard to health.
> This list of literacies also includes academic literacy (critical use and experiences of writing for academic purposes), information literacy (locating, using, and critically evaluating diverse information sources), visual literacy (being able to design, identify, and critically evaluate images), media literacy (critical analysis of mass media messages), and multicultural literacy (cultural competence with diverse written narratives)...financial literacy (ability to critically evaluate and use economics in daily life).... (Cuban & Cuban, 2007, p. 95-96)

The Cubans' ideas capture a wide array of different aspects of literacy, most of which are pertinent to the discussion here. By including environmental, health and financial literacy, the Cubans lean toward that "other" literacy, i.e. skill or ability. On the other hand, their varied definitions bring in digital, media and so on, and they generally tie these other types of literacy to reading and writing. Librarians work especially with information literacy as the Cubans define it, an increasingly necessary component of critical literacy.

Picking up on the broader and specifically sociocultural aspects of the definition, another perspective comes from the work of British literacy scholar Brian Street, an advocate of a view of literacy as a social practice, a view likely shared by adult education specialists and librarians. The social practice view sees, "literacy practices as multiple and culturally varied" (Street, 2011, p. 2). Street proposes that from an ideological perspective, "Literacy, like culture, then, is an active process of meaning making and contest over definition, including its own definition" (2011, p. 3). He goes on in this work on literacy inequality to summarize the views of Jack Goody about literacy and power, noting that having literacy gives people or cultures power. Moreover, he argues that seeing literacy as a set of practices rather than a single autonomous entity offers a more comprehensive picture of what literacy is.

An ethnographic perspective, Street says, offers the advantage of shifting from a view of the absence of some features as a "deficit" to support a more concrete analysis without judgment. It also moves away from the broad statistical analysis of literacy that can arise if an autonomous definition is used for purposes of assessment and judgments of those who "have it" in contrast to those who don't (Street, 2011, p. 5-6). Two other literacy scholars present a series of questions that might be asked which help to clarify the advantage of the ethnographic/social practice perspective. Stierer and Bloome suggest these questions:

> How are people in different situations using written language? What are people using written language for? How do people use written language to interact with each other? What social values are associated with the use of written language? In what ways do people interpret written language? Implicit in these questions is the proposition that the answers will not be generalisable [sic] or universal, but specific to a cultural group, a social institution, or perhaps even limited to a particular situation or event. (Stierer & Bloome, 1994/2007, p. 54)

These questions lead to a view of literacy as much more than a set of intellectual skills that exist in isolation from the circumstances in which they might be used, but rather as an array of processes that develop over a lifetime, in school and out. The definition of academic critical literacy presented at the beginning of this chapter integrates this view.

The advantages of this ethnographic, social practice view of literacy are especially clear in the highly-regarded work of Scribner and Cole (1978/2007), who studied the Vai people of Liberia and offer an analysis of their various literacy practices. The Vai are literate in English, Arabic and a written form of their own language, Mande, which is a created or invented phonetic writing system used entirely for personal communication. Scribner and Cole's original report of their work with the Vai (1981) is often cited because the Vai's widely used writing system co-exists with other languages and is not taught in a school-type setting. Moreover, Scribner and Cole did not find any evidence of superior memory, language integration or other related abilities among Vai literates than among those without literacy skills. So, though literacy may change the brain in ways that Dehaene (2009) has found, as discussed earlier, it does not necessarily lead to superior intellectual skills or performance. There are some clear advantages to keeping both the autonomous and social practice definitions of literacy in mind.

The object of presenting all these definitions from these many and varied perspectives is not to suggest that there is one simple or right answer to the problem of defining literacy. Instead, the goal is to present a range of definitions and perspectives and draw from them to offer a focused concept of literacy. This concept then serves as the basis of the discussion in the rest of the book. To review the definition that I propose:

> Academic critical literacy is best defined as the psycholinguistic processes of getting meaning from or putting meaning into print and/or sound, images, and movement, on a page or screen, used for the purposes of analysis, synthesis, evaluation and application; these processes develop through formal schooling and beyond it, at home and at work, in childhood and across the lifespan and are essential to human functioning in a democratic society.

My goal is to capture the many features and aspects of both autonomous and social practice views of literacy suggested by the organizations, agencies, and scholars whose work has been discussed to this point.

Multiliteracies and literacy

At this point in the discussion, it might be easy to think that these various definitions and distinctions seem to be framed around traditional reading and writing on printed pages, and not at all focused on all things digital. Surely, students using digital devices of all kinds are doing more reading and writing than ever before, both in and out of school. And yet, careful measures of their performance suggest that while they can update status on Facebook efficiently, when it comes to finding, reading, evaluating and using material they find on the Web, students' performance is in fact rather poor. Two instruments designed to measure students' abilities in these areas were both developed using the Association of College and Research Libraries' Information Literacy Competency Standards for Higher Education (Association, 2008). The ACRL is the major professional organization for research librarians. The Educational Testing Service, an organization with long experience creating standardized tests created an instrument called iSkills to measure students' abilities to meet the ACRL information literacy standards (Katz, 2007). A group of faculty and librarians at Kent State University have also designed an instrument using the ACRL standards and tested it widely in Project SAILS (2009). Both measures show that students seldom score better than 50%. Thus, careful consideration of digital literacy definitions is warranted.

Writing about literacy education for the digital age in the context of a discussion of literacy, drawing on principles from the United Nations, distinguished international literacy scholar Robert Tierney writes that learners must be:

> -capable information technology users
> -information-seekers, analyzers, and evaluators
> -problem-solvers and decision-makers
> -creative and effective users of productivity tools
> -communicators, collaborators, publishers, and producers
> -informed, responsible, and contributing citizens (Tierney, 2009, p. 293)

This list on the one hand provides a good working definition of digital literacy which will be expanded next with the work of Stuart Selber. On the other hand, a careful reading of these goals shows that information seeking, analysis, evaluation and communication, are the essentials of academic critical literacy as I have proposed it. Indeed, Tierney goes on to say that while digital literacy is highly collaborative, it still requires use of analysis, synthesis, evaluation and application (2009, p. 292-94). The venue (i.e., page or screen) is really moot; it is the abilities that are of prime concern.

Combining the impact of technology and the social views, Wagner and Kozma, writing on the UNESCO Literacy Decade project (2005), expand the definition of literacy along similar lines to those offered by Tierney. Wagner and Kozma point out that "technology is changing what it means to be a literate person" (2005, p. 79). They go on to note that in addition to basic reading and writing skills,

> …new skills are needed to: search for, organize and manage information; interpret and analyse [sic] data; work with distributed teams; communicate with others; and to use information to solve problems and create new knowledge and cultural artefacts [sic]. With these skills, citizens of today's world will be better prepared to search for, create and use information to extend their education, and to advance their economic, health and living conditions. (Wagner & Kozma, 2005, p. 79)

These abilities build from the basic ability to read and write. While these new venues offer new opportunities, they still rely on fundamental skills as a starting point.

Integrating Tierney's description with the specific skills needed because of technology enumerated by Wagner and Kozma, Stuart Selber, Pennsylvania State University rhetorician and scholar on computer literacy and human and computer interaction, also explores the definitions of literacy in his discussion of multiliteracies (2004). He views multiliteracies somewhat differently than others, framing his discussion around three categories of literacy: functional, critical and rhetorical (2004, p. 25). He argues that students need to achieve, first, functional literacy, by which he means that student users should have the ability to use computers as tools to attain effective employment. In addition, students should understand computers as cultural artifacts that they can question through processes of informed critique. Finally, like Tierney, Selber suggests that students should be able to see computers as a resource of hypertextual media they can produce and understand through processes of reflective practice (p. 25).

His description of functionally literate students expands this idea in a productive way. He argues that there are five major parameters to functional literacy. Students who are functionally literate can use computers to achieve their educational goals, can follow the social conventions of computer use, can know and make use of the special discourse of computers, can manage their "online world" (p. 45) effectively, and can resolve technological problems efficiently. To broaden this description to include print is quite simple; it can be done easily by adding "printed language" to the description wherever "computers" appears. Thus, functionally literate students can also use written or printed language to achieve educational goals, follow social conventions of written language, use the special discourse of writing, manage their "offline" world effectively and address technological problems easily (replacing pens that run out of ink, perhaps?).

Turning to critical literacy, Selber (2004, p. 96) proposes four parameters for critical literacy. Students who are critically literate can examine "the perspectives that shape computer design cultures and their artifacts" (p. 96), can use context to understand how computers are used, can be aware of institutional factors that affect them, and can evaluate how computers are understood by the public. Here again, written texts can be included easily to expand this definition of critical literacy to include print as well as electronic media. The critical literacy Selber describes is also pertinent to written language, so readers of printed texts should be interested in and aware of books, newspapers, magazines and other kinds of printed material in terms of design requirements, contexts of use, institutional factors affecting print and public response to printed material. Much of the discussion in the remaining chapters of this book examines these issues from both print and digital perspectives.

Finally, in rhetorical literacy, Selber argues that here again there are four parameters: persuasion, deliberation, reflection and social action. Rhetorically literate students "understand that persuasion permeates interface design contexts in both implicit and explicit ways and that it always involves larger structures and forces" (p. 147). Design problems, for rhetorically literate students, require deliberation concerning the nature of the problem and possible solutions. Reflection allows rhetorically literate students to make conscious choices about design and use, as well as critical assessment of actions and practices. Finally, design and use of computer technology is, for rhetorically literate users, a way to address social problems through action, not just technical expertise (Selber, 2004, p. 146-166). Persuasion, deliberation, reflection and social action are all very close to classical rhetorical strategies that date back to the Greeks and apply equally to print as they do to digital forms. Whether the object of creation is a website or a printed essay, these parameters apply. Selber's discussion broadens the idea of functional literacy and adds in critical and rhetorical literacy. Selber's exploration captures the expertise of meta-readers and writers. The definition of literacy I propose attempts to integrate the ideas of Selber and others by presenting literacy from both print and digital angles.

Expanding literacy: Generation 1.5 and L2 learners

A further challenge to defining literacy has to do with the language base for literacy. The challenge arises in the sort of situation I might be in if I were attempting to live and work as a user of Hebrew. If I were trying to get a job or an education in Hebrew, I would have significant difficulty. My ability with the language allows me to call words off the page, albeit slowly, but I can't really do anything essential like complete a job application or read a book. Suppose I really didn't know the language at all, not to speak it or read or write it. Or suppose I was someone who did know the language well enough to understand and speak to the needs of daily life but had little or no written language ability or academic writing ability. This latter situation describes the position of members of the group now referred to as Generation 1.5 (Harklau, 2003). An examination of this group in terms of critical literacy issues provides another dimension of understanding the definitions and possibilities of literacy.

Linda Harklau, a second language researcher at the University of Georgia, describes this population as follows:

> An increasing number of U.S. high school graduates enter college while still in the process of learning English. Referred to as generation 1.5 students because they share characteristics of both first- and second-generation immigrants, they do not fit into any of the traditional categories of nonnative English speakers enrolled in college writing courses, nor have they been the focus of much research on students learning to write in

> English as a second language. …There is great diversity among them in terms of their prior educational experience, native and English language proficiency, language dominance, and academic literacy. …One of the most common traits among generation 1.5 students is limited or no literacy in the first language. (Harklau, 2003)

In terms of critical literacy, these students are one of the most challenging groups to teach because of their complex characteristics and varied learning needs. They may have achieved some level of communicative competence in spoken English and they may be able to read with minimal comprehension, but their critical reading and especially their writing abilities are non-existent or sharply limited. They make an interesting test case for the development of critical literacy because they may or may not be able to read and write in either their native language or their second language (English or any other).

As Harklau (2003) points out, the key point is that these students are distinct from both *international* ESL (English as a Second Language) students and *immigrant* ESL students. International second language students are those who come to the U.S. to earn a college degree with the intention of returning to their native countries to live and work. They are usually literate in their L1, though perhaps not critically literate, and have often had extensive instruction in English in their native countries as well as intensive ESL instruction in special programs prior to or concurrent with their U.S. college enrollment. They have had ample instruction and practice in literacy development in both their native language and in English.

By contrast, immigrant second language students are those who may have had public education in their native countries to some level but now live in the U.S. and may be American high school graduates and/or American college students. They expect to spend the rest of their lives in the U.S. They may or may not be literate in any sense of the term in their native language. Or they may be literate in their L1, but such literacy goes unmeasured in the U.S. and certainly doesn't "count" when literacy is evaluated, especially when the measures are exclusively in English, as pointed out by Huot, an American literacy and assessment scholar who has critiqued various standardized measures measures of literacy (2007).

The problem is not that the U.S. population is linguistically diverse, but lies rather in how we define literacy to exclude those who are linguistically different:

> …literacy problems do not result from language diversity; rather, the perception of a literacy crisis is magnified by ignoring literacy in languages

> other than English and by blaming those who have not had an opportunity for a meaningful education. On the national level, the literacy "crisis" in the United States is largely invented and re-invented as cover for an economic system that is unable to employ all who can work and for the failings of an educational system that is neither adequately funded nor designed to meet the educational needs of all its students. (Wiley, 1996, p. 197)

This evaluation continues to be an appropriate assessment, even years after it was written, and seems particularly apt when attention is focused on the Generation 1.5 group.

Generation 1.5 students are different from both L1 and L2 learners, especially with regard to literacy; they may not be literate in either L1 or L2 as Harklau has observed. Thus, they might be seen as having special literacy needs, but in fact, careful examination shows that like others, they need to develop critical literacy skills from the same base of cognitive and linguistic capacities described later in Part I of this book. Generation 1.5 learners, like international and immigrant ESL students are literacy novices and are working toward expertise like native-speaking novices.

Summing up definitions and distinctions

The problem of defining literacy has sent scholars back to ancient times and forward to the digital age, trying to provide a precise description of what it means to be literate. As we have seen in this chapter, there have been a variety of attempts to define and measure literacy, generically in the dictionary, specifically among college students as well as adults in the general population in the US and elsewhere, in community settings, and among second language learners as well as those in Generation 1.5. These measures, whether self-reported, surrogate, or direct, fail to address critical literacy levels and fail to address the practices of literacy on paper and on computer screens. All of the work on definitions reviewed here reveals one key point clearly: far too many people lack the critical literacy skills to function in contemporary society.

It's important to keep in mind the methodological issues that bear on the varied definitions presented here. Reading and writing are enormously complex activities that involve the interaction of readers and writers as they meet in and through a print or digital text. These activities are for most people transparent, such that highly skilled readers get meaning directly from the text with very little or no attention to the mechanics of the visual array of letters, words, punctuation and so on. Expert writers likewise rarely attend to the mechanics of writing. Because of the transparency of these processes, it is a challenge to access exactly what is happening as text production or comprehension unfolds. Published studies discussed in the Introduction rely variously on self-report data (United States, 2007; Jolliffe & Harl, 2008), multiple choice tests of comprehension (American College, 2006), think-aloud reporting of text processing (Bazerman, 1988), brain scans (Dehaene, 2009) or other measures; every strategy has strengths and weaknesses and none provides a complete picture.

There might be better ways to think about this very complicated problem. Suppose that the focus in literacy is on just what it is that readers and writers need to be able to do to function in contemporary society: to live and work, to get educated, to participate fully in a democratic system of government, to take care of themselves and their families. To achieve these goals, critical literacy is simply essential. My definition offers a focused description of the key aspects of literacy presented in all of the preceding definitions:

> Academic critical literacy is best defined as the psycholinguistic processes of getting meaning from or putting meaning into print and/or sound, images, and movement, on a page or screen, used for the purposes of analysis, synthesis, evaluation and application; these processes develop through formal schooling and beyond it, at home and at work, in childhood and across the lifespan and are essential to human functioning in a democratic society.

Using this definition, which moves far beyond being able to call words off a printed page or write one's name, it is clear that self-report and schooling data do not help to establish who is or is not literate.

Yet another way to think about the definition problem is to look directly at what ordinary people actually do with respect to literacy. For example: about half the students who start college in the US don't finish (Bowen, Chingos & McPherson, 2009). What role does the lack of critical literacy play in that situation? The No Child Left Behind legislation in the United States has created a cottage industry in testing and evaluation. How many of those measures directly examine students' skills in critical literacy? At least one attempt to focus specifically on college students' reading and writing abilities suggests that post-secondary education in the US is not helping students develop these essential skills (Arum & Roksa, 2011). The NALS data suggest that a major of those in prison for serious crimes lack literacy skills (Kirsch, et al., 1993). What is the role of literacy in their problems? These practical questions suggest that there is a very serious problem with weak literacy abilities in school and out, as well as around the world. This review of extant definitions helps clarify what literacy is and sets a clear goal for the entire population to achieve it. To achieve this goal, I offer in the following pages evidence from case studies with novices and experts to support a theory of meta-reading and writing, and practical suggestions for how those who teach and support literacy might help novices achieve it.

CHAPTER TWO

CASE STUDIES OF EXPERTS AND NOVICES

Introduction

As digital texts and electronic searching increasingly dominate the reading landscape (Battelle, 2005; Kelly, 2006), it is becoming more essential for educated citizens to be critically literate and ever more challenging to achieve this goal. Recent studies also show that only half the students in the US who begin college manage to complete a degree (U.S. Dept. of Education, 2005). The resulting view of this situation as a reading "crisis" according to the Alliance for Excellent Education (2006) warrants attention. This chapter presents close analysis of the reading strategies of expert and novice readers; it helps to reveal the differences between these groups in terms of their awarenesses and skills, leading to my proposal that experts are meta-readers and writers.

Statement of the Problem

As I noted in the Introduction to this book, faculty members I work with on college campuses are increasingly concerned about students "don't, won't, can't" problems with reading. That is, students don't do the assigned reading and they won't do it unless there are going to be consequences in terms of course grades. Moreover, and perhaps most importantly, many students really can't read in the ways faculty require and expect. The issue is not being able to call words off the printed page and it is certainly not whether anyone can read and process a Facebook status update. The problem with reading is that students don't, won't, and can't read continuous texts such as books or substantial articles in journals, i.e. extended nonfiction prose, well or at all, for the purposes of analysis, synthesis, evaluation or application. This chapter explicates this problem by reporting a series of case studies with expert and novice readers, revealing the differences between these two groups. What struck me as I collected this case study data over the course of several years was the difference between these groups in terms of their awareness of texts and their skills in reading.

Some background studies

The studies discussed in the Introduction and opening chapter of this book make clear that students and many adults in the United States and in many other countries lack the awarenesses and skills needed to analyze, synthesize, evaluate and apply what they read to their writing or to their lives in school or outside of it. Novices need to be able to do these things in order to work well with printed material, whether it appears in published books, magazines, journals, newspapers and so on or whether it appears on a website or in some other electronic form. That is, roughly half or more of the population of the nation at large cannot comprehend effectively, as measured by the U.S. adult literacy surveys; the International Adult Literacy Survey (IALS) and Adult Literacy and Life Skills surveys suggest these dismal results can be found in many of the first world countries, raising a further concern about the rest of the countries as well.

American college students perform only a bit better. For example, relying on NSSE, the well-regarded National Survey of Student Engagement and other studies, Rebekah Nathan (aka Cathy Small, Professor of Anthropology at Northern Arizona University) has carefully documented students' unwillingness and inability to read and her own resistance to completing reading assignments during her participant-observer study of the culture of first-year college students reported in *My Freshman Year* (2005). The most recent U.S. National Endowment for the Arts study (2009) mentioned in the opening chapter, shows a small recent uptick in literary reading, but it is quite small and the finding is based chiefly on self-report data. The ACT (2006) and Pew (2006) studies, also discussed in the first chapter, show that about half of the students entering college lack the skills to be successful and they are not much better off when they leave. Problems with reading and writing are further illustrated in the much-publicized report *Academically Adrift*, which relies on the Collegiate Learning Assessment, a standardized test of critical reading and writing (Arum & Roksa, 2011). Though this most recent study is criticized by some for flaws in methodology, approach and claims, it does raise some questions about reading, writing and critical thinking (Haswell, Gunner, Calhoon-Dillahunt & Redd, 2012).

The point here is not to criticize the public schools in the U.S. or elsewhere for their work or to criticize colleges and universities for theirs.

The point is that many people do not have the literacy skills needed to be successful in their education or in their lives, their work, or as citizens. Students and all citizens need reading skills that incorporate new technologies because they are essential to reading in all venues. For example, University of Connecticut reading scholar Donald Leu and his colleagues show that the new digital literacies require foundational reading skills:

> It is essential, however, to keep in mind that the new literacies… almost always build on foundational literacies rather than replace them. Foundational literacies include those traditional elements of literacy that have defined almost all our previous efforts in both research and practice. These include skill sets such as phonemic awareness, word recognition, decoding knowledge, vocabulary knowledge, comprehension, inferential reasoning, the writing process, spelling, response to literature, and others required for the literacies of the book and other printed material. Foundational literacies … will become even more essential because reading and writing become more important in an information age. (Leu et al., 2004, p. 1590-91)

Print-based reading forms the basis for any and all work in our increasingly digital world; moreover, the essential awarenesses and skills used by experts are the same in print and digital environments.

All of this prior work shows a significant weakness in novices' reading abilities and reveals the need for greater understanding of their reading problems and better strategies for addressing them. The lack of meta-textual, meta-contextual and meta-linguistic awarenesses is clear among the novices when their reading habits and strategies are set side-by-side with those of experts in the following set of case studies. While not every participant shows every awareness in the data, the contrasts emerge across all the cases; in addition, the experts all show a full range of skills while the novices have only some skills and do not always use them effectively.

Methodology

The theory of meta-readers and writers being proposed here arose from this series of case studies completed with experts and novices in a format reviewed and approved by my institution's Institutional Review Board for the use of human participants in research. Each case includes some baseline data, an interview and two reading/writing tasks completed by each participant. The interview methodology to draw self-report data was loosely based on the kinds of questions asked by University of Wisconsin literacy scholar Deborah Brandt, discussed in *Literacy in American Lives*

(2001). I asked readers about their personal reading history and their current uses of reading of various kinds, including online reading and textbook reading. With participants' permission, I either administered and scored the Reading portion of the ACT exam, or accessed their scores from their university records if they were students. The reading test is a 35-minute paper and pencil test with four reading passages followed by multiple choice questions about the passage (40 questions total). Some sample questions can be found at http://www.actstudent.org/sampletest/reading/read_01.html.

Then, taking an approach similar to that used by Bazerman (1988), I asked my participants to read two passages of non-fiction prose, one online and one on paper. Each text, when printed out without illustrations, ran around eight to ten typed pages. The task I set was for readers to suppose that they were going to write a report on this topic for school, so they would want to mark the text in preparation for writing a summary to be used in the report. To see their text marking, I asked them to either mark the text (for the paper passage) or to say aloud the first three words of any sentence or section they wanted to mark (for the online passage), which I then marked on a paper copy. I also asked them to say aloud why they chose to mark the parts they did. The reading was done silently, and after ten minutes, participants were asked to write a brief summary of as much of the passage as they had read. The summaries are presented exactly as written by the participants without any editing.

The participants thus provided a kind of think-aloud protocol while reading printed and digital materials drawn from two Wikipedia sites, one online on the history of Michigan's capitol building and the other on the summer Olympic games (these can be found at http://en. Wikipedia .org/wiki/Michigan_State_Capitol and at http://en.wikipedia.org/wiki/Summer_Olympic_Games respectively) These passages were chosen in part because they involved topics that might be of general interest to the participants and in part because they were listed by Wikipedia as "featured" sites, so labeled by virtue of having outstanding content and organization according to the editors. Half the participants received the printed material first and half received the online material first. All interviews and think-aloud sessions were audio-taped with participants' knowledge and consent. Student participants provided written consent for access to their university records for test scores and GPA information.

Participants

There are five Expert readers and eight Novice readers in the study. All participants were volunteers and received the informed consent letter describing this project (see Appendix A). The project was granted exempt status through my university's Institutional Review Board for research with human beings. The Experts were all known to me to be expert readers by virtue of my prior experience with them and by virtue of their careers. The Novices were invited into the study through their instructors in developmental reading, developmental writing or various Honors College courses, or were students in my own sections of these courses. While having one's own students as research participants raises some concern, it was made clear to all the Novices that their participation was entirely voluntary and would have no impact on their grades or class standing; if they were students of other instructors, they were assured that their work in the study would not be shared with their teachers.

Materials and procedure

Participants provided their scores on the Reading portion of the ACT exam and the results of a Myers-Briggs Type Indicator introductory quick survey online (10 minutes). The Myers-Briggs results were not revealing of any consistencies and are not presented in the case reports. If the participants did not have an ACT Reading score, they took the Reading test in 35 minutes, and I scored it, using a sample copy of the exam I obtained from ACT. I recorded all the baseline data on a demographic information sheet (see Appendix B). Participants then completed a 15-30 minute interview on personal reading history (learning to read, early reading in school and out, favorite books in early life and related questions) and current reading practices (time spent reading per day or per week, current reading interests/preferences, digital compared to printed materials and so on; see Appendix C) with me, or in some cases answered these questions online, and completed a short questionnaire on reading challenges on paper (see Appendix D).

The Experts

Introduction

The Experts were invited to participate individually. They are all readers known to me to be Experts by virtue of their work (editor, librarian, university faculty members) and interest in reading as a personal as well as a professional activity. I made some effort to balance these cases in terms of gender and age, though it will be clear that all of the Experts are considerably older than any of the Novices. The expert group is homogenous in terms of its racial composition as well.

Table 2.1. Expert participants' demographic baseline background.

Partipt	Age	Gender	Race	ACT-R
EAF	68	M	W	35
EBD	63	F	W	33
ECO	54	F	W	36
EDT	73	F	W	25
EEM	72	M	W	32

Participant EAF-Baseline data

EAF is a 68 year old college professor at a research intensive institution in the Midwest. His data was collected in December, 2009. His ACT Reading test score was a 35 (all scores are reported on the ACT 0-36 scale). He answered all the questions. On the Reading Challenges questionnaire, he marked understanding tone as a 4 (relatively harder) and reading quickly and efficiently a 3. All the other items were marked 1 or 2, easy for EAF.

Participant EAF-Reading background and current practices

On the background questionnaire, EAF recalled nothing about learning to read, nothing about problems with reading, and nothing about reading in school. He had an idea that he knew how to read before he went to school, but does not know for sure. He remembered that there were copies of *Time* in his house, which he read, as well as a set of encyclopedias, almanacs and atlases which he browsed for facts. He especially liked the atlases. He grew up in New York City and lived a few blocks from a public library branch at 51st and Lexington Avenue to which he could and did go alone.

In elementary school, he remembered liking stories about talking animals, such as a book about Freddy the Pig, a detective story. He also liked science fiction, such as the work of Robert Heinlein.

In terms of current reading habits, he estimates spending about two hours per day reading on paper and about an hour reading online. He reads newspapers, magazines, student work, journal articles and fiction. His preferences tend to run in streaks, as he may read several books by an author he particularly likes. At the time of the conversation, he was reading books by Haruki Murakami such as *The Wind-Up Bird Chronicle*. In terms of textbook reading for teaching purposes, he tends to read quickly for overall goals and structure, then re-reads more carefully looking for details to cover in his teaching. He adds marginal notes and makes separate notes in the second reading. He finds there is much fluff in textbooks these days and not much meat.

Participant EAF-Think aloud comments on Olympics

EAF read the Olympics passage first and read it online on the laptop computer I had brought along to our meeting. In his comments, he mostly responded to facts and new information that surprised him. I neglected to say that he was welcome to follow any links in the passage that he wanted to pursue, but he did not choose any links and did not ask about this option. When he got to writing the summary after ten minutes of reading, which he did on the laptop by choice, he asked if it was timed; he said he could have gone on writing beyond what he provided.

He said there were lots of details on the cities that had hosted the Olympics but that he would not mark these as this was information he could look up easily. He wanted to mark the information about the Wenlock games as this was new information for him, and wanted to mark the fact that there were no women initially but one did get into the Olympics. He marked croquet as an Olympic sport as this was new information for him. He noted Jim Thorpe's achievements and also the stripping of his medals. He marked the 1928 Amsterdam games as having commercial sponsorship, finding it interesting that such sponsorship had not always been true as it appears to be now. He marked the 1936 date of the Berlin games as those are famous, and the 1948 exclusion of Germany and Japan as he did not know about this. He marked 1964 as the first TV year. He was interested in when things started, especially those now taken for granted. He marked the 1972 games as a black mark on the Olympics because of the killings in Munich. He marked also the 1980 and 84 boycotts mentioned in the article.

Participant EAF-Summary of Olympics passage

Modern Olympic Games have their origin in the late 19th century. A major force behind their creation was a Frenchman Baron de Coubertin. The first games were held in Athens, with mostly Greeks competing. Only men were officially allowed to compete at first with the inclusion of women in some sports not sanctioned till after WWI. Various sports have been included and then dropped from the games, for ex. I was surprised to learn that croquet and golf were once Olympic sports. Games are held every 4 years but were suspended during war times (1916, 40 & 44). Most venues have been in European capitols such as Paris, London, Helsinki Athens and the infamous Berlin games of 1936. (118 words)

Participant EAF-Think aloud comments on Michigan capitol passage

EAF read the Michigan passage second and on paper. He also wrote this summary on the laptop. When he began the Michigan passage, he looked through it first to see that it was about history and architecture. He marked little asterisks at various points in the passage and put in a few words in hand-written notes. He noted that the Executive is in the capitol and that it is the 3rd building for the capitol. He was surprised that Michigan's capitol had ever been in Detroit and marked that, along with the move to Lansing. He marked the Toledo controversy as part of the "desire for statehood" and was surprised also that Michigan was forced to accept 3.4s of the Upper Peninsula as part of the deal. The second capitol was built at the time that Michigan was becoming the 26th state.

EAF brought in much prior knowledge to this passage, as with the Olympics where he knew a lot about the Berlin games in 1936, for example. Here, he noted the similarity of Michigan's capitol history to Brasilia as the capitol of Brazil in that there was competition for where the new capitol would be. He marked the use of a tax to fund the capitol as new information, thinking that in general, taxes in 1870 would be unusual. He circled the mention of Myers as an "interesting factoid." He got to the Capitol Today section but said he would not mark the building details even though he found them of interest. Similarly, he found the mention of the muses on p. 4 of interest.

Participant EAF-Summary of Michigan capitol passage

I read an article on the History of Michigan. The capitol of the Michigan territory was originally in Detroit., Michigan Terriotory was established in the first years of the 19th century, having been initially just a part of the northwest territory. When Michigan sought statehood a dispute arose over the boundary with Ohio, specifically regarding the inclusion of Toledo in Michigan. This was resolved about 1835 in Ohio's favor with the proviso that Portions of the Upper Peninsula be included in the state of MI, an idea the Michigan legislators initially rejected for reasons that were not explained in the text.

In the 1840's a decision was made to move the capitol away from Detroit. Two reasons motivated this: Concern over vulnerability to invasion by the British (this had occurred during the war of 1812 when Detroit was occupied). The second reason for a move was to promote the development of the hinterland. Several towns competed for the new capitol (Marshall for one believed they had this sewn up and went so far as to build a governor's mansion) before Lansing was chosen. The article spends considerable detail describing the structure of the various buildings that housed the government of MI both in Detroit and in Lansing, culminating in the current structure designed by Myers around 1870. (213 words)

Participant EBD-Baseline data

EBD is an editor at a commercial book publishing house. She is 63 years old. Her ACT result on the Reading test was a scaled score of 33, with answers to all questions. In her responses to the Reading Challenges questionnaire, she marked only analyzing parts of a text and understanding tone as 3s (a bit more difficult) and all other items a 1 or 2 (easy). This information was collected in February of 2009. Because this participant does not live nearby, she completed the reading background and current practices portion of the study by email.

Participant EBD-Reading background and current practices

Part 1

1. I don't remember learning to read.
2. No problems.
3. Pleasant. Most years I took the basal reader home the first day and read a lot of it--in elementary school.
4. Continuous. Sometimes spent time with friends reading (each of us our own book).
5. Books: The first series I read to myself was The Bobbsey Twins. Later, I loved Nancy Drew, Maida's *Little House*, The Boxcar Children, the Hardy Boys, Trixie Belden, and numerous other series. At nine I read *Little Women*, which was the first book to make me cry. In 5th grade my teacher read the *Little House* books aloud to us. In 6th grade, my teacher read us Edgar Allan Poe stories, including "The Tell-Tale Heart," and "A

Cask of Amontillado," etc. I loved Louisa May Alcott (esp. *Eight Cousins, Little Women* and its sequels, *An Old Fashioned Girl*) and read bios of her and Amelia Earhart around the same time (5th grade?). I loved my friend Eileen Murphy's Catholic school basals (which she owned and I borrowed). My favorite book of all was *Whoa Ginger*, the only thing I ever stole. (The school librarian made fun of me for taking it out so often; the next time, I didn't bother checking it out. I still have it.)

Part 2

1. Reading on paper: 2—4 hours/day. Online: most of the work day--6 hours.
2. see above
3. Newspaper—about 1/2 hour a day; magazines 1/2 hour every third day; books—all the rest, not counting online. Books: theology, philosophy, popular science, modern fiction--junk only (mysteries, thrillers); classic fiction.
4. I don't use textbooks.

Participant EBD-Think aloud comments-passage 1

Looked at no links in the Michigan state capitol passage, read first, online. In this passage, EBD was reading online and reporting aloud the portions that she would have marked had she been reading on paper. She marked National Historic Landmark and third building in the first paragraph. In the second paragraph, she marked the locations, saying that the history was just interesting and that it helped explain why there was a third building built. She marked Neoclassical style, in case she might be asked about its architecture. In the First state capitol section, she marked the Toledo War, finding this new information and somewhat amusing (i.e. that there would be a fight over Toledo). She marked the conditions for Michigan's recognition as a state, accepting much of the UP in lieu of Toledo, noting this might have been a good deal. She marked Detroit as first capitol. In the third paragraph, she marked the first sentence, noting that it was the first of three that the author was setting out to explain. She marked Greek revival as the style of the building. Second state capitol, the heading, was marked, and she noted that this was the second of three in the passage. She marked that Detroit was occupied during the War of 1812, noting this was information about why the capitol needed to be moved. She mentioned that she looked at a picture here in this online passage. In the next paragraphs, she marked several points reflecting her understanding of the appeal of the Lansing location, the relationship of the Lansing structure to the first building and the date, plus the mention of the fire, as it explains why this is the second of three buildings/sites for the capitol. In the Third state capitol section, she marked the date and the words "permanent capitol," along with the style (like the US Capitol building) and the date, noting the time of completion. In the final paragraph of this section, she marked "extensive historical restoration" and Landmark status, noting that these items gave general information about the Capitol and about its design. At the end of ten minutes, she had read about two and half pages.

Participant EBD-Written summary-passage 1

Mich Capitol bldg. is third capitol bldg--a national historic landmark (designated in 1992). First capitol was in Detroit--Italianate in style (neoclassical)--built after the Toledo War which was resolved by MI giving up claims to Toledo in return for getting the western UP (good deal), as a condition of receiving statehood. Statehood was granted in 1837. Detroit had been occupied during the War of 1812, and that contributed fire to the argument to move the capital/capitol instate and away from the Canadian border. Argued for by a state senator b/c he wanted to move it to Lansing, which was pretty empty and more centralized. That was approved and construction of the wood frame 2-story bldg began in 1847. The third bldg, a permanent one, which was dedicated in 1879, was modeled in part after the US Capitol and the 2nd one was made into a factory. Landmark status was awarded in 1992. (154 words)

Participant EBD-Think aloud comments-passage 2

EBD read the Olympics passage second and on paper. She read about as much of this passage as she read of the Michigan capitol passage in the ten minutes of reading time. She misread the opening paragraph as being about the winter Olympics, but marked quadrennial, gold, silver and bronze and the date, 1904. She marked much of the first sentence of the second paragraph, saying that it tells about the Games now, how many there are and what they do. She noted that the passage, making reference to the Beijing Olympics, set for 2008, was old, since she was reading this passage in 2009.

In the fourth paragraph, she marked the first sentence, commenting on American patriotism and noting also that we have hosted the most because we have the most. She skipped all the material on other countries, saying it was of no interest. She marked five countries in the next paragraph, commenting that this part was somewhat unclear in its mention that Greece competed under its own flag—who else's flag would they use? She marked the paragraph on qualification rules saying it explains the rules for the Games. In the last paragraph of this section, she marked the sentence beginning "Nations qualify…" saying that this was more general information that was more interesting than the information about individual sports. At the end of this section, she asked if the writer read this, a comment in response to a note in the passage indicating that a citation was needed at this point.

In the History section, she marked the first sentence up to the date, saying it begins the history, then "promote international understanding" as it explains the purposes. The next paragraph mentions the 1896 launch of the modern Games—a point she marked as giving more of the history. She marked this same information where it is repeated in the following paragraph. To account for continuing the modern Games, she marked the facts about participation rates and the German wrestler who won the most medals. In the next paragraph, she marked the information about the 1900 Games and also 1906 as these are the next points in the history. In the next paragraph, she marked the facts about 11 women, saying women proved themselves worthy to be in the Games. In the paragraph on 1904, she marked the decline information and the whole opening sentence, noting that it explained the smaller size. In the final paragraph she read, she marked the first sentence "A series of smaller games…" without making any comment about why.

Participant EBD-Written summary-passage 2

Summer Olympic games happen every 4 years--org. by International Olympic Committee with the medals (gold, silver, bronze) for winners. Winter games created b/c summer games were so successful. Many more games now included--began w/42, now 302 (roughly) w/10,500 athletes competing. US has hosted 4 times--more than any other country. Five countries have been at all of the games since modern inception, but only Greece in every single one under its own flag (?--not sure what this means). Rules set for athletes competing by International Federation and qualifying tourneys eliminate all but best athletes on national levels. First organized games in Athens in 1896 organized by a Frenchman...(de Coubertin). Big success! Best athlete was a German wrestler. 1900 games held in Paris and women were included (11 of them). After that in St. Louis in 1904 games held but not well attended (too far for most Europeans). Smaller games held in Athens in 06, but these weren't official. (161 words)

Participant ECO-Baseline data

A 54-year-old female librarian is the next participant. She works in a suburban public library in an upper middle class community. Her ACT Reading test scaled score was a 36, based on her answers to all questions and passages. On the Reading Challenges questionnaire, she marked only Analyzing parts of a text as somewhat more difficult (circling a 3) and all the other items as 1 or 2 (easy). This material was collected in May of 2009.

Participant ECO-Reading background and current practices

Participant ECO was a late reader, learning to read in perhaps second grade. Parents read to her and modeled reading as well as supporting school work, but ECO found basal readers boring. In fourth grade she had help as a slow reader. She does not recall exactly what her problem was with reading or how it got solved, but she recalled getting *Little House on the Prairie* as a gift in about third grade, and her interest in that as a story was a key to her success. Her teacher read the book aloud in school, and that also helped.

She also received *The Incredible Journey* as a gift; she recalled reading that and enjoying it, though the ending made her cry.

On the whole, school was limited and under-funded in Steilacoom, Washington on Puget Sound, where ECO grew up. There was a town school through eighth grade, then kids took the bus to HS elsewhere. In school, there was SRA (a box of materials for reading that students could work on independently, including longer passages to build comprehension and higher level skills, known as "Power Builders," and shorter passages that were done as class exercises to build reading speed, known as "Rate Builders." SRA is now owned by McGraw-Hill; the boxed sets of materials are still available; see https://www.mheonline.com/program /view/5/1/109/0076021122). ECO admitted cheating on these to get to a higher level. At home, her father read aloud and told stories. Her parents were older and very focused on the children. They read themselves. There was a daily newspaper. *Little House* books came from the library; newer editions had good illustrations by Garth Williams. Books ECO remembered from elementary school: *Little House* series, the Alcott books, *Five Little Peppers*. There was limited Young Adult (YA) material available, but some in the school library. ECO recalled reading a YA novel called *The Pink Dress*. In eighth grade, she read *Gone with the Wind* and then went on to read other "adult classics."

In her current reading, she is happy if she has a book going, as she has "an alternate universe." Currently, ECO reads the *NY Times* for 45 minutes or so in the mornings, and finds time to read at lunch (30 min.) and in bed at night (30 min.). Many magazines at home, including the *New Yorker, Harper's, Atlantic,* and *Free Inquiry*. ECO reads mostly nonfiction in *New Yorker* as those stories stay with her in contrast to the fiction which she says has weird endings. Most reading at work is online and is in the form of search requests for patrons. ECO's reading preferences include new nonfiction and memoirs. She does not read best sellers unless a book group she is leading has chosen one. ECO prefers challenging books, such as those that win the Booker Prize in Britain. She reads some fiction, memoir, biography and a limited number of mysteries. When a library patron says he or she can't find anything to read, ECO refers to this as "reader's block." Short stories are often a good antidote. Textbooks in school were often hard for ECO. She tried re-reading and/or reading aloud to deal with difficult material.

Participant ECO-Think aloud comments-passage 1

Participant ECO read the Michigan state capitol passage first and read it online. She marked very little and said very little as she was reading it. On the first screen of the Wikipedia article, there is a picture of the capitol building and a caption indicating that there is a statue of Austin Blair in front of the building. ECO was curious and wanted to know who this person was, so she marked the caption. Having been told she was welcome to pursue any link of interest in the online passage, she went to the link for the Toledo War to see that it was "not a real war." It seemed bizarre to fight about this. She marked the Toledo War after looking at the link, saying it was a "bloodless" war and that it seemed like a rotten trade to have gotten the Upper Peninsula in exchange for Toledo.

As she was reading the "Second state capitol" portion she commented that she was never a great marker of texts as she never felt she knew what to mark.

ECO got to bottom of p. 3 at 10 minutes, the end of the second paragraph of the "Capitol today" section.

Participant ECO-Written summary-passage 1

The Michigan State Capitol has been located in Lansing since the last half of the 19th century. The capitol was originally set in Detroit but the pressure of the British troops in Windsor during the War of 1812 and pressure from the western regions of the state led legislators to consider other towns and eventually choose Lansing.

The current building is in fact, Michigan's 3rd capitol building. The first in Detroit was later the city's only high school before being destroyed by fire. The second, a temporary structure in Lansing, was also destroyed by fire. The current capitol was built of fire-resistant materials, a building trend at that time. (109 words)

Participant ECO-Think aloud comments-passage 2

ECO read the Olympics passage second and read this one on paper. She found this passage much harder than the one on the Michigan capitol due to the number of dates and acronyms presented in it. Here again, she said very little and found few points to mark in the passage. She marked the date, 1904, and said it indicated when the current games started. In the printed version of these passages, I left in the underlining that indicates a link in Wikipedia. ECO asked if the underlining was for this purpose and I said yes. She marked nothing else on page 1 of the text.

On page 2, ECO marked "Wenlock Olympian Society" asking what this is/was and whether it was a place. Because she was reading on paper, she had no opportunity to click the link for this item to get an explanation.

At the top of p. 3, she marked croquet, noting it was a funny sport to have in the Olympics. Then she marked "Irish-Americans" commenting that the idea of having a separate competition for Irish-Americans was "weird."

In the paragraph beginning with "The 1908 London Games…" ECO read with her finger following the text on the page. She completed page 3 at just about 10 minutes. As she began writing the summary, she noted that this passage had too many dates and acronyms and was much harder than the first passage.

Participant ECO-Written summary-passage 2

The modern Olympic games started in 1896 in Athens, the idea of a French pedagogue. It was his wish that an international athletic competition would encourage understanding and cooperation between peoples.

The games are now held every 4 years. At both the 2004 and 2008 games, over 10,500 athletes from over 300 nations participated. (54 words)

Participant EDT-Baseline data

Participant EDT is a retired college professor of English who is 73 years old. She completed the ACT Reading portion with a scaled score of 25; she did not answer 5 questions due to careful and precise timing of the test. As this participant is not a student, neither the ACT composite nor a GPA for course work is available.

EDT completed the Reading History and Current Practices questionnaires on the computer on her own, as she lives some distance away. These responses were sent to me by email prior to the reading and think aloud portions of the study.

On the Reading Challenges questionnaire, EDT marked all items on the list of aspects of reading as 1, i.e. easy for her. Her comment about the list was this: "These are teacherly questions; it never occurs to me to factor out these aspects of my reading."

Participant EDT-Reading background and current practices

1. What do you recall about learning to read?

I have no memory of being taught to read; I simply read. No big deal. No fanfare. I know I read pretty advanced stuff well before first grade because I vividly recall a very thin, pale boy made to stand in front of my class and read aloud "The is-land is grrrrr…." The teacher made such fun of him that the kids laughed, and he wet his pants right there on the floor. I felt his embarrassment deeply and wanted to take him aside to explain that the words were "iland" and "green," but I said nothing. I never got up the nerve to talk to him or help him, which made me feel awful.

2. Did you have any problems with reading or learning to read that you recall? Describe these problems and how you solved them if you did.

None. Thing is, my parents paid no attention to my school work (or me), so I was on my own, assuming that was the norm. That was fine and dandy with me.

3.What was your reading experience in school?

Fine. No memories good or bad. I just read. If quizzed, I found the questions truly stupid. I answered as if I took them seriously—HA.

4. What was your reading experience at home or outside of school?

I THINK my mother took me to the local public library once and left in a huff when the librarian said she should not allow me to be looking at books outside the "children's book shelves."

I also recall—this is my only memory about my parents getting involved in my reading—that when I was about eight, I had just finished *Exodus* by Leon Uris (it was on a shelf in the room in our house called "the library"), and I asked my mother if *Battle Cry* by the same author was on some shelf because I wanted to read it. She handed it to me, said I was too young to read it, but then just walked away and said nothing when she saw me reading it. I remember one very raunchy scene that stuck with me for years.

5. Do you recall specific books or authors in elementary school? Which ones?

I only remember thinking that "Dick and Jane" books were beyond stupid and way too easy for me.

Part II: Current Reading Practices

1.How much time do you spend reading now on paper?

About 2-3 hours when I can, more if I have time (all day would be glorious), but less when I have to write to meet writing deadlines. On line? Maybe 15 minutes a day at the most.

2. How much reading do you do online as opposed to on paper?

Almost none.

3. What types of materials do you read?

Books and a few journals which I skim. What do you prefer to read? Novels.

4. How do you handle textbook reading? What strategies do you use? What problems do you have with textbooks, if any?

Heck, I write the things. I try to keep the reading levels easy for college students.

Participant EDT-Think aloud comments-passage 1

EDT read the Olympics passage online first, from the Wikipedia website. She took the description of the task to mean that she needed to read the whole text in 10 minutes, but when I corrected this impression, she slowed down a lot. Because of some difficulty reading on the screen, she copied the text to Word and enlarged it. All the links remained live and I invited her to access any links of interest, but she chose not to look at any.

For the online reading, I was looking at a printed copy of the text. The task was to read silently but to say aloud the first three words of any sentence she would mark with an eye toward writing a summary of this passage to be used in a report on this topic. What she did was to give me a kind of think-aloud of her reading, going much beyond simply indicating what sentences or parts she wanted to mark. She said she would underline various things, figuring there's a topic sentence that gives general idea. She went back to the beginning to see the distinction of summer vs. winter Olympics. Qualification rules: she notes this is an important section that she will need to know to see how nations qualify teams. She marked "For individual sports" and "Nations qualify teams." She marked "modern Olympics founded," saying she would definitely need this information. She said she was skimming this part with an eye toward the summary. She's not particularly interested in history, but she went back to this as a key piece of the text. In the History/Early years part, she skimmed but marked "first edition" and "1896 Summer Olympics" and "Despite many obstacles" as this last piece explains why things happened. She marked "Four years later" and then skipped the next two paragraphs saying she didn't care about it. She marked "1908 London" as this part provides some details. She marked Stockholm 1912 as reflecting growth of the Games. She marked the sentence about the 1916 Berlin games being cancelled, commenting that this was of interest and pertinent due to her Jewish heritage.

In the section on the interwar period, she said she knew things were "crappy," marking "This record only stood." She was developing a thesis about how the Games started, their flourishing, cancellations and restoration. She marked "1928 Amsterdam" and the word females, saying this is important. She marked the 1936 Berlin games re: Hitler. She noted that the passage presents a quick history of WWII, and she marked the paragraph indicating that everything was cancelled due to the war. She skipped the paragraph on the first post war Games in Helsinki, after marking the city, since the rest did not seem important. She marked the paragraph on the 1960 Games in Rome, said she cared about Cassius Clay due to the obvious racism and due to her own early relationships with African Americans. She skipped the Mexico City paragraph. She marked "Politics again intervened..." saying this was very important. I stopped her at End of the 20th century, page 6 of single spaced text.

Participant EDT-Written summary-passage 1

Idea of Olympic games came from ancient Greece but were not started in modern times until 1904. The "idea" of Olympic games was appreciated across nations but the success of the actual games didn't catch on until about 1896. From then until the 1930s, the numbers participating in and attending the games varied greatly.

The games consisted of athletes from various countries competing against each other every four years. Each participating nation established its own criteria for qualifying athletes sent to compete. Soon the winning of medals became a point of national pride. Indeed, when the games were held during the Hitler era in Germany, they were considered proof of the supremacy of the Germanic race.

After WWII, the Olympic games became a dominant site for competition and for advertising, especially once television was ubiquitous, and its related entertainment value. Various succeeding years became known for the various athletes who stood out for their prowess and their popularity. In 1972 tragedy soiled the games because a terrorist group from a Palestine freedom organization assassinated nine Israeli athletes—and five terrorists were also killed in the fire fight. The shadow of this tragedy haunted the games for a few times, and security has been tight. (204 words)

Participant EDT-Think aloud comments-passage 2

Participant EDT read the Michigan State Capitol passage second, on paper. Her initial response upon seeing the topic was to say "boring topic!" She said she'd skip the first part, not caring about the first state capitol. She said she knew she would need to know a little about the history, having to write something about the MI state capitol. She marked the sentence "Michigan began applying" as the fact that it was rebuffed is important. Knowing that Michigan became a state later, so it was "unbuffed," making this part important. She was making a guess about what is coming up in the passage. At the end of the following paragraph, she marked the sentence "Michigan became the 26th state," commenting that it took five years and negotiation to get state status.

She marked "The first building" saying that though this was boring, she knew she had to care about this. In the Second state capitol section she marked nothing but said she knew Detroit was important. She asked aloud what IS the capitol of Michigan? She peeked ahead to see that it is Lansing. By looking through the text but not marking any of it, she saw that the goal was to get the capitol to the middle of the state.

She said it was important to pay attention to the 3rd state capitol. She said she was trying to trace the building development as it seems to be important to the author. She didn't care about measurements. She marked "The cornerstone was laid" and the rest of that paragraph as well as the first sentence of the next paragraph, noting that it was important that it was fireproof. At the end of that paragraph, she marked the sentence about the capitol being a Historic landmark; the third one never burned down.

In The capitol today section, she skipped the first couple of paragraphs about measurements and doorknobs, saying this was information she did not care about. She marked the use of gas and then electric lights as signs of progress. And she marked the "pine that has been wood grained" commenting that it was crafty and dishonest like most politicians. In the Muses section, she marked a sentence about the first floor and one about the second floor, commenting that the pictures in the "Gallery of Governors" would be "ugly pictures of white men" but that she would need this information in the summary.

In the State Senate section, she raised the question of where representatives meet, noting that the passage did not seem to say. Then she went back and did not mark but did find references to the "chambers," that is, meeting rooms for House and Senate, on the 3rd floor. She commented on the fact that both houses appear on TV. She marked the last part of this section, describing each of the chambers. I stopped her at the heading "Grounds" at the top of page 5. She offered many side comments while reading, noting that this passage was quite boring.

Participant EDT-Written summary-passage 2

The Boring Story of the Michigan State Capitol (MSC)

The building of the MSC is located in Lansing, MI. Declared as a National Historic Landmark in 1992.

The "idea" of a capitol started in Detroit in 1837. It took 5 years for the state of M to be accepted as one of the US states, which happened only after the old white men agreed to accept land in the Upper Peninsula and let Toledo go to Ohio.

Various buildings for the MSC were erected. The third survived fires, etc. and is to this day the capitol building. It has been updated (e.g. gas lights were replaced by electric lights in 1900). Within the MSC, there are floors. The first for visitors to see the dome; the second for offices; the third for the galleries for each of the two branches. The senate has 38 members and the House of Reps has 110 members. Each gallery is decorated very differently. (159 words)

Participant EEM-Baseline data

This participant is also a retired college English professor. He is 72 years old. EEM took the ACT Reading section for this project and scored a 32. Since he is not a student, he has no GPA. On the Reading Challenges questionnaire, he marked all of the items in the list a 1 or 2, finding all aspects of reading quite easy. This data was collected in February of 2012.

Participant EEM-Reading background and current practices

EEM completed the reading autobiography and current reading practices questions on his own and gave me a printout of them. He remembered learning to read in kindergarten under the instruction of a beautiful young nun, and had no difficulty learning to read, liked it and was good enough at it to be sent to the Principal's office to read aloud for her. He did not read much at home until fifth grade when he had a teacher who read aloud to the class from the Hardy Boys series. EEM and his classmates became fans and read all the books in the series. In grade school he recalls reading adventure books for boys like the Rick Blaine series, but not reading "real novels until high school—when I fell under the spell of Conan Doyle and Poe."

In his response to the current practices portion of the questionnaire, EEM reported that he reads 2-3 hours per day on paper, and while he writes for a few hours each day, he does almost no "real reading" online beyond checking email or looking up information through search. His reading preferences range from poetry and Shakespeare, to criticism to novels. He often has projects that require reading, such as leading a film discussion group; for these projects, he will read from a variety sources focused on a topic such as a film director or an actor. With regard to textbooks, he no longer uses them as he has retired from teaching, and said that he used textbooks very minimally when he was still teaching, chiefly as sources for terminology or history.

Participant EEM-Think aloud comments-passage 1

This participant read the Michigan capitol passage first and on paper. He was the only participant in this research (including both novices and experts) to complete this passage in the 10 minutes of reading time used in the study. He checked the overall length of the passage before starting to read, but when I saw him do this, I reminded him that he was to go as far as he could in the time allowed. His marking consisted of putting vertical lines in the margins next to things he found interesting or important. In his summary writing on both passages, he looked back at the text.

He marked the last sentence of the first paragraph, noting it was the 3rd and saying he thought this fact was reasonably important. In the History section, he marked the mention of statehood and the dispute over Toledo, saying that the conflict with Ohio was significant historically because it needed to be resolved prior to statehood for Michigan. At the top of page 2, he marked the date of the move of the capitol to Lansing, saying it was an important milestone. In the Second state capitol section, he marked the last sentence of the first paragraph, saying it explained the two reasons for the move. In the next paragraph, he marked the second sentence concerning the city of Marshall, commenting that there was some whimsy about the location of the capitol; Marshall makes the most sense based on location. In the third paragraph of this section, he marked the sentence describing the cupola as a matter of art history; a cupola seems to be required for government business. He reached the top of page 3 after about 5 minutes of reading time. He marked the first sentence of the last paragraph in the Third state capitol section, saying it was just interesting, particularly the fireproofing. He also marked the sentence in that paragraph about the restoration of the building and noted the effort to make the building accessible for the disabled, part of a "nice historical development," he said. In the Capitol today section, he marked the first sentence in the first paragraph about the Muses, saying that the information about the ceiling was interesting and that he was surprised that such work would appear in a government building. The fact that this information seems odd jogged his attention. He also commented on the first sentence of the second paragraph on the Muses, saying he would not mark it as it was expected that the building would have government offices. In the Grounds section, he marked the first and second sentences, saying that the Native American representation of the state was interesting as it indicated official recognition by the state. He marked the first sentence of the third paragraph, concerning the Eastern White Pine and

Martin Luther King trees as this was new information for him. About 10 minutes had elapsed and EEM had completed the passage.

Participant EEM-Written summary-passage 1

There have been three state capitols in Michigan.

The first was in Detroit, owing to its defense-ready position across the river from Canada and was erected after Michigan became a state in 1835 after a border dispute with Ohio, over the Toledo River [sic], was satisfactorily resolved.

The second state capitol was erected in 1847 by which time a decision to move the capitol from Detroit to then-unoccupied Lansing had been made. Lansing provided a more central location and it was thought the move would spur development throughout the state. It did.

The first capitol, still in Lansing, was begun in 1871—a suitably grand structure to house the state government and reflect the state's greatness.

Originally, it housed all state governmental offices—a condition no longer possible.

Two noteworthy items are, inside, portraits of the 8 muses on the ceiling, and, outside, interesting trees—the Eastern White Pine, the state tree, and a tree dedicated to the memory of Dr. Martin Luther King, Jr.

Finally, it is noteworthy that 'Michigan' is personified, in a painting, as a Native American female. (181 words)

Participant EEM-Think aloud comments-passage 2

EEM read the Olympics passage online, following the Michigan passage. He marked the first sentence of the second paragraph, saying that the numbers of events and participants was huge and surprising. He marked the first sentence of the third paragraph, about the US hosting four times, saying this was new information. It was clear by time he got to the bottom of the first page that he was reading the online passage much more slowly than the one on paper. At the end of page 1, he marked the last sentence about Britain being the only country to win a gold medal in every summer games as it was a "factoid." In the History section, he marked the last sentence in the first paragraph, and then went to the link for Much Wenlock, finding out that it was a small town in England. He read a little bit of the linked material and then returned to the Olympics passage, probably less than 2 minutes total. (No other reader looked at this link in this passage.) He marked the last sentence of the second paragraph in the Early years of the history section, where a woman entrant is mentioned, saying "That's the spirit!" And he marked the first sentence of the next paragraph on the 1896 games, saying that it was interesting that these were not international, but a Greek revival. In the fifth paragraph, he marked the last sentence about Greece's role, saying it was interesting. In the next paragraph, he marked the numbers of women and the mention of croquet as recognizing women's "official" role and as new information, respectively. In his comments, though he did not get to the section that mentions the 1936 Games, he noted that he knew a lot about the 1936 Games because he knew about the Nazi influence and had studied the films of Leni Riefenstahl and read about her life and work for a film group he leads. In the paragraph on the 1908 London Games, he marked the comment about the winner of the first marathon, a Greek water-carrier, saying that the run would surely have built up his legs. He also marked the sentence about the change in the distance and rationale for that, commenting that there was a relationship between sports and politics. At the end of this paragraph, 10 minutes had elapsed and so EEM stopped reading and wrote his summary of this passage.

Participant EEM-Written summary-passage 2

The revival of the ancient Greek games began with I Olympiad in Athens in 1896—the brain child of a French aristocrat and "pedagogue," Baron de Coupertin.

They were based, surprisingly enough, on annual games held in Much Wenlock, a British town in Shropshire, founded in 698 (or so).

So, the 1896 games already had ancient and international roots.

The modern marathon distance was increased by slightly over 2 kilometers so that the finish line would be right in front of the British royal family. This alteration occurred in the 1908 games.

The games became a great success—today, ten thousand [sic] athletes compete in over 300 games—and they are held every four years.

So great is the success of the games that all the great cities and countries compete avidly for the honor of hosting them.

And the Winter Games also testify to the great success of the Olympics. (151 words)

The Novices

Introduction

Table 2.2. Novice participants' demographic baseline background.

Partipt	Age	Gender	Race	ACT-R
NFW	19	F	C	31
NGZ	18	M	AA	18
NHS	18	F	C	n/a
NJL	20	M	C	34
NKT	18	F	AA	18
NLW	18	F	C	21
NMJ	19	F	AA	12
NNW	20	M	Asian	17

Participant NFW-Baseline data

NFW is a 19 year old female. Her ACT scores include a Reading score of 31 and a composite score of 28. Her college GPA is 3.68 as of November, 2009 (university record accessed with student's express consent). She is enrolled in the Honors College program and is a college sophomore. On the Reading Challenges Questionnaire, Participant NFW marked most items a 1 or a 2 (easy), circling a 3 for "Putting together ideas from different texts" and for "Knowing an author's purpose or intent" and "Noticing a writer's bias, preferences or opinion." Thus, some of the higher order critical reading skills present a bit more of a challenge for this reader.

This material was collected in November of 2009.

Participant NFW-Reading background and current practices

In the reading history interview, Participant NFW reported no recollection of learning to read; she went to school already knowing how to read. She had no problems with reading or learning to read and enjoyed it. In school, she liked reading aloud; in particular, she recalled the whole class reading the *Frog and Toad* stories together and enjoying that experience. There were many books at home and from the public library. She recalled reading Goosebumps, and liking other mystery/horror types of books. She remembered *Goodnight Moon*, Grimm's fairy tales, the *Narnia* books and *Bridge to Tarabitha* among other fastasy works. She did not read series books such as those about horses or the *Babysitters' Club* series. In high school, she recalled reading books by Anne Rice and a number of classics such as *East of Eden*, and *The Great Gatsby*, as well as more contemporary books such as *The Kite Runner*. Commenting on the popular vampire stories in the *Twilight* series, NFW said shc thought of those as books for people who don't read or like to read—too easy. She also said she did not like to see movies based on books she has read and liked because in general, "movies ruin books."

In terms of time spent, Participant NFW reports reading about three hours per week online, chiefly for an online class. In addition, she reports spending five to six hours reading textbooks for school. Her current preferences for personal reading are fiction, including science fiction and fantasy.

To deal with textbook reading, this subject sets up a schedule so that reading time is structured by breaks and snacks. She plans this time carefully. She takes notes following the structure or plan provided by the book she is reading, but does not make use of questions or other apparatus provided in texts. If the material is difficult, she will take a break and then re-read more slowly. If she still has difficulty, she will ask about the material in class.

Participant NFW-Think aloud comments-passage 1

Participant NFW read the Michigan State Capitol passage first, online. She marked the first sentence because it is the intro and explains the passage and gives the location. In paragraph 2, she marked the first sentence as important new information and because it gives the rationale for the move. Then she marked the "The present capitol…" because it was moved and had a new form. In the History section, she marked "Toledo Strip" noting that there was a "squabble" that developed into a war. She marked "By 1835" as it was the first step to the capitol. In the paragraph "The dispute culminated" she marked the last two sentences. The one on the Upper Peninsula she found ironic, since she knew there are important resources in the UP. The last sentence she also marked because it was about Michigan becoming a state and was important for that reason. She marked "The first building…" in the next paragraph as it shows the evolution. Then she marked the part "until 1848" (top of p. 2) because it explains why the Capitol was moved. She then reported skimming the whole article to see that it included History, 1st, 2nd, and 3rd now—she scrolled up and down in the text while noting this order of the information. In the "Second State Capitol" section, she marked the paragraph that begins “Prior to 1847” –first sentence because it provides the reason for the 2nd capitol, the security issue. And she marked the last sentence saying that it was also about security (it isn’t, but that’s what she said).

At ten minutes, she was halfway down page 2 on the printed version of the passage.

Participant NFW-Written summary-passage 1

The Michigan State Capitol was originally located in Detroit in a Greek-style brick building used previously as a courthouse. Felt the need to move due to growing economy/activity on western side of the state. Lansing chosen as cite [sic], hastily-constructed wooden building. Renovated in 1992. Also moved due to security threat from Canada and its British troops. (57 words)

Participant NFW-Think aloud comments-passage 2

In this reading on paper, NFW got about as far as she did on the State Capitol passage. Since she was reading this one on paper, she marked various parts with underlining using a pen. In paragraph 1, she noted that the text provided background and info on the medals and 1904 as the start. There was no system. The winter games were started because of summer’s popularity. In paragraph 2, she marked the numbers. She said that going from 42 to 300 shows expansion as does the addition of women. The mention of Beijing also shows the expansion. In paragraph 3, she marked NOC and “recognized nations” because these points explain that entrance is done by committee and how the athletes are chosen to participate. In paragraph 4, she marked the US hosting 4 times as showing the US influence, then also marked the UK and others as hosting most in order of their influence. She marked the mention of China as important because of its economy and power. In paragraph 5, she thought that 5 countries in all Olympics competitions was interesting. She also marked the mention of Greece as the original location. She also marked the fact that Britain won gold in every Games and was surprised that this was not true of the US. On page 2 under Qualification she marked “International Federation” at the top and then the rules in the paragraph “For individual sports” noting that there are rules and it is not random. The IF ranking tells how athletes get in. She thought the NOC choices and selection process were interesting. In “Nations qualify…” she underlined the sentence “The host nation…” and said the automatic qualification makes sense. Under “History” she only read the first paragraph. She circled 1894 and underlined the first sentence. She said this was important as it tells the founding date. She was surprised that the goal was international understanding and that the person who started the games was not interested in sports and was not Greek.

Participant NFW-Written summary-passage 2

> Summer Olympics started in mid-late 1800s by French guy for international cooperation/understanding. Medals awarded. Gold, silver, bronze awarded later in early 1900s. US hosted Olympics 4 times (most), then Great Britain, three times. Great Britain only country to win gold medal every year. Has expanded significantly from less than 100 events to over 300 and from 250 males to 10,000 of both sexes. Committee decides which athletes compete if benchmark limit has been reached. Host country gets automatic ins. (79 words)

Participant NGZ-Baseline data

NGZ is an 18-year-old male student new to the university, so he did not have an overall GPA. His ACT composite score was a 17 and his Reading test score was an 18. He was enrolled in the "Reading and Critical Thinking" class by recommendation at Orientation, due to the Reading score being below 19. In the Reading Challenges survey, he marked only drawing inferences and putting ideas together from different texts as 3 on a 5 point difficulty scale (5 is hard). He marked 2 for speed, summary, analysis, author purpose, and bias and 1 for vocabulary, use of reading in discussion and understanding tone. The data is this case was collected in October of 2011.

Participant NGZ-Reading background and current practices

In his reading autobiography questionnaire, NGZ remembered that when he was learning to read, he was told to sound out words and move slowly through the text. He definitely learned to read in school. He had some problems with learning to read in school and was involved in a program through Title 1. He took a test in second grade that sent him to the Title 1 program for help with comprehension. It definitely was helpful. He found reading in school was some fun, but avoided reading aloud if possible. Reading at home helped him. Although he had no public library experience at home, he did choose to read when he could and got books as gifts. The only book or author he could recall was Dr. Seuss. No series or particular reading experiences or favorite authors or re-reading. Whatever book was available he picked up and read.

In terms of his current reading, he spends an hour a day reading textbooks for his classes and his ten pages per day, required for reading class, and about 3 hours reading various items online, including social networking. Given time and a choice, he prefers to read autobiographies or life stories. He was reading *Gifted Hands* about pediatric neurosurgeon Ben Carson and was looking forward to starting a book by Hill Harper, the *CSI* star on television.

To deal with textbooks, NGZ tries to summarize sections in his head as he reads. He uses a highlighter, makes notes on paper, or uses sticky notes, a strategy learned in class. He finds these strategies very helpful. Reading with strategies improved his grades from a D to an 82, with doing reading and using a strategy as opposed to not at all.

Participant NGZ-Think aloud comments-passage 1

NGZ read the Michigan capitol passage first, on paper. Dates are always important, relevant to capitol. He marked the description of how it was made ("The present capitol"). He marked the Toledo war sentence as a "detail about the passage." Date 1835 plus info about the Constitution. He highlighted this because it's a good detail about the capitol and the constitution within the capitol.

This participant did not say much or mark much of this passage.

He marked more description (bottom of p. 2) of capitol that was built. He marked Texas on p. 3 but did not give a reason.

At the end of 10 minutes, he was at end of first full paragraph on page 3.

Participant NGZ-Written summary-passage 1

In today's society we all are aware of where our state capital Building is located. In recent decades, Michigan State Capital was not located in Lansing but in one of the poor Urban Cities we know of today. Detroit Michigan was the City where our State Capital and government workers was located. In the middle 1800s, Canada and Michigan began to have a dispute because the governor wanted to move the Capital Building to Lansing. Citizens in Detroit didn't agree, nor did Canada. Canada felt that if the Capital Building was in Detroit they would be right next to each other. Michigan governor said NO because it would increase our economy if we moved to we did. Now as we look today, Michigan State Capital is in Lansing Michigan. (128 words)

Participant NGZ-Think aloud comments-passage 2

NGZ read the Olympics passage second, online. He marked first sentence as definition, then 1904 as a key date. He did not say much or mark much of this passage as he read it online. He did not pursue any links, though he was invited to do so. He marked "The modern Olympic games…1894" for the date. He marked the Intl. Olympic committee, saying it defines what it was. He marked nothing else. He stopped after 10 minutes near the end of the Interwar era section.

Participant NGZ-Written summary-passage 2

> To this day many people don't understand where the World Olympic's come from. The World Olympic's comes from another Country Greese. The Olympic's is a searies of games ranging from swimming, Track all the way to snow boarding. In the past decades, the Olympic's have reached Paris, Winsor Canada and the United States. Along with a searies of games there are many of great prizes. The prizes are medals (Silver, Gold, Bronze). Many people enjoy playing these games not for the medals but, for the fun and excitement. The Olympics happen every year, So when you hear about it go and attend. (102 words)

Participant NHS-Baseline data

Participant NHS is a female student who was enrolled in a first-year writing course at a medium-sized public university in the Midwest. She had no ACT scores at admission to the university. Her overall GPA was a 3.5. On the Reading Challenges questionnaire, NHS marked only "Putting together ideas from different texts" as a 4 (relatively difficult), and marked four other items as a 3: inferences, analysis, tone and purpose. All other items were marked as 2s. This data was collected in October of 2008.

Participant NHS-Reading background and current practices

NHS read a lot as a child and recalled that she knew how to read before school. She did not recall being taught by her parents, but was read to a great deal and thought she just "figured it out" in those parent reading sessions. She had no problems with reading in school. Like most students, she knew that she was in the more advanced reading group and she also worked with a different teacher in a special group for more advanced students. She enjoyed reading and while her parents didn't take her to the library that she remembered, there were always books at home; she also received books as gifts from her grandparents. She remembered reading *Amelia Bedelia* as a child and also the books in the *Babysitters' Club* series.

In terms of current reading practices, NHS claimed to spend about three hours per day reading, with very little of that time spent online. She read information for her classes and spent a little time on Facebook, but overall, did very little reading online. If time allows, she prefers to read something like *The Guardian*, a suspense novel, and also romance novels like *The Sisterhood of the Traveling Pants*. For textbook reading, NHS uses skimming, highlighting and annotation as strategies. If the material is boring, she finds it hard to focus, so she re-reads or just keeps going.

Participant NHS-Think aloud comments-passage 1

NHS read the Olympics passage first, on paper, and made extensive annotations on the text as she was reading. In the margin of the first paragraph, she wrote the word definition, and underlined "quadrennial" saying that she was not sure of the meaning. In the second paragraph, she noted in the margin #s (facts) and said that the specifics of numerical information caught her attention. She underlined the last sentence of paragraph 3, writing the note "why?" at the end, and also wondered about and noted the first sentence of paragraph 4, writing "why?" in the margin there as well. The next paragraph summarizes places the Olympics have been held, so she wrote in the margin "places hosted." She circled "IF" saying that she was not sure what this was. She marked the last sentence of the first section, noting that it was unfair for the host nation to be able to qualify any athlete; host nations should also have to qualify. She said at this point that she liked to write about her opinions. In the History section, she marked the name of de Coubertin, saying that the name of the founder was important for overall understanding. In the following paragraph, she underlined the information about female athletes, noting the margin "NOT fair!" She marked the quote from the woman marathoner, commenting that she was the only woman in the Games. In the last paragraph on page 2, she circled Panathinaiko Stadium, and wrote in the margin "where? Why largest crowd?" and had also underlined those words in the text. On page 3 in the second paragraph, she marked "11 women" and wrote in the margin "what allowed this many women?" asking what changed to cause this participation. In the third paragraph on page 3, she underlined the first sentence, put a star in the margin and noted "first time in the United States." At this point, ten minutes had elapsed and she stopped reading to write the summary. As she was writing, she looked back at the passage.

Participant NHS-Written summary-passage 1

The summer Olympic Games have been an important part of nations being able to come together to accomplish something. The Olympics are an athletic competition of mostly recognized nations and some sovereign disputed nations. They compete in events that range from track and field to swimming. Many different places have hosted the Olympics from when it started in 1894 to the present. (62 words)

Participant NHS-Think aloud comments-passage 2

NHS read the Michigan capitol passage second and read it online. She got about as far with this passage as with the Olympics passage, about the middle of the third printed page of the passage. In this reading, she provided a commentary, indicating what she would mark and why, with a bit more detail since she was looking at the text on a computer screen.

In the first paragraph, she marked the first sentence and the last, noting that the opening described the government to define the capitol, and that the last sentence offers further explanation. In the second paragraph, she marked "for easy defense" because it gives history. In the History section, she marked "Toledo War" and clicked that link to see what it was. She said that this eventually leads to the University of Michigan/Ohio State rivalry in sports, a point of interest from her prior knowledge of sports relationships. Having read about the Toledo War, she returned to the Michigan passage and continued reading. In the third paragraph, NHS marked the first sentence as an example of courthouse use, and circled the $24,500 figure on the last printed line of the text on that page, commenting that it is not what it would cost now. She marked "burned in 1893" because it explains the second state capitol. In the Second state capitol section, she marked the first sentence of the second paragraph "Contenders seeking designation…" saying that the meaning of this part was not clear and she would have put a ? in the margin if she were reading this passage on paper. In the next paragraph, she marked the first sentence, with the comment "Why this?" and noting some conflict or confusion about the various dates as there was an earlier mention of 1893. In this part of the reading, she scrolled up to review this section of the text. Then she moved on to the Third state capitol section, marking $1.2 million, noting that this is a big jump from the prior dollar figure. In the next paragraph, she circled "Tuebor" finding it interesting and by way of summary at this point said design, architecture, why chosen—these are words she would have written in a paper margin. At the end of the section, she followed the link to the "National Register of History Places" to get an idea, she said, of what this is and what others are in it. In the link, she moved directly to the section marked "Criteria for selection." At this point, the ten minute time frame ran out and she did not go back to the Michigan passage. She said she followed the link to see specifically how buildings were chosen.

Participant NHS-Written summary-passage 2

> Any states [sic] capitol building is an important part of the state due to the fact that it houses the legislative and executive branches. There were three different capitol buildings that were built over the years, ranging in costs. The uses for this building differed some, depending on the time period, but for the most part the reasons have stayed the same. The third capitol building was a part of the National Register of History Places, which is difficult to gain the criteria to do so [sic]. (87 words)

Participant NJL-Baseline data

Participant NJL is a 20-year-old male student who was enrolled in the Honors College program at my institution. His ACT Reading score was 34 and his overall GPA a 3.4. On the Reading Challenges questionnaire, he marked as relatively difficult summary, analysis, synthesis, and use of material in writing or discussion, as well as noticing bias or opinion. All of the other items he rated as relatively easy. This data was collected in October of 2008.

Participant NJL-Reading background and current practices

NJL's reading background begins with his knowing how to read when he went to school. He was praised a lot for reading when young; in the early years he liked literature and short stories and read with his parents. He recalled no problems with reading as a child. In elementary school, his reading was encouraged by books from the school library and a reading program that allowed him to earn points toward prizes. His reading preferences included the *Harry Potter* series through book 4, but he said he might continue to read those in Japanese, the language he was studying at the university. He also recalled reading *Brave New World* and *The Fountainhead* along with fantasy books in high school. NJL's current reading practices included about 30 minutes per day of online reading, and about 45 minutes per day of school material, read on paper. His current reading preferences included fantasy novels such as the *Dragon Lance* series and a book called *Song of Fire and Ice*. For textbook reading, if he had difficulty, his strategy was to re-read the text and sometimes to look at but not make use of questions at the ends of chapters. He did make use of a Glossary if there was one in the book and reported trying to follow and fill in the steps if he was reading math.

Participant NJL-Think aloud comments-passage 1

NJL read the Michigan capitol passage first and read it online. He found the passage difficult and stopped early on to ask what the task was and to have some context for what he was supposed to do. He also made the observation that Wikipedia condenses the most important information about a topic. He used the cursor, moving the mouse to follow the text while reading. He marked the first sentence saying it provided a definition and gave the branches of the government. He marked the first sentence of the second paragraph, commenting that the capitol had not always been in Lansing. He marked the first and second sentences of the first paragraph under the "First state capitol" section, saying it was about state creation and why the capitol was needed, as well as the establishment of the Michigan Territory preceding the need for a capitol. He followed the link for "Michigan Territory" to find out what this was and returned to the text after just a few seconds. He scrolled up and down in the text a bit, seeming to have trouble following it. In the second paragraph of the First state capitol section, he marked the last sentence, commenting that it indicated when Detroit was the capitol. He marked the first sentence of the next paragraph because it indicated when the capitol was first built. At 10 minutes, he was just up to the Second state capitol section, and stopped there.

Participant NJL-Written summary-passage 1

The capitol was originally located in Detroit and build in 1832. The capitol was moved to Lansing. (17 words)

Participant NJL-Think aloud comments-passage 2

NJL read the Olympics passage second and on paper. In this passage, he marked the very first sentence, saying it gave a summary and tells the time frame. He also circled the word "quadrennial" and said he would look it up if he were reading online. He marked the first sentence of the second paragraph, again because it tells the time and more about the development of the Games. In the third paragraph, he marked the first sentence again, looking back at this part after reading further in the passage. In the fourth paragraph he marked the first sentence saying that this information might be important if he was asked who has hosted the Olympics the most. In the last paragraph on page 1, he marked the "Five countries" sentence, the "Summer Olympic Games" phrase and the reference to Great Britain without any particular comment other than it was important content and because Britain got a medal in every round of the Games. NJL looked back at page 1 after he turned to page 2, having seen how competitors enter. On page 2, he marked "individual sports" and "major international event," asking aloud "How do they qualify?" In the last paragraph of the section, he marked "Nations qualify teams" and most of the rest of that line, saying that it was how *teams* qualify while the prior paragraph was on how individuals qualify. In the History section, he marked "modern" and the date and name, saying this information told him the year and who started the Games. In the next paragraph, he marked "Athens in 1896, saying that this information indicated when the first of the modern Olympics was held. In the third paragraph he marked the official name and date, saying that this was what the title was. At 10 minutes of reading time, he was almost to the bottom of page 2.

Participant NJL-Written summary-passage 2

Individuals qualify by getting NOC approval from the nation they will be representing. The summer Olympic Games went from a 45 event, 205 person event to over 300 events and 11,000 participants. Great Britain has gotten a gold in every summer Olympic Games. Countries that have been in every game: Great Britain, Greece, Switzerland (there were 5). Founded in 1894, first one in 1896. (64 words)

Participant NKT-Baseline data

This participant is an 18-year-old female whose ACT Reading score was an 18, so she was just below the score at which the university recommends students take the Critical Thinking and Reading class in which she was enrolled. Her university GPA was a 3.15 when this data was collected, in October of 2008. On the Reading Challenges questionnaire, she marked putting together ideas (synthesis) and purpose as 4s, and five items as 3s: speed, inference, analysis, tone, and bias. The other items were 2s, relatively easy.

Participant NKT-Reading background and current practices

In the interview on her reading history, NKT reported that she learned to read in school and that she had no problems with reading in school, though she read faster at home. She was not always a good reader, partly because she is a very social individual. In 5th grade, she was in a separate group of some kind due to a low score on the Michigan Educational Assessment of Progress (MEAP) test. This help entailed some kind of separate class. She did not recall specific details about it. She recalled learning the alphabet at home; her sister made her a tape for help. She did not do much reading at home but looked occasionally at library books. She recalled reading nursery rhymes and Dr. Seuss books such as *Green Eggs and Ham* and *The Cat in the Hat*.

In her current reading, she claimed to spend 3-4 hours per day reading school material. Online, she thought she was probably spending 2-3 hours per week. In terms of choices, she preferred reading fiction and about politics, so she read the *New York Times* online or on paper for this interest. In dealing with textbooks, she was trying a new approach of reading her class notes first and then the text, and really working on vocabulary. She said she also tried reading a chapter summary first before reading a textbook chapter, but did not use the textbook questions or other apparatus. In her Biology class, she was enrolled in a Supplemental Instruction session (study support led by a trained peer in the discipline) but found that the leader's use of textbook questions was not always helpful to her.

Participant NKT-Think aloud comments-passage 1

NKT read the Olympics passage first online. In the opening paragraph, she marked the last two sentences, about medals and the winter Games, saying these parts explained how athletes place and why the Games were created. The first sentence of the next paragraph was marked as it explains how many events there are. The first and last sentences of the next paragraph were marked also, as NKT said that these explain why and how the bigger countries are involved. In the next paragraph, she marked the first sentence, saying it showed that the US had more than others. In that same paragraph, she marked the sentence listing the cities that have hosted twice, to show where the Games have been. She marked the whole of the next paragraph (the last on page 1) because it tells all the countries involved, shows how Greece is distinctive, and tells about every round of the Summer Games. NKT marked the first sentence under the Qualification heading, as it tells who runs and governs the events. She also marked the first sentence in the "For individual sports" paragraph, saying it explains the International Federation requirements to get into events. In this section, she marked the very last sentence about host nations automatically qualifying, noting that this was important. In the History section, she marked the first sentence about the founding as it gives the important reason to promote the Games. She marked the first sentence of the next paragraph (second paragraph in History section) as it shows the numbers and which countries were involved, as well as the last sentence on the role of women, saying this was important history. She finished the end of this second paragraph in the History section at 10 minutes of reading time.

Participant NKT-Written summary-passage 1

> The summer Olympic Games were created to promote international sporting events from every country. The Games, originally called, did not go that well. Today the games are hosted by big cities around the world. To qualify for the Olympics you have to meet the IF's standard. The country that hosts the games are automatically qualified into each event. The US has hosted the games more times than any other country. The most recent city to host the Olympics was Beijing in 2008. (82 words)

Participant NKT-Think aloud comments-passage 2

NKT read the Michigan capitol passage on paper as her second passage. She marked the first and second sentences of the passage as explaining why it is the building for the capitol and its location. She also marked the first sentence of the second introductory paragraph as indicating the location and why it was changed. She marked the last sentence, which offers an explanation for the re-dedication of the capitol. In the History section beginning with the First state capitol, she marked the section beginning "Michigan began applying…" and much of the rest of that paragraph, saying it explained the dispute with Ohio over property. She marked the last sentence, with the comment that the state was formed without authorization. In marking "The dispute culminated" she said that this part tells about the Toledo War. In that paragraph, NKT marked the last sentence as it reports when Michigan became a state and when and where the capitol was at that time. On page 2, she marked all of that rest of the paragraph ("…until 1848") as it explains when the capitol was moved and how the old building became a high school and burned down. In the Second state capitol section, she marked the "reasons for moving inland" section, noting the need to get away from Canada due to the War of 1812 and the Detroit occupation during that time. In the following paragraph, she marked the first sentence, saying Lansing was not the only city contending for the capitol. And she marked the second to last sentence in that paragraph, saying it explained why the legislature decided the location. At this point, ten minutes had expired.

Participant NKT-Written summary-passage 2

> Michigan wanted to become a seperate [sic] state in the late 1800s. The independence of Michigan struck a war between Michigan and Ohio. The dispute was mainly over territory, who would get Toledo and other surrounding cities. Michigan set up its own government before it was agreed upon by Congress. The original capital of Michigan was Detroit. Citizens thought that to westernize the state we should move the city over. There were many other cities who wanted to be the capitol but the legislature decided on Lansing. The state also wanted to be freed from proximity with Canada. At the time, a war was going on at [sic] with army camps set up, the distance from Detroit and Windsor was less than a mile. (124 words)

Participant NLW-Baseline data

This participant is a female who was enrolled in the Critical Thinking and Reading course even though her ACT Reading score was 21 and so was above the level at which the university recommended students take the reading class. Her overall GPA was a 2.8 in October of 2008 when this data was collected. She was 18 at the time of the study. On the Reading Challenges questionnaire, she marked only tone as a 4, but speed, summarizing and using material in writing or discussion as 3s and the rest of the items as 1 or 2.

Participant NLW-Reading background and current practices

Participant NLW learned to read in school and knows she is dyslexic. In school, she read words backwards and said this sometimes still happens. However, in school she had more difficulty with math than with reading as a result of her dyslexia. She got extra help from a teacher after school as well as from her parents, but did not recall and specific strategies that were helpful. She remembered reading Dr. Seuss books and liked the sounds and rhymes. Overall, her reading is quite slow.

In her current reading, NLW estimated that she spent about an hour a day reading printed material and 30-45 minutes online. She preferred to read humor material, magazines and library books. In dealing with textbooks, she felt that her level of motivation was key. She made no use of textbook questions or apparatus but used a strategy of re-reading and highlighting so that she would re-read highlighted material on the second pass. She also made flash cards to learn key concepts.

Participant NLW-Think aloud comments-passage 1

NLW read the Michigan capitol passage first, and read it on paper. She underlined the words "Michigan State Capitol" which appear in bold type on the print out, saying that they tell the topic of the passage. She marked the date at the end of the second paragraph, saying that the dedication might be on a test. In the History section, she marked the Toledo War sentence as an explanation of what happened. Because it "seemed important," she underlined the last sentence of the Toledo War paragraph concerning the date of statehood and mentioning Detroit as the capital. She also marked the phrase "territorial courthouse" at the bottom of the page, though she said she was not sure why, but that it might appear on a test. She moved on to page 2 after about 6 mintues. At the top of page 2, she marked the date of the move of the capital to Lansing as a big fact. In the Second state capitol section, she marked only the last sentence of the second full paragraph about the legislature renaming Lansing, and then changing the name back, saying she would need to know why this happened. At the end of 10 minutes, she was at the bottom of page 2 of the passage.

Participant NLW-Written summary-passage 1

> Detroit went through many state capitals. They had a war on where to set the capital, which ended up in Lansing. They had to rebuild it twice because of a fire. (31 words)

Participant NLW-Think aloud comments-passage 2

NLW read the Olympics passage online as her second reading. For the online passage, readers were asked to say the first three words of any sentence or part they wanted to mark, and as with the paper passage, to explain why they chose that part to mark. NLW marked the first sentence of the passage, saying that it provided a definition. In paragraph 3, she marked the name of the National Olympic Committee as important because it showed that there *is* a committee. She marked the fact that the

US has hosted four times, saying the number was of interest. She marked the mention of the International Federation, explaining that this group was needed for qualification. She got to the History section after about 4 minutes of reading time. The first sentence of "The early years" section accounted for how the Olympics got started, providing background. In the third paragraph of that section, NLW marked "Ancient Greece was the birthplace" noting that this section explained where the Games were formed. In the seventh paragraph, she marked the first sentence, "Numbers declined for the 1904…" as it explains why the US had a lower turnout. At the end of 10 minutes, she was up to "The interwar era" heading and stopped there. NLW read almost twice as much of the Olympics passage as she had of the Michigan passage.

Participant NLW-Written summary-passage 2

> The Olympics started off out of the US in Greece. When it did move to St. Louis one year, the numbers decreased. They said right from the start it was a big hit, which has grown to thousands of people now. (41 words)

Some additional data

Two additional novices warrant discussion here. One of these is a participant with an unusual personal history that had a definite impact on her reading abilities. The second is a participant who is a native speaker of Vietnamese, and who did not arrive in the United States until he was seven years old. He is fully bilingual in Vietnamese and English.

Participant NMJ-Baseline data

Participant NMJ is a 19-year-old female with an unusual personal history. Her ACT Reading score was 12 and her overall, composite ACT was 13. Her university GPA based on her first term in college stood at 2.4.

Participant NMJ-Reading background and current practices

When she was asked about learning to read, NMJ said that she had some problems with reading because she moved around frequently as she grew up in foster care and had aged out of the system (that is, she reached the age of 18 without having had a permanent home). She had a hard time learning to read without phonics instruction and thus could not pronounce many words. She also claimed that she is a poor test-taker, but willing to work hard to learn. She found the reading course in which she was enrolled helpful in terms of developing better reading and study habits, but still found reading such as the book *Arc of Justice*, assigned in her class, very difficult. She noted that like all readers, her level of interest in the assigned material is a key factor in whether she can read a particular text. She reported very limited reading experience at home or in school, and no contact with libraries at home or in school. About the only book she recalled was one called *Antoine Fisher*.

In her current reading, Participant EMJ reported spending much more time reading online than on paper, including email, and news as well as sports material. Altogether, she said her reading time is about 2-3 hours per day, with more than 50% of that devoted to online material. She likes to read sports reports; she reads no magazines. She had textbooks in several of her classes but did not read them at all except in the case of one chapter for one class that was the basis of an in-class debate.

On the Reading Challenges questionnaire, EMJ marked only writer bias or opinion as relatively easy, and only two items as neither hard nor easy (a 3 on the Likert scale of this instrument): analyzing parts of a text and using reading materials in writing or discussion. All the other items on the list were marked a 4 or 5, with speed, vocabulary and summarizing main ideas all marked a 5. This data was collected in November of 2007.

Participant NMJ-passage 1

NMJ read the online passage on the Michigan state capitol first. She was an early participant in my studies and at the time, I was following a slightly different procedure, stopping readers after 3, 6, and 9 minutes to summarize orally what they had read. At the end of the first 3 minutes, she identified the topic of the passage and said she was surprised to learn from the reading that the first capitol of Michigan was in Detroit and then it was moved to Lansing. She reported re-reading the first paragraph for comprehension, but did not need to re-read any other part.

After 6 minutes, she was able to report on the development of the capitol building in Detroit and the problems there (including a fire) that caused the move of the capitol to Lansing. She reported re-reading in several places due to problems with such vocabulary items as *militia* and *duress*. She found the material neither hard nor easy, and felt she had some prior knowledge that was helpful to her understanding.

After 9 minutes, she had reached the discussion of the third state capitol. In her summary, NMJ noted that there were two capitols for the state of Michigan, one in Detroit and then a second in Lansing due to a fire in 1882. There is discussion in the passage about the branches of the state government. Much of this was new information to her and she learned something new about Detroit from the passage. She reported at the end that she saw a link in the passage to material about the Upper Peninsula, but did not actually go to or look at that link.

Participant NMJ-passage 2

Participant NMJ then went on to read the paper passage on the Summer Olympics. At the end of the first reading period, she identified the topic of the passage and said that there were a number of variations in the Olympics, including the numbers of participants and the differences in locations and the amount of time involved. She did not re-read the first paragraph or any other part.

When she was stopped a second time in her reading, she did not recall much from the passage. She read the rules and qualifications sections in the early history and the part about women participating in the Olympics. This latter point was of interest to her. She found the passage easier than the one on the capitol as she has some interest in and knowledge of sports and also of women's history.

At the end of the reading, she had reached the bottom of the second page of the passage. Her summary at the end included a number of facts she said she had learned from the reading, such as that there were 900 people involved in the Olympics in 1904 and that women were not considered good enough to enter, though there was a woman in the marathon. In 1900, women began to compete. She reported having watched the Olympics on television and would have liked to compete herself. She said that some people are forced into sports participation and this is not a good thing, but with good coaching, sports could be good.

Participant NNW-Baseline data

NNW is an immigrant from Vietnam who moved to the US at the age of seven. His spoken English is somewhat accented, and he is a fluent speaker Vietnamese as well as English. Though he forgot most of his Vietnamese early in his American experience, he attended a Vietnamese school in his teen years and re-learned the spoken language. He said he cannot read or write in Vietnamese now, but he understands the spoken form pretty well. In Vietnam, he remembers that he mostly read from newspapers as there were no books in school or at home. The school focus was on math, so books were less important. When he came to the US, he was placed in first grade, even though he was seven. He had no English when he arrived. The family lived first in Missouri, then in California where there were some relatives in the Sacramento area. His ACT Reading test score was a 17.

Participant NNW said the Vietnamese writing system is similar to English, i.e. it uses much of the same alphabet, with some letters omitted and some that have several alternative forms. A good explanation and description can be found at *Bathrobe's Chinese, Japanese and Vietnamese Writing Systems* (2012).

On the Reading Challenges questionnaire, he marked vocabulary and main ideas as relatively easy (both 2) and all other items somewhat more difficult. Inference, tone and bias was marked as a 5, with the rest of the items marked as 3 or 4. Thus, much critical reading is challenging for this reader. This data was collected in February of 2012.

Participant NNW-Reading background and current practices

NNW had bilingual or ESL instruction in his elementary school experiences, largely because his work was below grade level, and recalled learning to read in English in second grade. He mostly liked to read short works at home, and recalled Dr. Seuss from early reading, and then *Death of a Salesman* and the work of Mark Twain in middle school and high school.

In terms of his current reading practices, NNW estimates that he spends about 5 hours a week reading on paper and at least double that reading online. He prefers short works as he prefers to learn visually; he often gets lost in long works of any kind. Given a choice, he prefers to read short stories or plays, things he can visualize easily. He also likes horror stories as a genre, mentioning Stephen King. A title that came to mind is *Don't Be Afraid of the Dark* which is a movie, but a good example of this genre. When dealing with textbooks, NNW likes to look at pictures first if there are any in the material. If there are no pictures, he finds the reading much harder. If the material is math or science, he likes to do the problems or exercises first before reading the chapter. He also does pre-reading, using a chapter outline, glossary or other apparatus in the book, and will re-read if he feels it is necessary for understanding the text.

Participant NNW-Think aloud comments-passage 1

NNW read the Olympics passage first and read it on paper. He did not say much as he read, so the taped record of his comments is not particularly revealing. He marked the first two sentences of the second paragraph, saying these were cool facts he should remember. He marked the first sentence of the fourth paragraph, about the US hosting four games, also a cool fact. Similarly, he marked the sentence about Britain winning gold in every summer games noting it also as a "cool fact." In the History section, he marked the first sentence about the date of the founding, saying that if he were writing a paper, he should mention this information. He marked the first sentence of the next paragraph, concerning the 1896 Games, saying this would be a good fact for a paper. In the following paragraph, he underlined the sentence about Athens being the birthplace of the Olympics, saying it was a good fact. On page 3, he marked the section on the 1900 Games, saying that it showed that at this time, women could play in the Olympics. He marked nothing else on that page. In the "Interwar era" section, he marked the second paragraph, saying the information about women's participation was a good fact. The ten minutes of reading time ended as he got to this section, so he stopped reading there.

Participant NNW-Written summary-passage 1

This article was talking about the Olympic game and the history behind it. The first Olympic game was held in Athens in 1896 with about 245 competitors. As time progressed more competitors had join in. In the 2008 Olympic game in Beijing, there were 10,500 athletes competing. The first Olympic that included female was the 1900 Summer Olympic in Paris, which included 11 women. In addition, in 1928 Olympic game in Amsterdam, female were also included in games such as track and field. Each country that are entering the Olympic games are represented by the National Olympic Committee (NOC), which represent their country of citizenship. Their National Anthem and flag are shown and played when they enter the game. Every games has a metal awarded for first, second, and third place. First place was awarded with a gold metal, followed by a silver and a bronze metal. Great Britain was the only country to win at least one gold metal in every Olympic game. (164 words) [Note: this is an exact transcript of NNW's handwritten summary]

Participant NNW-Think aloud comments-passage 2

Like NNW's reading of the first passage, there are relatively few comments here. He marked the second sentence of the first paragraph about the location of the capitol, saying it was an interesting fact, and thought that the first sentence of the second paragraph, on Detroit as the first capitol was also a good fact. In the History section, he marked the first sentence of the second paragraph, on the Toledo War, saying it seemed pretty interesting. He marked the last sentence of that paragraph about the year of Michigan's statehood saying this was a good fact to know. He marked nothing more until the "Third state capitol" section, where he marked the first sentence, saying again that it was a good fact. Then, he marked nothing further until the last paragraph of the Building section, saying that the description suggested a Neoclassical style. When he finished this paragraph, 10 minutes had elapsed and so I ended NNW's reading at this point.

Participant NNW-Written summary-passage 2

> This article was talking about the Michigan State Capitol. The capitol building was originally build in Detroit, which was the capitol build at the time. Due to easy def. from British troops from Ontario, the capitol building was moved to Lansing; being that it is in the middle of the state. The old capitol building was built based on the Neoclassical style. During the time of the old capitol building, Michigan was also in a war with Ohio known as the Toledo War. After this war, Michigan became the 26th state. After the capitol building moved to Lansing, the old capitol building was converted into high school. After a short amount of time, the building was burnt down.
>
> The new capitol building in Lansing is also built based on Neoclassism. Instead of being built with woods, it was built with marble and limstones. The capitol building today is home to many offices. When the building was first built, it cost about $1.2 million. (163 words) [Note: this is an exact transcript of NNW's handwritten summary]

Cross Case Analysis and Interpretation

These cases provide rich and varied data, but like any case study material despite consistencies in the protocol I followed, there is considerable variation among the participants. I have looked at this data repeatedly; the theory to be proposed in detail in the next few chapters arose from my examination of the cases from a variety of angles and perspectives. Most experienced researchers are familiar with this process of looking over data many times until the patterns in it become clear. In the following discussion, the commonalities are reviewed to show similarities across the cases and the differences are examined to suggest differences between Experts and Novices.

Observations across baseline data

All of the Experts score much higher on the ACT Reading test than the Novices except for two of the Honors College students; the third Honors College student is not a native speaker of English and may have a lower score as a result of his ESL background.

As noted previously, there does not seem to be any particular consistency in terms of MBTI type preferences for any of the readers in the study; for this reason, the MBTI results are not presented in any of the cases. All of the Experts work in professions that entail a great deal of reading, all are older, and all are highly educated. They are also all white. The Novices as a group are more mixed in terms of their ages, education, and majors or areas of interest (not asked for in the baseline data, but true of all the students known to me).

In terms of their responses on the Reading Challenges questionnaire, no Expert finds any item on that list difficult, with the highest response of difficulty a 3 (neither easy nor hard) and very few of those. The Novices commonly report difficulty with the higher order critical thinking/reading skills that entail synthesis, evaluation and application.

Commonalities across reading background questions

Virtually all Expert readers have no recall of learning to read and report no difficulties with reading early in life. As is well-established in the research literature, all had extensive access to books and other written materials (newspapers, magazines, libraries) and reading was a valued and common activity. While not all had positive experiences with school reading, school often exposed them to good books and classics they might not have found on their own. Most recall many books from early reading. By contrast, the Novices have much less early reading experience except for the Honors College students, who resemble the Experts on this point as they do on many others.

Commonalities about current reading practices

All Expert readers continue to read extensively on paper despite the ubiquitous presence of computers, e-readers and other electronic forms of text and distraction. Is this behavior a function of age rather than true preference? Nothing in the data collected gives an answer on this point. However, it may be worthy of note that in Hillesund's (2010) study of experts reading printed and online materials, he found that the experts preferred to read on paper. Like Hillesund's readers, my Experts read books and other kinds of texts on paper for both personal and professional purposes, i.e. for both pleasure and work. Some Experts read textbook material (if teaching) but do not have any difficulty with it, so they have no special strategies for it. They do not report particular difficulties with reading online as opposed to reading on paper, though none of the questions ask about this aspect of reading. Most Experts do not read extensively online, even though their work often calls for extensive computer use and most do at least some writing, using a word processor for this purpose. While the Novices report spending more time online than the Experts, their responses on the Reading Challenges questionnaire do not reveal more or less proficiency online than on paper.

Commonalities that arise from the reading exercises, think-aloud reports and summaries

Taken together, the Experts have a higher level of awareness about text structure. They see what the writer is doing, explicitly or implicitly, reporting on structure ("the writer is setting up three points…") or making clear what is important in the passage. They read quickly and purposefully and will sometimes move ahead or look back in the text to see key words ("chambers") or to answer questions. They set expectations and read to answer their own questions ("where do they meet?"). When reading for writing, they are thinking ahead to how they will be able to capture the content in a summary. They bring much prior knowledge to bear, reporting on aspects of history that bear on the text (the 1936 Olympics), or on dimensions of their personal lives that account for their interest in the text. These insights suggest a meta-contextual awareness not shown by the novices. These commonalities reflect these readers' meta-textual, meta-contextual and meta-linguistic awarenesses as they read.

The Experts all get through much more of the text than the Novices do. Almost all of the Experts read more than half of each of the two passages in the study, with some of them getting all the way or almost to the end or more than halfway. The summaries suggest that they get much more of the content, just at a basic level of comprehension. The summaries contain content that reflects Experts' skill in analysis. They bring in inferences and conclusions beyond the text, putting what they know together with what is presented in the text.

Expert readers read in a very focused way, often task oriented. EDT provides an especially strong example of this level of focus. She was very focused on the summary writing task and was reading with an eye toward the writing. In general, Expert readers (like Bazerman's physicists, 1988) read this way and Novices do not. Experts see the whole text much more clearly than do the Novices: "I read a story about the Michigan state capitol" or "There have been three state capitols in Michigan."

Participant EDT was very focused on the writing task and what she might need for the summary she was going to do at the end. She mentioned issues of race and heritage, affecting her knowledge of Hitler and her sense of compassion for Cassius Clay. In her response during the reading, she did more of a think-aloud than most participants in this research. Her reading of the passage was very fast and selective, like Bazerman's physicists. While writing her summary of this passage, she looked back at the text. Also, while doing the summary, she put in several editorial comments and then took them out. My notes on her comments while marking suggest that she was reading very selectively.

She said out loud at a number of points "I don't care about this part." She was not particularly interested in the history, but did mark some of the general background information about how often various countries have hosted the Games, and the way qualification for the Olympics is handled. She got through the history, marking the start date for the modern Olympics and problems over time. She paid attention to details on the 1908 London games and the growth described in the paragraph on the 1912 games in Stockholm. In the "The interwar era" section, she observed that things were "crappy" but saw that the passage was describing the historical development of the Games. Her comments reflected her developing sense of a thesis for her own written summary. She marked the paragraph on the cancellation of the Games of 1940 due to the war. In the After World War II section, she marked the paragraph about Cassius Clay, highlighting the racist episode that is mentioned there. Then she marked the first sentence of the paragraph on the Munich Games of 1972 saying it was very important. At 10 minutes, she was at the heading "End of the 20th century," page 6 of the printed text.

Unlike most readers, EDT was very focused on the writing task and was thinking ahead to see what she would want to include or exclude. Her "I don't care" comments at various points were a reflection of her looking to see her thesis and plan for the writing. No other reader read this way. She skipped things and went back to them as she saw the text unfold and as her writing plan was taking shape. While participant EBD saw the text structure unfolding and said so ("he's setting out three points"), she did not comment on the use of this observation for the purpose of writing the summary. One Novice reader (NHS) was also obviously predicting, asking questions and working at analyzing the text, but she is an Honors

College student and like the other more prepared students resembled the Experts to some degree.

It should be clear just from the length of the summaries that the Expert readers stand in sharp contrast to the stronger and weaker Novices, who are all still students. However, several other key insights arise from the results. It isn't just the length of the summaries that indicates the difference between the Expert meta-readers and the Novices. There are other features of the Experts' reading that reveal their stronger awarenesses and skills: they almost all read at least a full page more than any of the Novices. They read with questions in mind and noticed the overall structure of the text.

The beginnings of the theory

By looking across the cases, then, some general features of the theory emerge. In terms of awarenesses, the Experts' cases suggest meta-textual, meta-contextual and meta-linguistic awareness. They get far enough into each passage and are good enough readers to see the text structure as it begins to develop. Several of them provide a meta-contextual commentary, drawing on their knowledge of history, their knowledge of the Olympics, or other information or experiences to be able to see the text in a larger context. And they are sensitive to the use of language, so that "chambers" and "muses" for instance elicit specific responses from them. None of these awarenesses appear in the data of the Novices. None of the Novice readers got far enough in either text to see much of the overall structure and development of ideas unfolding in the discussion. All of these readers got some of the key ideas of the passages, but not all had both the awareness and the skill to read effectively and efficiently. A key difference between the Expert meta-readers and Novices, then, is that Novices have little awareness but do have some skills, while the Experts have both awareness and skills.

Turning to the skills, the Experts clearly have the skills to read and analyze, getting the main ideas of each passage. And some of the Novices are able to get the key points as well, as indicated in their summaries. The Novices who are in the Honors College program read more of both passages and get more of the key ideas than do the students who are not in the Honors program and they write longer and more complete summaries of as much of the material as they cover in the 10 minutes of reading time allowed on each passage.

A further point that arises from the analysis of the data from all the cases concerns the relationship of the theory to the tasks readers were asked to do in the protocol that I used. Readers are asked to read and summarize for content; the hypothetical task is to read for the purpose of writing a school report. The focus, then, is on main ideas and details, essentially analysis. Readers are not asked to synthesize as needed, for instance, for a typical college research paper and they do not need to evaluate or apply the information that they get from the reading in any kind of real life situation beyond the writing of a school report. The task I set, then, elicited the awarenesses readers have, even though I did not ask for that directly, and it shows some of the skills.

The idea that experts can and should be able to synthesize different texts arises in part from my work as a teacher of reading and writing. In first-year writing courses, as well as in other kinds of school-based writing, synthesis is a common requirement. Students may read multiple sources on a topic or issue and the expectation is that they will synthesize this information to support their own ideas or arguments. The task I set in the study does not call for such work.

However, an indirect way of looking for readers' ability to synthesize is to examine the performance on the ACT Reading test more closely. The reading skills that ACT purports to measure suggest that Novices show limited ability to work with these key features of complex texts identified by the ACT test writers:

> **Relationships**: Interactions among ideas or characters in the text are subtle, involved or deeply embedded.
> **Richness**: The text possesses a sizable amount of highly sophisticated information conveyed through data or literary devices.
> **Structure**: The text is organized in ways that are elaborate and sometimes unconventional.
> **Style**: The author's tone and use of language are often intricate.
> **Vocabulary**: The author's choice of words is demanding and highly context dependent.
> **Purpose**: The author's intent in writing the text is implicit and sometimes ambiguous. (American, 2006, p. 17)

These features are ones that Expert readers generally do with ease, while the Novices struggle. The differences in ACT Reading test scores suggest that the experts have the relevant skills for synthesis while the Novices are lack them. Table 2.3 shows the differences in ACT Reading test scores. While the ACT has a number of weaknesses, such as the fact that it does not address the skills of people whose native language is not English and it does not address reading skills online, the ACT findings show that many Novices' skills are weak in contrast to those of Experts.

Table 2.3. Expert and Novice ACT Reading scores

Experts

Partipt	ACT-R
EAF	35
EBD	33
ECO	36
EDT	27
EEM	32

Novices

Partipt	ACT-R
NFW	31
NGZ	18
NHS	n/a
NJL	34
NKT	18
NLW	21
NMJ	12
NNW	17

Of the Novices, NFW, NJL and NNW are all Honors College students, but NNW is the participant who is not a native speaker of English, which may account for his lower ACT Reading score. While the ACT is not a perfect measure of all reading skills, it does give some indirect evidence of overall reading ability, and it suggests that skill in synthesis is one area where Experts clearly have superior ability.

Just as the task in the study does not call directly for synthesis, it also does not call for evaluation. However, at least one of the Expert subjects produced marked evaluative comments even though these were not specifically requested. EDT entitled her summary on the Michigan capitol passage "The boring story of the Michigan state capitol." While Novices make comments like "this is a good fact," the Experts comment on what they find interesting, on what they can connect to what they know (EEM says about the muses pictured in the capitol, "Aren't there nine?"), and otherwise show that they are making judgments as they are reading. Little in the Novices' responses suggests much evaluation.

Finally, the task of the study does provide application of the information, since the summary or notes participants take are for a specific purpose: to be used for writing a school report. Here again, EDT was perhaps the most focused reader, sorting the ideas and information by thinking about the writing task. Her selective reading of each passage was a mission to find the most useful material for the writing task assigned. None of the Novices' comments point to a focus on the application of the material for the task at hand.

The case studies, then, gave me a lot to think about as I considered how Experts and Novices read non-fiction prose. Taken together, the cases did suggest that Experts have a level of awareness of the text itself, its context, and its language that does not appear in the reading responses of the Novices. And while both groups have some analytical skill, it appeared to me that Experts have skills beyond analysis that Novices do not show in their responses. Framing these cases against the backdrop of psycholinguistic theories of literacy makes their differences come into sharper focus, as the next two chapters make clear.

Appendix A: Informed consent letter

To: Reading Strategies Research study volunteers

From: Investigator

Re: Study information and informed consent

You are invited to participate in a research study on the development of critical reading skills among twelve adults, the purpose of which is to understand the similarities and differences among expert and novice readers of printed and digital documents. The study will take about 60-90 minutes of your time, in a single session devoted to several different activities.

Your participation will first involve completion of two instruments unless you already have reasonably current results: the Reading portion of the ACT exam (35 minutes) and a Myers-Briggs Type Indicator introductory quick survey online (10 minutes). You will also be asked for permission to access your university record to find out your current university grade point average (if you are a student). You will then be asked to complete a 15-30 minute interview on your personal reading history (learning to read, early reading in school and out, favorite books in early life and related questions) and current reading practices (time spent reading per day or per week, current reading interests/preferences, digital compared to printed materials and so on) with me, and to complete a short questionnaire on paper (5-10 minutes to complete). Finally, you will be asked to complete two ten-minute think-aloud protocols while reading printed and digital materials. All interviews and think-aloud sessions will be audio-taped with your consent. I will be the only person to listen to and transcribe these tapes; once the transcription is complete, the tapes will be kept on file for two years. Short excerpts may be played anonymously as part of conference presentations about this work. After two years, I will destroy the tapes.

The study may help you be a better reader in several ways. First, the activities of the study will encourage you to think more carefully about how you read different kinds of material on paper and on a computer screen and may help you become a faster and more efficient reader. You will learn something about your personality preferences and their impact on your approach to reading. The activities may help you understand any difficulties you have with reading and ways you might resolve those difficulties.

You may find the study activities uncomfortable in a few ways. My questions and the other activities may be awkward or difficult for you to complete. You may prefer not to be taped. You may ask any questions or raise any concerns at any time during the study activities.

Your ACT score, Myers-Briggs results, GPA, questionnaire responses and transcripts of your think-aloud work will be kept confidential. My written or oral reports on this research will not reveal any identifying characteristics that would link you to the data. Your participation is entirely voluntary; you may choose to leave the study at any time without penalty. You may also choose to skip any questions during the interview without penalty.

If you agree to participate in the study, please sign and date the space below and give it to me. By signing below, you give me permission to access your university record to learn your current GPA and to use your materials and data anonymously in oral or published research reports. Your signature also gives me permission to audio-tape your interviews and to present taped material publicly. Any presentation will be anonymous; you will not be identified and will have the opportunity to review any taped material prior to public presentation.

For questions about this study, you may contact me by phone at 248-370-4134 or by email at horning@oakland.edu. For questions regarding the rights of human participants in research, you may contact Oakland University's Institutional Review Board at 248-370-2762.

Print your name:_________________________
[university] ID:___________________________
Signature:______________________________
Date:__________________________________

Appendix B: Interview questions

Reading Strategies Research demographics questions, to be completed prior to data collection:

1. Age
2. Gender
3. ACT Reading exam score
4. Composite ACT score
5. Overall OU GPA (if available)
6. Verified MBTI type preferences:

Permission to access OU records for this information if student does not have it available?

THIS PAGE WILL BE SEPARATED FROM OTHER MATERIALS AND KEPT CONFIDENTIAL.

Appendix C: Reading Autobiography Questionnaire

(to be completed orally with the investigator and/or independently on paper)

Part I: Reading History

1. What do you recall about learning to read?
2. Did you have any problems with reading or learning to read that you recall? Describe these problems and how you solved them if you did.
3. What was your reading experience in school?
4. What was your reading experience at home or outside of school?
5. Do you recall specific books or authors in elementary school? Which ones?

Part II: Current Reading Practices

1. How much time do you spend reading now on paper? On line?
2. How much reading do you do online as opposed to on paper?
3. What types of materials do you read? What do you prefer to read?
4. How do you handle textbook reading? What strategies do you use? What problems do you have with textbooks, if any?

Appendix D: Reading Strategies Research

Reading Challenges Questionnaire (to be completed by each subject individually and privately on paper)
What aspects of reading are most challenging for you? Please circle the appropriate number for each of the following areas of reading ability, using the following scale:

1—Very easy for me
2—Fairly easy for me
3—Not easy or hard for me
4—Fairly hard for me
5—Very hard for me

	Easy←------------→ Hard				
Reading quickly and efficiently	1	2	3	4	5
Understanding vocabulary in texts	1	2	3	4	5
Drawing inferences	1	2	3	4	5
Summarizing main ideas	1	2	3	4	5
Analyzing parts of a text or argument	1	2	3	4	5
Putting together ideas from different texts	1	2	3	4	5
Using reading material in writing or discussion	1	2	3	4	5
Understanding a writer's tone	1	2	3	4	5
Knowing an author's purpose or intent	1	2	3	4	5
Noticing a writer's bias, preferences or opinion	1	2	3	4	5

CHAPTER THREE

THE MENTAL CAPACITIES FOR CRITICAL LITERACY

Introduction

Human language ability, usually thought of as the ability to speak and understand, serves as the basis for expert critical literacy. While most discussions in linguistics that describe language ability assume the spoken form as primary, some research has attended to written discourse, such as the work of Halliday and Hasan (1976) on cohesion and other issues. The normal course of language acquisition focuses on spoken forms as well, perhaps partly because most linguists believe that the development of language is a process of "acquisition," i.e., a first language is not taught directly by such conventional means as imitation, memorization or stimulus-response techniques. The outcome of this acquisition process is fluent spoken language production and comprehension for all normal individuals and for many of those with physical or mental disorders of some kind. So the spoken form is generally considered primary. However, I propose that proficiency with the written form of language, and especially critical literacy is the most sophisticated level of human language ability. By describing the mental capacities that underlie this ability, we can account for how experts work as meta-readers and writers.

Expert literacy relies on both general cognitive capacities and linguistic capacities. To keep this somewhat detailed discussion organized, they will all be referred to here as mental capacities. Taken together, there are seven of these mental capacities that are essential to expert literacy. They include the cognitive capacities of identification, categorization, discrimination, and prediction. A key limitation on them lies in short term memory, which is restricted, according to classic psycholinguistic research, to seven plus or minus two items. In addition, they include two human linguistic capacities, the use of syntax and the use of the fundamental psycholinguistic redundancy of language. The following synthesis of the research on these mental capacities makes clear their relevance for meta-readers and writers; the capacities rely on vision for input, so understanding the operation of the visual system provides an essential backdrop for a discussion of the mental capacities.

The Visual System

In his book *How the Mind Works* (1997), Harvard cognitive psychologist Steven Pinker discusses human mental functions of various kinds. Certain parts of his discussion bear particularly on abilities important to language. Key features of our mental functions, our capacities, relate specifically to language and help account for how it is that we are capable of expert critical literacy. Pinker's description of how the mind works shows that only a few key visual and perceptual mechanisms help account for the mental processing that supports expert critical literacy. He provides an exploration of visual processing and the making of meaning that is essential our capacities for literacy. Although reading is only "incidentally visual" (Kolers, 1967), it relies at least in part on the visual processing of what is on the page, and writing requires the creation of a visual array to be read. So it seems appropriate to start with visual matters. Vision happens when light images enter the eyes and are passed along to the brain for processing (Pinker, 1997, p. 215). Perception is the process of making sense of visual stimuli, including the ability to sort illusion from reality and to insure that we perceive what we see (Pinker, 1997, p. 215-241).

Vision works under some key constraints that affect literacy. First, "vision is not a theater in the round" (Pinker, 1997, p. 257). That is, the eyes focus on what is in front of them and everything else, though generally perceived through peripheral vision, is unfocused and much less clear. In reading, this feature of vision means that readers see only the patch of text in focus at any given moment. A series of focus points or fixations on a line of text provide the sense of reading continuous text, but that is not how text processing actually happens. French cognitive psychologist Dehaene's (2009) report of brain imaging studies confirms these physiological mechanisms in reading.

Second, humans do not have x-ray vision. It is not possible to see what is inside a box. Vision works strictly on the surface of the world, a sort of "what you see is what you get" in the sense that what we see is all we see, and all we see is two dimensions, not three (Pinker, 1997, p. 257-258). We may intuit or guess what is in a box, but we don't actually see it or perceive it. Perception can be fooled into seeing what isn't actually there (Pinker, 1997, p. 259), as in the well-known Rubin face/vase image of a vase that can also be two faces in profile which can be found at psylux.

psych.tu-dresden.de/i1/kaw/diverses%20Material/www.illusionworks.com/html/figure_ground.html (Figure/Ground, 2011). Perception also relies heavily on redundancy (discussed in detail later in this chapter) to make assumptions about what might be there, even though we don't see it.

These characteristics of vision account for much of how reading works. We don't actually look at or see or need to see much of what is on the page, hence Kolers' claim that reading is only "incidentally visual" (1967). This phenomenon explains how it is possible to read more than 200 words per minute with good comprehension. The more prior knowledge we have, the less we need to see to get meaning. The interaction of what is on the page or screen with what is already in our heads explains why most of us can read best sellers much more quickly than theoretical physics.

An additional important feature of vision is that it has perspective and a sense of the boundaries between objects. As a result, we can see and perceive (i.e. make sense of the sights) only one thing at a time. In the faces/vase image or others like it, if we see one possibility, the other is gone. The brain simply cannot process two images at once; the visual system does not allow it (Pinker, 1997, p. 259, 293). As psycholinguist Frank Smith explains, reading capitalizes on this feature of the visual system. Smith contends that literate humans actually look at or see only a sampling of letters or words in reading, but perceive through them the meaning of a text (Smith, 2004, p. 156-161).

Pinker describes some other features of how vision works that are not crucial to reading, such as the fact that most of vision is two-dimensional, with depth functioning as .5 of a third dimension because it is somewhat less important in overall perception and because it requires so much space in the overall system. Pinker's analogy is to computer systems; he points out that graphics take much more computer storage than text, consuming more memory and taking longer to load to the screen (1997, p. 260-261). The visual system tries to limit demand by taking in depth in a limited way, to reduce the load of information; shifts in the frame of reference as we look around the visual world make the discounting of depth possible without a loss of information.

Expert meta-readers and writers read and write by using the visual fixations, the surface nature of vision, the lack of need to look at everything, the sense of perspective and boundaries and the limited use of depth. In addition to using the visual system, albeit only incidentally, expert meta-readers and writers use a total of seven mental capacities, all of which are essential to literacy: the five general cognitive capacities of identification, categorization, discrimination, prediction and limited short-term memory; these five along with the linguistic capacities of using syntax and redundancy round out the capacities experts use in meta-reading and writing.

Mental Capacities for Critical Literacy

Mental capacities 1: Identification/recognition

It may not seem that identification or recognition is important to literacy. One of the great debates in the teaching of reading and writing concerns whether it is necessary for readers and writers to identify, that is, to label, letters and words at all; this issue plays out in arguments over phonics vs. "whole language" approaches to teaching reading, for example. Although Frank Smith, author of one of the definitive textbooks on the nature of the reading process, now in its sixth edition (2004), argues that letter and word identification are not necessary to reading, he does concede that when readers cannot get meaning directly, mediated letter or word identification is an alternate approach through phonics or other strategies (Smith, 2004, p. 138-155). Thus, identification does play a role, albeit limited, in literacy.

The first of these capacities, then, is the human ability to recognize and/or identify letters, words and other written forms, such as punctuation. Recognition, in psycholinguistic terms, includes both remembering, i.e. "conscious recollection of seeing the item previously" (Knowlton, 1998, p. 254), and knowing, i.e. "recognition in the absence of such recollections" (Knowlton, 1998, p. 254). These general abilities apply not only to letters and words but also to meanings in written language processing. Identification makes it possible for us to look at A and a and *A* and label all of them as letter 'A'. Identification refers specifically to the ability to name the letters, words or other literate forms.

The process by which recognition or identification occurs in literacy is simply a specialized form of a more generalized ability to recognize shapes. This more generalized ability is described by Pinker, building on the work of Biederman (Pinker, 1997, p. 270). Biederman specifies a core set of twenty-four shapes he calls geons and a small set of methods by which they attach to one another. Like the grammar of language, the small set of shapes and attachments accounts for human ability to recognize thousands of shapes. Moreover, Pinker notes that "language and complex shapes seem to be neighbors in the brain. The left hemisphere is not only the seat of language but also the seat of the ability to recognize and imagine shapes defined by arrangements of parts" (Pinker, 1997, p. 271). The proximity of these functions in the brain suggests a relationship between them. It is a fundamental processing capacity that makes critical literacy possible. Dehaene's studies of brain anatomy support these claims with recent findings through various types of scans (Dehaene, 2009, p. 137-39).

Geons and their connections are one part of recognition and identification, but some other basic principles are needed, as Pinker points out. The main principle is mental rotation ability, along with awareness of left/right relationships and the idea of an axis on which a figure might turn (Pinker, 1997, p. 274-284). These are all part of the basic set of visual principles that make literacy do-able for humans. And there is one final principle of the visual system to be considered. Pinker describes the "Perky effect," named for Cheves Perky who discovered it in 1910 (Pinker, 1997, p. 288). The principle is that a mental image wipes out fine visual details, and often people merge images and what is actually seen. The implications of the Perky effect for reading are quite important: readers mostly don't see what is on the printed page, but have images, certainly of letters and words, in their heads. This phenomenon further accounts for the high speed of proficient reading.

Identification/recognition is a key feature of our perceptual abilities, making literacy possible. Readers can identify or recognize letters, words and meanings. According to Smith, however, after beginning reading, readers don't need the ability to identify extensively under ordinary conditions. One exception might be those developing literacy in a language with a different writing system, or those moving from a spoken language with no writing system to one that has a written form. Research suggests that the ability to deal with orthography changes the brain in clear and specific ways, so these abilities are tied to real physical changes (Petersson, Reis & Ingvar, 2001; Castro-Caldas & Reis, 2003). But once readers have learned to identify the letters and words, identification per se is only needed if readers cannot get meaning.

On the production side, again beyond the learning stage, the actual identification of letters and words is completely automatic and requires no conscious attention. For example, unless I am typing numbers or symbols, I never think about the individual letters my fingers are touching on the keyboard. While my typing speed does not approach my reading speed, I am pretty fast and I suspect I am typical. Handwriting is necessarily slower, but is the same process wherein writers do not think about individual letters or words but are processing meaning directly. Identification, that is, being able to label particular items with their conventional names, is a fundamental tool. It is mostly needed for learning to deal with written forms in the first place, for a new language if the writing system is different, and for the occasional mediated approach to meaning.

Mental capacities 2: Categorization

A second capacity is the ability to categorize a range of possible shapes as belonging to the same group. Categorization is not the same as the first capacity, identification, which specifically refers to labeling ability. It is categorization that allows us to read bad handwriting, or distorted print like a smeared newspaper or different type faces. Categorization is a second fundamental tool for literacy. My own attempts to learn Hebrew, for instance, were easily thrown off by trying to move from the primer text I was using to learn the letters to other books which had a smaller font size and slightly different shapes for the letters. Categorization is part of the reason why story books for beginning readers are printed in large type fonts.

Categorization has uses in many aspects of daily experience. McGill University neuroscientist Daniel Levitin (2006), for example, writes about it in terms of responses to music. Levitin points out that "Categorization is a basic function of living creatures. Every object is unique, but we often act toward different objects as members of classes or categories" (2006, p. 140). It is a matter of interest to philosophers as well as psychologists and literacy scholars. Wittgenstein wrote about categorization as did Eleanor Rosch, and Levitin notes that Rosch's work on categorization and the idea of prototypes (i.e. typical features that mark a category) to capture the nature of categories has "changed the way we think about categories" (Levitin, 2006, p. 141).

Both Pinker and Smith discuss the ability to categorize. Pinker shows how the process works, and why it is relevant to critical literacy, while Smith demonstrates how categorization makes literacy possible. Pinker explains where the ability to categorize fits in human cognitive ability:

> People think in two modes. They can form fuzzy stereotypes by uninsightfully soaking up correlations among properties, taking advantage of the fact that things in the world tend to fall into clusters (things that bark also bite and lift their legs at hydrants). But people can also create systems of rules—intuitive theories—that define categories in terms of the rules that apply to them, and that treat all the members of the category equally. ...Law, arithmetic, folk science, and social conventions...are other rule systems in which people all over the planet reckon. The grammar of a language is yet another. (Pinker, 1997, p. 127)

So having categories is a general thinking strategy humans use, and they use it particularly with sets of rules, notably those of language. Expert meta-readers and writers categorize letters, words, sentences and other bits of language in terms of rules that they follow.

Pinker makes a further point about the usefulness of catcgorization as a process. He notes that categories allow us to make inferences about how the world works. This ability to draw inferences is clearly pertinent to language. As Pinker says "obviously, we can't know everything about every object. But we can observe some of its properties, assign it to a category, and from the category predict properties that we have *not* observed" (Pinker, 1997, p. 307). This ability to predict based on categories is part of what is going on in the ability to process written language, both understanding and producing. We use the rules to do language, and the rules specify how categories of language behave or are used.

Categorization is such an essential cognitive ability relevant to language learning and use that humans apparently come into the world wired to sort sounds from birth. There are many variations in sound, for instance, that arise as a by-product of dialect variation, and speakers must be able to categorize those sounds in order to understand spoken forms. There is substantial evidence that babies come into the world with a specific ability to categorize sounds into phonemes; the data on categorical perception of sound among infants across languages and cultures is well established (Eimas, et al., 1971). Dehaene's work (2009) suggests that we have a similar kind of ability with written language forms; the forms that are basic for letter shapes resemble those essential in the environment "coded deep in the primate visual cortex" (p.179).

Categorization ability described by Pinker has implications for reading and writing discussed by Frank Smith. Smith says that identifying letters or words is not that hard, as it entails only labeling. Putting items into a category is more complex since it entails knowing the features of the category. He makes the distinction between these two abilities clear as follows:

> Two aspects of letter identification can be distinguished. The first aspect is the establishment of categories themselves and especially the allocation of category names to them, such as "A," "B," "C." The second aspect of letter identification is the allocation of visual configurations to various cognitive categories—the discrimination of various configurations as different, as not functionally equivalent. The great part of perceptual learning involves finding out what exactly are the distinctive features by which various configurations should be categorized as different from each

> other, and what are the sets of features that are criterial for particular categories. (Smith, 2004, p. 119)

Identification, he goes on to say, is different from the ability to categorize or discriminate between categories. By using the sets of features, both processes are possible. He further points out that the exact feature list is not essential to either identification or categorization, suggesting, I think, that the features may well be intuitions. Dehaene's research shows that the shapes used in written language "evolved to fit the cortex" capitalizing on basic extant human abilities to categorize (2009, p. 150). He shows some of the features quite clearly (2009, p. 151). For now, these findings show that the ability to name (i.e., identify or recognize) and the ability to group like items together (i.e. to categorize) are basic tools of human thinking ability that make expert critical literacy possible.

Mental capacities 3: Discrimination

A third mental capacity that works together with identification and categorization is discrimination. Discrimination does not require either identification or categorization, but is a separate kind of ability. It is not necessary to be able to identify (i.e. label) two items in order to discriminate between them. It is also not necessary to categorize two items in order to discriminate between them. Discrimination is the ability to perceive two items as the same as or different from each other. This ability is important in a number of different kinds of cognitive processing, including literacy.

The idea that two letters might be the same or different from each other may not seem terribly significant. All of these cognitive abilities, taken one by one, do not seem as though they are very important. However, each capacity plays a role in expert critical literacy. When we use discrimination beyond letters to distinguish words or ideas, the significance of the ability to judge similarity and difference becomes more clearly relevant to literacy, and especially to critical literacy. In reading two editorials on the same topic for instance, perhaps in different newspapers, the ability to judge the positions of the writers may be very important. It is one kind of ability expert meta-readers and writers have and novices need for success in education and in their personal and professional lives.

The differences among discrimination, identification and categorization are made clear in the following explanation by University of Maryland developmental psycholinguist Grace Yeni-Komshian:

> In many perceptual domains, discrimination is better than identification. We can usually discriminate between two different stimuli much better than we can label or identify two different stimuli. Consider the following example from the visual domain: Let us imagine a series of photographs of two men who look somewhat alike. We could photograph each standing up with arms pressed against his sides. We could then take a second, third and fourth photograph of each individual, asking each of them to raise his arms about 20 degrees for each photograph. The discrimination task would be to ask the viewer whether a pair of photographs were identical or not. The identification task would be to label the identity of the person in the picture. In this example you would not find it difficult to tell whether any two photographs of the *same* individual were identical or not (discrimination). (Yeni-Komshian, 1998, p. 133)

In this example, the categorization task might be to sort the photos of men with their arms down from those with their arms raised, while discrimination pertains to same or different judgments. These are distinct kinds of processing abilities, all of which serve as the base for the development of critical literacy.

Yeni-Komshian goes on in her discussion of speech perception to discuss the importance of the ability to discriminate among different speech sounds in order to comprehend spoken language (1998, pp. 134-136). Moreover, the work of Eimas, Siqueland, Jusczyk and Vigorito (1971), investigating newborn children's ability to perceive the major phoneme categories in spoken language, demonstrates clearly that humans come equipped with this essential processing capacity, as noted previously. Yeni-Komshian also makes one further point: the ability to categorize is not limited to speech perception, but appears to be a more general processing or perceptual ability (1998, p. 135).

The relationship of discrimination to identification or recognition and the differences between these capacities can be clarified as follows: "Object recognition involves two aspects, discrimination and naming. The first is essential whereas the second is not… We perform many discriminations for which we have no verbal categories" (Wade & Swanston, 2001, p. 5). We also perform many discriminations for which we DO have verbal categories and this capacity, which allows us to distinguish among the letters b, d, p, and q, is an essential component of expert literacy.

Mental capacities 4: Prediction

A fourth mental capacity is the ability to predict. Prediction is a powerful mechanism because it allows us to create expectations. We predict based on our prior knowledge of the world and to some extent, our knowledge of language. Prediction relies chiefly on our knowledge of the world and how it works. Psycholinguists describe this ability in part with the concept of a schema. We have schemas for many different kinds of experiences in the world. Mention a child's birthday party, and many predictions immediately come to mind: cake, ice cream, presents, pin-the-tail-on-the-donkey, singing "Happy Birthday," and so on. Mention lunch at McDonald's, and some menu features (Big Macs, fries) along with the general plan of ordering at a counter, picking up and paying for the food, and related matters will come up. Among the Experts whose cases are discussed in Chapter 2, the one who saw the writer as setting up three points was clearly predicting the structure of the text and marking it accordingly.

One of the early writers on schemas is educational psychologist Richard Anderson. Pointing out that his definition draws on work by Bartlett, Kant and others, Anderson provides a clear, helpful definition of a schema:

> ...mental structures that incorporate general knowledge...Schemata summarize that which is common to a large number of things or situations. Because of its generality, a schematic representation must be more abstract than the representation of any particular thing or situation. ...Schemata ...give generic characterizations of things and events. (Anderson, et al., 1978, p. 434)

A schema helps readers predict what will come next in a text and writers can capitalize on them to help readers understand their ideas.

In written language, there are many schemata: "Once upon a time" calls up a schema of damsel in distress, knight on a white horse and "they lived happily ever after" with a possible dragon or troll thrown in for good measure. Another one emerges from predictable text structures, such as the one suggested in headings like these: Review of the Literature, Methods, Results, Discussion, Conclusion. Mostly, though, prediction draws on our knowledge of the world, its conventions, and how it works rather than specifically our knowledge of language and how it works.

One example of the process of prediction comes from the opening sentence of a story by British author Roald Dahl. Dahl's story "Poison" opens with the following sentence:

> It must have been around midnight when I drove home, and as I approached the gates of the bungalow, I switched off the head-lamps of the

> car so the beam wouldn't swing in through the window of the side bedroom and wake Harry Pope. (Dahl, 1990/1953, p. 411)

When I have used this text following a strategy offered by psycholinguist and reading scholar Kenneth Goodman, I ask readers of it to draw a picture of the scene described. I also ask them to indicate, in their pictures, the gender of the speaker. Discussion of the pictures shows that many readers in the US provide only one gate, and render the bungalow as a one or one-and-a-half story simple house. They are surprised to learn that in the next paragraph, the speaker gets out of the car and crosses a veranda to enter the bungalow. Even more interesting is that the gender of the speaker has changed over time. Perhaps 15 or 20 years ago, the speaker was always male, but more recently readers are more evenly split between males and females.

Readers often suggest that only a woman would think to turn off the lights so as not to wake Harry; seldom do current readers say only a man would be out alone at midnight. Readers have a variety of ideas about the relationship between the speaker and Harry Pope. The discussion of this passage can often go on for 10-15 minutes even with a small group of readers. When I use this exercise, I end by asking readers to notice that the entire discussion is based on just *one* sentence of the story. This sentence really helps both novice and expert readers see how quickly and in how much detail they predict what is coming in a text; the predictions are based almost entirely on their real world schemata.

Mental capacities 5: Short term memory: A limitation

A fifth mental capacity that plays a key role in expert literacy is the limitation on the content of short-term memory. This limit is well-established at the "magical number seven" give or take two items, as reported by George Miller in a landmark study more than fifty years ago (1956). Miller's research showed clearly that humans can hold about seven unrelated items in short-term memory before they are lost. His finding is firmly established in the research on human information processing.

I usually think of short-term memory as the time between when I put the phone book back in the front closet and get to the phone to key in a number I've looked up in the book. Many things come in batches of seven because of this limit: phone numbers, days of the week, dwarfs, among others. And even with the advent of area codes on most phone numbers in our increasingly wired world, I'd suggest that the area codes most often needed are processed as a unit, making eight items to hold in short-term memory for telephone purposes. This generalized limit on our memory capacity in the short term constrains literacy in fundamental ways.

Human beings, then, have these five mental capacities that have evolved to make literacy possible: identification, categorization and discrimination along with prediction ability and the short-term memory limitation. All of these capacities play a role in literacy as they make it possible for human beings to comprehend and produce written language. The mechanisms discussed thus far are underlying cognitive abilities, essential to literacy. In addition, we have two kinds of basic linguistic capacities, the use of syntax and redundancy, that make expert literacy possible.

Mental capacities 6: Syntax

The sixth mental capacity, then, is the general cluster of syntactic ability. Human linguistic ability with respect to syntax entails a number of interrelated phenomena: knowledge of the rules for sentences that allows us to judge strings of words to be sentences and assess a string's grammaticality and acceptability; productive use of a small set of these rules that allows us to create an infinite number of possible sentences; recognition of the arbitrary relationship of symbols and meanings that allows us to adapt language to any need that might arise; disconnection of language from context that allows us to discuss matters unrelated to the immediate context. Each of these syntactic abilities, usually discussed early in basic texts in linguistics and psycholinguistics (Fromkin, Rodman, & Hyams, 2011, p. 5-11; Bernstein Ratner, Berko Gleason & Narasimhan, 1998, p. 5-6) is tied to literacy in easily recognizable ways.

The following passage from the work of Kenneth Goodman illustrates the extent to which readers rely on the rules of syntax to understand written language, allowing them to easily answer the questions following:

> A Mardsan Giberter for Farfie
>
> Glis was very fraper. She had denarpen Farfie's mardsan. She didn't talp a giberter for him. So she conlanted to plimp a mardsan binky for him. She had just sparved the binky when he jibbled in the gorger.
>
> "Clorsty mardsan!" she boffed.
>
> "That's a croutish mardsan binky," boffed Farfie, "but my mardsan is on Stansan. Agsan is Kelsan."
>
> "In that ruspen," boffed Glis, "I won't whank you your giberter until Stansan.
>
> Quiz
>
> 1. Why was Glis fraper?
> 2. What did Glis plimp?

3. Who jibbled in the gorger when Glis sparved the binky?
4. What did Farfie bof about the mardsan binky?
5. Why didn't Glis whank Farfie his giberter? (Goodman, 1996, p. 43)

In my experience using this passage to talk about reading, English-speaking readers make a kind of sense from this passage, easily producing correct answers to the quiz, as they rely strongly on their knowledge of English syntax to do so.

We use this knowledge of the rules of language for instance when we read poetry, where the rules may be broken for artistic purposes. We use productivity when we generate new texts in written form. We use the arbitrary connection of symbol and meaning when we make up new words, such as for new products or new phenomena in the world. We use the absence of context to read or write about people and events happening around the corner or around the world or in imaginary worlds.

Mental capacities 7: Redundancy

In addition to syntax, there is another linguistic ability that meta-readers and writers make use of, the capacity to process a text by drawing on the inherent redundancy of language. Redundancy is usually thought of as a negative characteristic of language, simple repetition. But psycholinguistically, redundancy constitutes an essential feature of language because it is the feature that insures that the message sent by one person is the same as the message received by another. Redundancy operates largely below our conscious awareness like the other mental capacities, but in its absence, communication is difficult, if not impossible. Redundancy's importance to written language is increasing because of the Web, as written language is so often presented in combination with visual arrays of various kinds.

The use of the fundamental redundancy of language is in some ways more complex than the preceding six basic tools because it affects a number of different aspects of written language. Redundancy, the information overlap built into language, pervades written language, from the configurations of letters to the overall structure of a text. It plays a role in our ability to recognize various aspects of written language, supporting both recognition that is based on both remembering and knowing (Knowlton, 1998, p. 260-261). As I have argued elsewhere (1993), without redundancy, the connection of readers and writers through a text would be much more difficult. The ability to tap into various kinds of psycholinguistic redundancy is a seventh processing ability of human beings that plays a key role in critical literacy.

Redundancy is one manifestation of our basic perceptual mechanism, and is part of what Steven Pinker suggests is a paradigm for how the mind works in a larger sense (Pinker, 1997, p. 241). In his discussion of stereo vision, the way in which our two eyes work together to provide mental images, Pinker suggests that it is from the overlay of the two slightly different images in our two eyes that we get an accurate description of the world. This mechanism of "stereo vision" makes depth perception and actually, all accurate perception, possible (Pinker, 1997, p.219). This biological mechanism, Pinker suggests, plays out in various mental functions, one of which is the human capacity for literacy.

In language, the simplest and sometimes most annoying type of redundancy is simple repetition. When this form of redundancy occurs, readers are likely to be bored or annoyed by it. One of my expert readers, EDT, found much of the Michigan history passage redundant in this way, leading her to say often "I don't care about this part." From a psycholinguistic perspective, though, redundancy is a much more sophisticated feature of text, essential to communication of all kinds of information according to former *New York Times* writer James Gleick (2011). In *The Information: A History, A Theory, A Flood*, Gleick points out that English (and mostly likely virtually all alphabetic languages) is about 50% redundant, based on mathematical calculations by information theorist Claude Shannon (Gleick, 2011, p. 217). Because of redundancy, we need much less to get the essential information in a text. This psycholinguistic feature plays out, for example, in the 140 character limitation on Twitter, where a great deal of information can be conveyed in very condensed form; processing tweets simply draws on the essential redundancy of language. (I am grateful to my colleague Lynn Quitman Troyka for pointing out the psycholinguistic features of Twitter.)

Pinker (1994) discusses this attribute in the context of the sound system, but his observations apply equally to the written form of the language. He writes:

> Phonological rules help listeners even when they do not exaggerate some acoustic difference. By making speech patterns predictable, they add redundancy to a language; English text has been estimated as being between two and four times as long as it has to be for its information content. For example, this book takes up about 900,000 characters on my computer disk, but my file compression program can exploit the redundancy in the letter sequences and squeeze it into about 400,000 characters; computer files that do not contain English text cannot be squished nearly that much. (Pinker, 1994, p. 181)

He goes on to show that the written form of the language also allows for compression:

> Thanks to the redundancy of language yxx cxn xndxrstxnd whxt x xm wrxtxng xf x rxplxcx xll thx vxwxls wxth xn "x" (t gts lttl hrdr f y dn't vn kn whr th vwls r). (Pinker, 1994, p. 181)

This example reveals that we can get meaning not only if we know the vowels' places, but also if they are absent. It might be worth noting that Pinker created this example long before text messaging became commonplace, but texting similarly relies on the inherent redundancy in written language.

There are some additional points to be made from Pinker's example, both pertinent to redundancy as a characteristic of written language. First, this example from Pinker, though I have used it before, is very difficult to type. My fingers expect vowels and resist their replacement with an "x"; it is a little easier to type the segment with no vowels, since then I can simply spell the letters in my head and order my fingers to move letter by letter, not trying to capture their patterns as words. A second point, though, is that some languages, notably Hebrew and Arabic, are normally written without vowels. Because of redundancy, readers have no problem getting meaning in their absence.

These examples show that redundancy offers insurance to language users that the messages they exchange will be understood successfully, despite the lack of conscious awareness of this characteristic of language. There are places, too, where redundancy is made more tangible. Beginning writers working on the infamous "five paragraph essay" are often told to repeat their main idea in the opening and ending paragraphs and tie each paragraph in the development explicitly to this point. It's the old "tell 'em what you're gonna tell 'em, tell 'em, tell 'em what you told 'em" strategy. This strategy has been around a long time for good reason; done well, it builds essential redundancy into a text at the discourse level. Stating a key term, giving a definition and then providing an example is yet another way that writers convey their ideas by exploiting redundancy.

Basic research on human perceptual processes such as that by Italian neuroscientist Gerbino shows clearly that redundancy "supports stable perception" (Gerbino, 1997, p. 151). Working from the perspective of understanding human and machine perception, Gerbino notes that "Generally speaking, experimental evidence about information fusion in human perception supports the conclusion that redundancy helps, while simplification leads to ambiguity" (Gerbino, 1997, p. 147). A study of scene recognition and object recognition further supports this claim

(Christou & Bulthoff, 2000). The experiments reported in this study show that recognition of settings and objects depends significantly on prior experience or learning. In addition, recognition abilities depend on the context in which the task occurs. In these experiments reported by vision researchers Christou and Bulthoff, changing the background against which a scene was viewed so that it was not a consistent source of information caused subjects to make recognition errors. The background provides redundancy that makes accurate recognition possible.

Research on redundancy in multimedia contexts suggests the ways in which a somewhat more sophisticated form of it can enhance learning. Redundancy in multimedia contexts arises when information overlap is produced by presenting the same ideas in different modalities (i.e., visual and auditory). Multimedia learning theorist Richard Mayer makes clear how the redundancy effect operates in such contexts:

> The redundancy principle seems to suggest that two modalities are worse than one, whereas the multimedia principle seems to suggest that two modalities are better than one. The apparent discrepancy can be resolved by applying the cognitive theory of multimedia learning. The redundancy principle is based on a situation in which presenting words in two sense modalities—as print and as speech—is worse than presenting words solely in one modality—as speech. A distinguishing feature in this situation is that the added on-screen text serves to overload the visual channel, which must also process the incoming animation. In contrast, the multimedia principle is based on the idea that learning can be improved when a narration is supplemented with corresponding animation. In this case, load on the visual channel is not increased because words are presented in the auditory channel. (Mayer, 2001, p. 158-59)

He goes on to say that in designing multimedia materials, it is usually more effective to present words in spoken form and pictures in visual form, but sometimes both spoken and written text can also be helpful (p. 159).

This finding by Mayer is supported by research with infants reported in the journal *Infancy* in 2001. A study of 7-month-olds showed that children use multi-channel redundancy to learn and remember word and object relationships (Gogate & Bahrick, 2001). Similar findings showing the positive effect of multi-channel redundancy on learning for adults were obtained by Bishop (2001). In her study, Bishop used information theory to suggest the beneficial impact of adding sound to instructional software for adult students. A third study, also using adult participants, found that audio-visual redundancy improved information processing and recall of news stories on television (Zhou, 2001), although visual potency of the images presented also had an effect on processing and recall.

Other studies also show the importance of information overlap from various modalities. For example, Paris, Thomas, Gilson and Kincaid (2000) looked at the role of prosodic cues (rising and falling sentence intonation patterns, for example) in how well people understand synthesizers reading printed text aloud. Prosodic cues apparently provide some redundancy and help people parse the text correctly; when such cues are missing or erroneous, they cause listeners to make more errors. These results have important implications for a variety of situations including education and consumer products as well as safety systems. Redundancy, however, is not a cure-all, since the effect of redundancy hinges on the prior knowledge of the reader or learner. Another multimedia learning theorist, Kalyuga (1999) finds that the positive impact of redundancy declines as learner expertise increases. Kalyuga examined the effect of text, audio input and diagrams at different levels of learner expertise. For more experienced learners working with diagrams for electrical wiring and soldering, multiple channels of information produced cognitive overload, though less experienced learners benefited.

One further study of cognitive load and the impact of redundancy for learners with different levels of expertise shows similar results. Yeung conducted three experiments on vocabulary learning by ESL students and native-speaking adults. Yeung (1999) found that

> In sum, vocabulary meanings presented in an integrated format may either increase or decrease cognitive load depending on the type of task and the readers' expertise. Yeung et al. (1998) demonstrated that when vocabulary definitions were presented in a separated format, younger native readers and lower ability ESL secondary school students performed better in vocabulary tests, but they performed better in comprehension with an integrated format. Adult native readers and higher ability secondary ESL readers, in contrast, scored better in vocabulary when vocabulary definitions were presented to them in an integrated format but did better in comprehension when the definitions were presented to them in a separated format. (Yeung, 1999)

Thus, the level of learners' expertise has an impact on their performance in terms of both vocabulary development and reading comprehension. In his studies, Yeung noted that

> although comprehension was improved by an integrated format, vocabulary learning was impeded. Vocabulary was learned best when the vocabulary meanings were separated from the text. Under those circumstances, the text

> acted as a redundant source of information imposing an extraneous cognitive load (Sweller, 1993). In contrast, the more experienced readers in Experiment 3 did not require the vocabulary meanings to comprehend the text. When presented in an integrated format, the meanings were redundant but hard to ignore; they were easier to ignore in a separated format. The redundancy effect increased cognitive load and decreased comprehension when the material was processed in an integrated format. Although attending to vocabulary meanings in the integrated format reduced comprehension for more experienced readers, increased knowledge of vocabulary might be expected and was obtained when compared with the separated format that permitted students to ignore vocabulary. (Yeung, 1999)

Redundancy, then, has different impacts, depending on the level of ability of the readers or learners, their knowledge of the subject matter, and the format of the presentation in the text—here, separated definitions in contrast to those integrated into text material.

It should be clear that, while redundancy doesn't always support literacy, there is solid evidence to suggest that it can be a useful element in many circumstances. Experts become experts in part by capitalizing on redundancy; in addition, it can be useful even to those with some level of expertise. The type of redundancy examined is also pertinent. The studies summarized here, with the exception of Yeung's work, do not examine psycholinguistic redundancy, but look chiefly at the overlap or simple repetition of material through different channels. The issue of the role and impact of redundancy across different channels or modalities will be considered more fully later this book.

Second Language Learners

Finally, it is easy to see how helpful redundancy can be to second language learners. The use of the inherent psycholinguistic redundancy of language helps insure that the message one person sends is the same as the message another person receives. Redundancy, the positive, essential information overlap that naturally occurs in language, exists in sound patterns, orthographic structure, word form and usage, syntactic structure and in meaning. Successful language users are always tapping into redundancy even though they are not often aware of it. All of these mental capacities are the building blocks of human language ability, including literacy. Pinker (1997) suggests that all people have them, regardless of what language they speak. And these capacities are essential for the development and use of expert literacy.

Summary

Expert critical literacy, then, is a highly complex and sophisticated form of human language ability. It entails the ability to put meaning into a text (writing) or get meaning out of a text (reading) for varied purposes. It is based on fundamental mental capacities that humans use in many aspects of daily functioning. These include the capacity for recognition or identification, which is necessary to get us to negotiate the world so that we know where we are in it. The capacity for categorization makes it possible for us to see things in groups or sets, putting like items together. Categorization is the basis, for example, of several of the rhetorical modes, but also helps us sort and make sense of the world around us. Third, discrimination, judging similarity and difference, is also essential to literacy. At every level of literate functioning, this kind of judgmental ability makes the critical part of critical literacy do-able. We also make predictions and rely on our short-term memory, limited though it is. Finally, the linguistic capacities that meta-readers and writers rely on, the use of syntax and redundancy, are pervasive, though largely unconscious. Despite the operation of all seven of these mental capacities mostly below our level of awareness, they are nonetheless essential to the processing of written language, both reading and writing. Experts have and apply these mental capacities, and they are used and essential for expert literacy in both print and digital environments.

CHAPTER FOUR

THE DISTINCTIVE FEATURES AND CRITICAL LITERACY

The mental capacities, both cognitive and linguistic, described in Chapter 3, operate on the language itself at a variety of levels. An analysis of these levels shows that written language has a defined, limited variety of features. These must be understood in order to see just what meta-readers and writers do with texts. Many linguists take the spoken form of the language to be primary and the majority of linguistic studies look at ordinary spoken language without reference to written forms. However, as increasing amounts of information come to us in written form on paper or, to an ever-greater extent on a screen, it is essential that our abilities to process and produce written text become a primary focus. The concept of distinctive features, even though linguists conventionally use it to analyze the sound system, is useful to examine the parts of the written form at rudimentary, basic, intermediate and advanced levels; features at each level account for meta-readers' and writers' abilities with text.

The distinctive features exist at the four levels of written language. They function through the use of the mental capacities discussed in Chapter 3, including the abilities to identify, categorize and discriminate. Like the phonological distinctive features, they make selective use of redundancy; they help to insure that readers and writers understand one another. These features appear in the orthography and graphology, a sort of rudimentary level of literacy, in the morphology and meanings of written language at a basic level, in the sentence patterns, discourse forms or genres at an intermediate level, and in the rhetorical modes and argument strategies of written text at the most advanced level. Meta-readers' and writers' critical literacy entails the ability to perceive and produce the distinctive features at each level.

Originally, in linguistic theory, distinctive features were proposed as characteristics of the sounds of a language that help speakers distinguish meaningful differences among sounds. Voicing or vocal cord vibration is one such feature in English, the distinguishing feature that separates /b/

from /p/ and allows speakers to determine whether ‘pat’ or ‘bat’ has been said. A more technical explanation is offered in an introductory linguistics text: “When a feature distinguishes one phoneme from another, it is a distinctive feature or, equivalently a **phonemic feature**” (Fromkin, Rodman & Hyams, 2011, p. 278). Distinctive features are important in the spoken form of the language because they help insure that speakers understand one another.

An additional recent finding about the phonological features supports their role in critical literacy I am developing. Peter Eimas and his colleagues (1971) have found clear evidence that babies come into the world with a capacity to hear the distinctive features of human language. Initially, according to Eimas, children can hear the full range of meaningful sound contrasts, but they quickly begin to pay most attention to those contrasts that are meaningful in what will become their native language. Thus, humans arrive prepared to pay attention to key features of language in the spoken form, and I am suggesting here, also in the written form. As meta-readers and writers, humans have the ability to process and produce these features for the purposes of expert critical literacy.

Although the phonological distinctive features have been discussed carefully by linguists and are generally accepted as a means of describing human language sounds, other kinds of distinctive features are not so readily apparent. Indeed, Smith suggests that it may be impossible to know what the distinctive features of letters actually are (2004, pp. 122-123). In what follows, I will suggest that we do know a great deal about the distinctive features of written language and will propose some for each of the four levels of literacy. In doing so, I will rely on Smith’s generic definition of what a distinctive feature is:

> …it is a property of visual information that can be used to differentiate some visual configurations from others. By definition, a distinctive feature must be common to more than one object or event, otherwise it could not be used to put more than one into the same category. But, on the other hand, if the feature were present in all objects or events, then we could not use it to segregate them into different categories; it would not be “distinctive.” In other words, a feature, if detected, permits the elimination of some of the alternative categories in which a stimulus might be allocated. (Smith, 2004, p. 115)

Though he intended for this description to apply chiefly to letter identification in reading, Smith’s description works well not only for rudimentary orthography, but also for the basic, intermediate and advanced levels of language essential to critical literacy.

The additional point to be made about the distinctive features in phonology is that there is a certain amount of redundancy built into the system. Some features are predictable from other features and are therefore redundant. For example, in English, all vowels are voiced sounds, since their production always entails vocal cord vibration. Thus, even in the spoken version of the language, there is some redundancy, though again, it is not part of speakers' conscious awareness.

Frank Smith supports this view in his analysis of the role of distinctive features and redundancy in reading:

> ...[I]t is just as appropriate to talk about distinctive features of speech as it is to refer to distinctive features of written language. In fact, the feature model of letter identification that was developed in the 1960s was inspired by a feature theory of speech perception published in the 1950s... . In both theories, a physical representation, acoustic or visual, is scanned for distinctive features which are analyzed in terms of feature lists that determine a particular categorization and perceptual experience. The number of physical features requiring to be discriminated will depend on the perceiver's uncertainty and other sources of information about the language (redundancy) that can be utilized. (Smith, 2004, p. 275)

According to Smith, then, distinctive features rely, in part, on those mental capacities discussed in Chapter 3, including categorization and access to redundancy. A look at the distinctive features at each level will clarify how they are used in reading and writing.

Rudimentary Level

The orthographic distinctive features at a rudimentary level include not only the components of written characters for both perception and production, but also the key features of graphology, the study of the written symbols of language. The geometric elements of print might include these: circle, square, triangle, vertical, horizontal, open, closed, diagonal, curve, positionality and sequencing. This set is similar to that proposed by psychology researchers Sadoski and Paivio (2001). It expands considerably the features observed by one of the great proponents of English writing/spelling reform, George Bernard Shaw, who suggested four types of letters: shorts, talls, deeps and compounds (Crystal, 1987, p. 216). Examples of the features can be drawn from diverse languages: English, Hebrew, Hindi, Japanese, Chinese, Braille.

Sadoski and Paivio (2001) address this issue in their discussion of the processing of written text in terms of individual letters and words.

Drawing on research on visual perception, they suggest that the brain has specific receptors for geometric shapes. When used in reading, then,

> print features include lines, angles, intersections, curvature, openness and so on, as well as the spatial orientation of features such as left, right, up, or down (e.g., *d, b, p, q*). ...Through neurological connections, activated visual feature detectors activate visual logogens of letters, common spelling patterns, (e.g., onsets, rimes, affixes), words, or even short phrases learned as visual units. (Sadoski & Paivio, 2001, p. 118)

Sadoski and Paivio (2001) account for literacy through their "dual coding theory" (2001, p. 42-66), which incorporates both verbal and nonverbal elements called logogens and imagens. The two coding systems work differently and can function independently, parallel to one another or in relationship and connection to one another. They claim that in dual coding

> all cognition including perception, memory, meaning, and knowledge must be accounted for by the operations of the representations within and between the two codes, and such an accounting can explain a great variety of literacy activities. (Sadoski & Paivio, 2001, p. 66)

For the present discussion, Sadoski and Paivio's findings are useful in supporting the basic claim I am making about distinctive features.

In graphology, British linguist David Crystal (1987) suggests that languages may have special writing systems to perform various functions. There are five of these functions that he identifies: orthography or standard writing, stenography or speed writing, cryptography or secret writing, paedography or instructional writing, and technography or specialized writing (Crystal, 1987, p. 194). Each of these functions draws on a different type of alphabetic symbol system.

While some of these writing systems are not alphabetic in nature, the vast majority of the world's writing systems are alphabetic. According to British historian John Man, "over 60 per cent of the world's total consumption of written material is in alphabets of one kind or another" (2000, p. 14). More recent research shows that alphabetic writing systems (as well as some syllabic and logographic systems) have key features in common. According to French cognitive scientist Dehaene, there are a relatively small number of features that distinguish among the letters in writing systems as diverse as Greek, Bengali, Tamil, Korean and Chinese (Dehaene, 2009, p. 174-77). The commonalities have to do with the way the brain works such that there are, Dehaene says, "universally shared deep structures" (p. 174). The features are those that our brains are designed to work with, and are close to those found in nature; moreover, they are the easiest to read (p. 178). Our neurons do a kind of double duty according to Dehaene's neuronal recycling theory, extending their ability to identify shapes in nature to identification of shapes in writing.

The alphabet allows a simple means of capturing, approximately, the spoken form of the language. It has advantages speech does not have, even in these high-tech times: transmission over time and space, potential for perfection, time for reflection and so on. Among the important advantages of alphabetic writing and perhaps its most important feature is that it is comprised of symbols that can be reduced to a small set of distinguishing characteristics, the distinctive features. Spelling and meaning work together in most writing systems according to Dehaene, a necessity since most languages have homophones like 'retch' and 'wretch.' If this were not the case, as he notes, reading would be much harder, like decoding the rebuses used in ancient Egypt: "it wood bee two in knee fish hunt" (Dehaene, 2009, p. 1890.

In a Hebrew text meant for beginners who are literate in English, for example, the 22 consonant letters are presented in an essentially contrastive pattern, putting together for instruction letters with similar distinctive features (Rothblum, Bergman & Band, 1987). In this volume, the letters in the second unit include [ד] dalet (similar to English 'D') and [ר] resh (similar to English 'R'). The sequence is not the ordering of the letters in the alphabet, but is based on the likely distinctive features of the letters. Maybe all primers work this way. The underlying principle is the same as noted previously in Sadoski and Paivio's (2001) discussion of English lower case letters b, d, p, and q. These are essentially the same shape, consisting of a circle and a bar, oriented differently in space and with respect to one another. The distinction hinges on whether the bar is to the left or right of the circle and whether it extends above or below the circle.

This example is meant to illustrate the larger claim I am making, that at a rudimentary level, there are distinctive features of written language that work in a way quite similar to the phonological distinctive features. That is, they are a relatively small list of characteristics that allow readers and writers to distinguish among the letters and words in a piece of writing and thus get the meaning of the text. Again, as is true of the phonological features and of the underlying mental capacities and redundancy of language, humans are not usually consciously aware of these features but do need them and rely on them to make meaning in language. To develop critical literacy, readers and writers must use these features of the written form for comprehension and production, and need them in both traditional and digital environments.

The challenges of learning and using written language are substantial but attainable for most people. But learning a new writing system, or learning literacy in a new language provides some distinct challenges for those often referred to as members of Generation 1.5. These students are the children of immigrant parents who arrive in a new country at a young age and attend school in the new country, learning a new language. To achieve any level of literacy, Generation 1.5 learners must know the writing system of the language in which they are trying to become literate; it may or may not be the same as that of their native language. And, as Harklau (2003) points out, Generation 1.5 students may not be literate in their native language anyway, even at this rudimentary level.

At this level, letters and words fall into basic patterns to which expert meta-readers and writers can apply their mental capacities. Literate users of English know such patterns and will quickly say that after 'q' comes 'u' and that words like 'czar' or 'Ngo' are not English. They can sort 'c' from 'o' and 'b' from 'd' from 'p' from 'q' quickly and easily, often at blinding speeds if they are reading meaningful text. They know the differences that make a difference to meaning, such as those between 'E' and 'F' and the differences of a similar kind, say between 'A' and 'a' that are not significant to meaning.

Generation 1.5 readers and writers, especially those not literate in their native language, face the challenge of learning the orthography and graphology, spelling patterns and writing conventions of whatever language they are learning, English or another. However, having skills at this rudimentary level is essential to critical literacy for all learners, whether children developing L1, adults developing L2, Generation 1.5 learners developing literacy in a new language, and whether the critical literacy is developing on paper or on the screen. Undoubtedly, there are rudimentary forms for the graphics, pictures, movements and sound patterns that might appear on a website as well.

Basic Level

At the second level, a kind of basic set of literate abilities, there must also be a distinctive feature set for words and meanings, following a similar pattern if the proposal of distinctive features as a mechanism is correct. At a basic level, the distinctive features address words and meanings. Word recognition features might include length, frequency, consistency with letter/sound sequential constraints for the language, and grammatical markers (plural, past tense, possessive, and the like), among others. Then there would have to be yet another set of distinctive features for meaning. These claims follow, again, Smith's general proposals in *Understanding Reading* (2004). The meaning features would be more complex, but still essentially at a basic level. Semantic feature theory as proposed by some linguists (Reeves et al., 1998, p. 185) offers the major meaning features.

Semantic feature theories capture key characteristics of words as components of meaning, such as human and animate and perhaps also such gender markers as male and female where relevant. As in graphology, we do not have a definitive list of what all the features are, but we do have an intuitive sense of them. In terms of syntax, we have a list of what might be features, the classic parts of speech: nouns, verbs, adjectives, adverbs, prepositions, conjunctions, articles, interjections. Notice that this is a fairly standard list of eight categories, within the mental limit of seven plus or minus two items.

The Dual Coding Theory of Sadoski and Paivio (2001) provides some support for these proposals. Their idea of logogens, drawn from various theories of cognitive processing, suggests that there are distinctive features for words, word sequences and meanings. Sadoski and Paivio define logogens and the corresponding nonverbal units, imagens, as follows:

> The morpheme *logo-* is Greek for word, speech or discourse, and the morpheme *imago-* for imitation, copy or image; the morpheme *–gen* means that which generates. Hence, logogens are language generators and imagens are image generators; both are also useful in recognition. More specifically, logogens are modality-specific (visual, auditory, etc.) units in the verbal system that are activated by external stimuli or internally by other, previously activated mental representations. Likewise, imagens are modality-specific units in the nonverbal system that are activated by external stimuli or internally by other, previously activated mental representations. (2001, p. 47)

They go on to say that logogens are word-like while imagens are scene-like, that is, visual in nature. Size, however, is not a defining characteristic of either logogens or imagens, so logogens can be letters, morphemes or words, punctuation, phrases, and so on (p. 47). A literate person's attention may shift between these various levels as necessary in the course of reading or writing.

In Sadoski and Paivio's Dual Coding Theory, meaning would be captured by the imagens or image generators, though some meanings do not have a visual counterpart, such as abstractions. It is important to keep in mind that Sadoski and Paivio see the two coding systems, verbal and nonverbal, as working either independently, in tandem or in relation to one another, as noted previously. Dehaene's (2009) research with brain imaging, discussed earlier, supports their view. In order for literacy to be possible, there must be some distinctive features like logogens and imagens that pertain to words and word sequences, and we must be able to perceive them and produce them.

A good example of the notion of distinctive features in the written form would be a text that is visually difficult to read: for example, one that is written in handwriting that is illegible, or printing that is unclear such as in a smeared page of the newspaper. If readers can make out the distinctive features of letters and words, it is probably possible to read the text in spite of the interference due to the lack of clarity. Distinctive features of not only the letters but also the words and sentences make literacy possible, even under difficult conditions.

Features of words might be roots, prefixes and suffixes, overall syllable structure, length, and sequential constraints. Speakers of English, for instance, know that 'q' will be followed by 'u' in English words, and that initial letter sequences in English words cannot be 'vl' or 'ng.' These are to some extent sequential phonological constraints, but not exclusively so. Features of words and word sequences entail the various types of phrases (noun phrases, adjective phrases and the like) and the main types of sentences, simple, compound, complex, declarative, interrogative, exclamatory, active, and passive, and also the main forms of meaning, figures of speech.

Support for this role for meaning on the path to critical literacy comes from the work of psychologist and rhetorician Alexander Bain (1866/1990). Bain's ideas rest on his understanding of psychology, supporting my proposal that the distinctive features I am suggesting function in cooperation with the mental capacities of the human brain, as discussed in Chapter 3. In his discussion of Figures of Speech, drawing from Quintilian, Bain sorts the major figures into three major categories:

> based on the operations of Intellect, or Understanding, that they have reference to. Now, our intellectual powers are reducible to three simple modes of working … DISCRIMINATION … SIMILARITY … RETENTIVENESS … (Bain, 1866/1990, p. 876)

The key figures of speech fall into these three categories. For Discrimination, the main figure of speech is antithesis or contrast. In Similarity, the figures of simile, metaphor and allegory are included, and Retentiveness is the category to which metonymy belongs. This approach to meaning sets up five major categories or distinctive features, a relatively short list that hinges on a key mental capacity, the limitation described by the magical number 7, plus or minus 2, as discussed in Chapter 3.

As De Paul University rhetorician Mulderig (1982) points out, Bain's work is important not only because it clarifies how the figures of speech work, but also because he relies on psychology to explain how rhetoric works more generally. Noting that Bain's scheme of contrast, contiguity and similarity is not new, as the general categories date back to Aristotle, Mulderig shows that Bain's unique contribution is to show their relationship to psychological processes. He writes:

> Observing at the start of the *Rhetoric* that "[s]everal of the more important Figures [of speech] have reference to the operations of the human Understanding, or Intellect, and may be classified accordingly," Bain introduces the mental properties of discrimination, retentiveness, and agreement as the framework for his classification. Under the property of discrimination he places figures of antithesis, under retentiveness come metonymy and synecdoche, and under agreement we find simile, metaphor, personification, and allegory (pp. 2-3). The arrangement is not simply ornamental. For Bain, it provides a way of using association psychology to explain how figures of speech acquire their rhetorical effectiveness and to suggest how they are generated. (Mulderig, 1982, pp. 97-98)

Bain's psychological explanation helps support his system of categories; it provides additional support for my proposal that there are underlying mental capacities, and they work together with the distinctive features to make critical literacy possible on pages and screens.

The distinctive feature idea also works for punctuation. For English and many other alphabetic languages, the marks of punctuation for major sentence units such as sentences, phrases and clauses are once again essentially a short list: period, comma, colon, semi-colon, apostrophe, question mark, exclamation point (seven items). While there are other marks of punctuation, such as dashes, quotation marks and parentheses and so on, the first list includes those used to mark sentence, clause and phrase boundaries and so are the most widely-used marks. While the question mark and exclamation point are considered somewhat minor in popular British writer Lynne Truss's (2003) hilarious discussion of the history and current use of punctuation, they do mark major structural boundaries.

It is interesting to note that most of these lists of distinctive features are fairly short. It may well be that the range of distinctive features at each level is itself constrained by the limits of short-term memory. This limit is well-established at the "magical number seven" give or take two, as reported by George Miller (1956) in his seminal study of human information processing. I usually think of short-term memory as the time between when I put the phone book back in the front closet and get to the phone to key in a number I've looked up in the book. Many things come in batches of about seven items because of this limit: phone numbers, days of the week, Snow White's dwarfs, Social Security numbers, computer passwords (usually suggested to be eight characters) among others. And even with the advent of area codes on many phone numbers in our increasingly wired world, I'd suggest that the area codes most often needed are processed as a unit, making eight items to hold in short-term memory for telephone purposes. So distinctive features at the orthographic level or the word or sentence level are constrained by this limitation. The major forms of punctuation, the major parts and figures of speech, and so on, all fall in this range of five to nine items. At the higher levels, the lists are again short (i.e. around seven items) for the same reason.

Letter sequences, word sequences, punctuation, and basic sentence patterns, in combination with the logogens and imagens of words and meanings must comprise the distinctive features of the basic level for readers and writers. Neither Sadoski and Paivio (2001) nor I argue for the idea that language users are aware of these matters or that they pay any conscious attention to them. However, these features must rely on the basic mental capacities that make critical literacy possible. The common patterns and structures are an essential feature of basic language skill. Second language learners will have to master the word structure of the language they are learning, English or any other. If they are already literate in one language, the underlying mental capacities and their use of syntax and redundancy are well established. If not, they face additional work to master the word structure, along with the basic patterns of graphics, pictures and so on. Again, both text and image have basic forms and patterns available for study and use by meta-readers and writers. Novices, whether second language learners or not, need these abilities to attain critical literacy, but certainly they may face additional challenges if they have not developed literacy in their L1.

Intermediate Level

Beyond these orthographic and morphological features, as well as the logogens and imagens, I propose that there is a third, intermediate level, again hinging on features of written language, for both perception (reading) and production (writing). The features here might be, for documents such arrays as tables, charts, graphs, diagrams, forms, and maps, and for prose, the various genres of text, including prose, poetry, drama, newspaper articles or editorials, textbook-type materials or basic legal texts like warranty statements. For both reading and writing purposes, language users must recognize these distinctive forms as distinctive, though again, not necessarily in a conscious way.

One attempt to make the features conscious arises in books designed to help novices read more effectively. A textbook for under-prepared college students, for example, addresses the types of documents and visual aids in texts quite directly. A whole chapter in Reynolds' *Reading for Understanding* (1995) examines visual aids, including discussion of tables, pie charts, line graphs, bar graphs, maps and diagrams (pp. 223-267). Most texts of this type also present these distinctive document forms and help students understand why they appear and how to read and understand them. Similarly, in the teaching of writing, the use of visuals may be taught directly, as it often is in texts on technical or professional writing. For example, in Kolin's textbook, *Successful Writing at Work* (2012), he discusses both visual document design and strategies for the use of tables, graphs, charts, pictographs, maps, photographs, drawings and clip art (p. 197-229).

The differences between prose and poetry, drama and news reports and such must also be distinctive. Some of the difference is visual in nature: readers know they are looking at poetry rather than prose because of the layout of the text on the page. The visual characteristics of a text are pertinent here as they are among the distinctive features that separate one type of text from another; these features will come up again later in this book, in the study of reading and writing for the World Wide Web. But some of the differences in types of prose go beyond page layout or other visual characteristics. These have to do with the various genres: prose, poetry, drama, news, biography or autobiography and so on. These are distinctive forms. Readers and writers may be more consciously aware of these distinctive features than they are of letter shapes or sentence patterns, but I propose that they are not a matter that most readers pay much direct attention to under ordinary circumstances, once they have learned the forms in school settings.

Text types, genres and structures are interrelated in a complex way. Washington State University reading and literacy scholar Stephen Kucer addresses this point in his discussion of the varied dimensions of literacy (2005, p. 5). Kucer's insights about the ways humans categorize language are particularly pertinent because his analysis addresses the ways that these abilities are taught and learned. He describes the interrelationships this way:

> The meanings that are generated to meet an individual's purpose are displayed through various text types, genres and text structures. ...Text types—narrative, exposition, poetic, dramatic—are expressed through particular genres and text structures and reflect particular features, patterns, and content....
>
> The meanings that are generated through text types and genre are expressed in a variety of corresponding structures—temporal order, adversative, response, attribution, and covariance. (Kucer, 2005, p. 27-8)

Note that Kucer uses the word "features" in his description of genre and structure, indicating that each has characteristic features, supporting my proposal. The structures he describes consist of more features, including some that specifically overlap with the rhetorical modes to be discussed below. Story grammars for narratives, comparison-contrast for adversative structures and so on all reflect the main principle here, that there are distinctive features that make literacy possible. The array of particular features described by Reynolds and Kucer clusters at an intermediate level of literacy.

Yet another perspective on this intermediate level of distinctive features appears in the United States government's adult literacy survey (NAAL) (Kirsch, Jungeblut, Jenkins & Kolstad, 1993), still considered a landmark study. The survey evaluated a representative sample of the American population, looking for skills at five levels of document and prose literacy. In this broad survey, the tasks in document literacy include locating pieces of information in a chart or graph, map reading, finding information in a table or map, creating a graph, and writing a summary of information from a table, or similar tasks (Kirsch, et al., 1993, p. 10). The tasks in prose literacy entailed reading short articles to find information, reading instructions from appliances purchased, comparing metaphors used in a poem, interpreting a phrase from a newspaper article, and writing a letter on a billing error, among others (Kirsch, et al., 1993, p. 10).

It is interesting to note that the Adult Literacy survey attempted to draw on both the various types of documents and the various genres of text that comprise the intermediate level of critical literacy. These tasks provide examples of the kinds of distinctive features and skills readers and writers must have to be critically literate. At the intermediate level, critically literate people can perceive and produce sentences and discourses in a variety of genres. Sentence and discourse features are consistent, whether they appear on pages or screens. Genres are also just as clear on websites as they are on paper—the websites of CNN.com or MSNBC.com as news sites are clearly different from a site like literacy.org, which is an information site, or amazon.com, a shopping site.

Critically literate individuals recognize the sentence patterns of their language as well as these genres. These abilities may not be conscious, but they are nonetheless present.

For second language learners, the intermediate level of skill may pose some challenges if they are not already able to read and write in their native language. However, there will undoubtedly be some carry-over awareness of the nature of sentences and discourse genres even from spoken forms if no level of literacy has been achieved. And while the types of genres may differ from those familiar in a learner's native language, the idea of genres should be constant and recognizable, in the same way that the idea of sentences as the basic units of written language would carry over from the first language. Second language learners need to learn the text types and genres of the target language for purposes of both reading and writing.

Advanced Level

The advanced level of language features for critical literacy requires an ability to perceive and produce the full array of rhetorical modes and the range of different types of argument. This level, again, must be based on a set of distinctive features. At this level, the features may include both the rhetorical modes and the forms of argumentation. The forms and features might vary from language to language and culture to culture as contrastive rhetoricians have pointed out (Kaplan, 1966). Critical literacy entails the ability to perceive and produce the various rhetorical modes and in particular, to use them to support an argument based on analysis, synthesis and evaluation.

In *English Composition and Rhetoric* (1866), Alexander Bain, a psychologist by training, established the definitions of the rhetorical modes that are still used in composition teaching now: description, narration, exposition, and persuasion. He also argues for the paragraph and paragraph unity. According to Bizzell and Hertzberg, "Bain's book settled the definitions of the modes of discourse for future textbooks and made paragraph unity a standard component of the rhetoric of composition" (Bizzell & Hertzberg, 1990, p. 861).

The modes of discourse enumerated by Bain will sound familiar to nearly any teacher or student of composition, since they persist, in one form or another, in many writing courses as well as in contemporary texts for the teaching of writing. Bain's major categories are description, narration, and exposition, including within these categories such familiar terms as definition, contrast, exemplification, classification, and process ("delineation of complex objects by the stages of their construction") (Bain, 1887, pp. xvi-xviii). Notice again that this is a fairly short list, falling easily within the 5-9 item range specified by the "magical number seven" mental capacity for short-term memory.

The idea of the modes plays out in at least one comprehensive theory of writing proposed by Grabe and Kaplan (1996). They offer a taxonomy of academic writing skills, knowledge bases, and processes, including the array of possible academic writing tasks. They distinguish narrative fiction and non-fiction from reports/(expository) essays and from argumentative essays. Among reports, they list the following: description, definition, exemplification, classification, comparison/contrast, cause/effect, problem/solution, and analysis/synthesis (note that there are eight types here). In argumentative essays, they list logical stances, ethical appeal, emotional appeal, empirical stance, appeal to authority, and counter-arguments (Grabe & Kaplan, 1996, p. 218). This list again is a short six items.

The modes and forms of argument are the most sophisticated forms of discourse for readers and writers and they appear in both traditional and digital environments. Perceiving them is a fundamental skill in expert meta-reading, and is again the subject of instruction in reading texts (Reynolds, 1995) and producing them is a key feature of expert meta-writing, as noted in Grabe and Kaplan's theory of writing (pp. 341-376) and in many, many composition textbooks (Huffman, 2010). Composition texts often provide examples in the form of readings that serve as prototypes or exemplars of the modes or types of argument (Levitin, 2006, p. 144-45).

Expert literacy also entails critical thinking capabilities; argument, finally, rests on the ability to make judgments and to marshal or recognize logical evidence in support of those judgments (Smith, 1990). In doing so, expert meta-readers and writers rely on the rhetorical modes and the forms of argumentation. Turning back to the work of Alexander Bain, we find an analytical scheme for the types of argument resting again on psychological principles Bain set forth in his textbooks in psychology that were major texts in the field for half of the nineteenth century (Mulderig, 1982, p. 96). Writing on oratory or persuasion, Bain relies heavily on Aristotle's rhetorical scheme of deliberative, forensic, and epideictic rhetoric (oratory of law, political oratory, sermons, and moral arguments). These distinctive features apply to both traditional and printed texts and have for centuries; Bain's use of them provides further support for the notion that digital reading and writing are not essentially new or different from these activities using traditional texts on paper.

Bain deals briefly with ethical argument, and expends most of his energy on persuasion by argument or especially, emotion. In the latter category, Bain suggests that persuasion works chiefly in one of three ways: pleasure or pain and its sustenance or alleviation, sympathy most notably in the form of pity, and the range of human emotions that move people beyond rational thought (Mulderig, 1982, p. 99-102). Here again, there are about seven categories of argument, consistent with the underlying limitation on human mental capacity. And while these categories are certainly fluid in contemporary writing, they are nonetheless a set of distinctive categories or features that mark critical literacy at the advanced level both on paper and on screens.

The idea of the rhetorical modes and strategies for argument naturally varies across different cultures, an observation made in the classic "doodles" article published years ago by University of Southern California applied linguist Robert Kaplan (1966) and pertinent to both first and second language learners. The article is usually referred to as the "doodles" article because Kaplan used small sketches to illustrate the differences in modes of thought and patterns in written forms in different cultures. Users of Arabic, for example, will tend to go around their point, as illustrated by concentric circles in Kaplan's doodles, rather than arguing it explicitly as westerners might. Here again, second language learners may have some additional work to do, but ultimately, like all those moving toward critical literacy, they must understand the rhetorical modes and forms of argument in order to perceive and produce texts. This understanding is essential to critical literacy.

Summary

Meta-readers and writers draw on these four levels of distinctive features for their expert work with texts on paper and screens. The concept of distinctive features carries over from spoken to written language. The distinctive features appear at four levels of literacy, from rudimentary, through basic and intermediate to the advanced form that entails being able to produce and comprehend the various modes of discourse and logical argument. Meta-reading and writing on the Web may entail a few more mental capacities and a few new features, but it is based on the same set of skills used with written language in printed form. There is a detailed discussion of the few additional processing skills and distinctive features in the later chapters of this book that examine writing and reading in digital environments.

There is a lot to literacy, and as UCLA education scholar Mike Rose has pointed out (1989, p. 188), ours is the first society to expect so many people to do so much with literacy skills. The whole "information economy" relies on literacy, and increasingly, on the expansion of literacy skills to digital forms. However, the fundamental skills involved are not different in these different venues and they are not any different for second language learners than they are for other individuals, whether they are developing expertise in their native language or in a second language. While there may be some additional features (like sound and juxtaposition of images) in a digital environment, the essential mental capacities and levels of language are constant and meta-readers and writers have them and use them consciously and/or unconsciously.

CHAPTER FIVE

META-READER THEORY AND THE AWARENESSES OF EXPERTS[1]

Introduction

In the summer, I'm always reading for new courses I am teaching in the coming academic year. The texts are informational prose, some textbooks per se and some not. As always when I read this kind of material, I am marking the text in a very particular way, following a strategy used in medieval texts. I sometimes underline or draw boxes around important ideas, but for key points, I draw a little hand in the margin with the index finger pointing to the passage. When I review the text, the little hands make it easy to find the key ideas without re-reading the whole text. I've been reading this way since I studied with a medieval literature scholar in college who told me about this text-marking scheme; the little hands are called manicules, according to Renaissance scholar William Sherman of the University of York in Britain (Sherman, 2005, p. 28).

Part of what makes me a meta-reader is that I know what to mark and where to put the little hands. It is this ability and related skills in reading that distinguishes experts from novices. In this chapter, the focus is on the awarenesses experts have about texts: meta-textual, meta-contextual and meta-linguistic awareness. A key question concerns how experts develop their abilities. There are four areas of research that explain the sources of expertise: research on the general nature of expertise in any area, proposals from schema theory in cognitive psychology, studies on the nature of implicit or incidental learning, and descriptions of academic voice. Taken together, experts' awarenesses and their sources help account for meta-readers' and writers' expertise with written language on pages and screens and reveal appropriate goals for novices.

Experts' awarenesses in the reading of nonfiction prose

The use of those little hands in text marking is quite pertinent to the theory of meta-reading and writing. Sherman points out that manicules help readers see the organization and structure of a text as they mark passages that are interesting and/or important (2005, p. 35). Medieval readers used them to flag passages they "considered worth noting" (2005, p. 38) for whatever specifically individual reason. Sherman says manicules "played an important role in the *personal* process of making a book meaningful" (2005, p. 43). For me, the symbol became just such a personally distinctive way of marking the text that has stayed with me since my college days. In the same way, Sherman's observations indicate that readers working with informational prose do have a specific and personal investment in the text. This individuality plays out in what experts read, how they read it, and how they use the marked text in their own writing and/or in their lives.

Meta-reader and writer theory

The theory proposes that experts are meta-readers and writers. The prefix 'meta' is drawn from the Greek, according to the dictionary ("meta," def. 1, 1966). It means after, along with, beyond, among, behind. Experts are able to do things with texts as they read, among the ideas presented and beyond them, so that behind, after and beyond the reading, they are able to get the essential meaning of a text. They can then analyze, synthesize, evaluate and apply, that is, engage with the text as expert readers and writers. This engagement occurs as experts bring these specific kinds of awareness and an array of skills to bear on their reading and writing experiences. The awareness of text may or may not be fully conscious. The three different kinds of awareness overlap a bit; these categories as described sound more separate than they probably are in actual practice.

Meta-reading awareness includes, first of all, *meta-textual awareness* of the organization and structure of the text. I had an expert reader tell me, for instance, in one of the case studies (in Chapter 2, EBD), that she was marking key parts of a text because the writer was setting out three points. She marked these 1, 2, and 3 as she saw the ideas unfold in the text. This meta-textual awareness allows readers to see the organizational structure of the text or how the ideas are presented, developed and exemplified. Meta-readers can easily see how they might use devices like graphic organizers (Grabe, 2009) to capture a text containing process analysis, or comparison-contrast, or classification, whether they actually take notes in any kind of graphic form. While this awareness may or may not be fully conscious, seeing the organizational strategy and structure of a text is one kind of awareness meta-readers have.

Meta-readers also have a second awareness, a *meta-contextual awareness* of where the text comes from and how it fits into the larger scheme of things—topic, research, author, disciplinary issues, and related matters. They are able to see the text as part of an on-going conversation about key issues or ideas in a discipline, drawing on their prior knowledge of the topic, the author's likely purpose and whatever else may bear on the text. Essays of literary criticism or Darwin's *Origin of Species* or reports of psychology experiments all arise from particular contexts and from long rhetorical and disciplinary traditions and genres. Expert readers know about and draw on this context, using their meta-contextual awareness. In rhetorician and education scholar Charles Bazerman's (1988) description of the physicists reading physics texts, for instance, the readers make choices about what and how to read based on their purposes, their prior knowledge of context, the author's other work and a range of other factors. In my case studies, a reader of a passage on the history of the Olympics marked the text's dates and filled in the history of the period in his summary through reliance on his prior knowledge (Chapter 2, EAF).

Finally, expert readers have a *meta-linguistic awareness* of the language of the text. Meta-linguistic awareness goes beyond individual words, though, to include various aspects of the language of the text, such as the sentence structures or patterns (parallel structure, for example), tone, register and other features of the language per se. Second language acquisition scholar Stephen Krashen explains that just as language learners must get what he calls the "din" of the target language in their heads, so expert readers are aware of the typical language forms of written language in their discipline (1983). The "din" refers to not only the sounds and sound patterns, but also other kinds of patterns in the text. Expert readers have an awareness of the typical patterns of vocabulary and other features of the language of informational prose in their discipline. In one of my case studies of expert writers revising (Horning, 2002), a writer with linguistics background reworks a sentence that has too much "puh" in it (i.e., too many words starting with [p]).

In addition to awareness of language per se, meta-linguistic awareness includes awareness of what University College London discourse scholar Ken Hyland calls metadiscourse. He examines the various aspects of metadiscourse in the informational texts of particular disciplines in *Disciplinary Discourses* (2000). More recently, Hyland has defined metadiscourse as "self-reflective linguistic material referring to the evolving text and to the writer and imagined reader of that text" (Hyland & Tse, 2004). Through metadiscourse, writers help readers see how the ideas of the text develop and connect by using their "interpersonal resources …to present propositional material" (Hyland & Tse, 2004). These three kinds of awareness, which may be fully or only partly conscious, meta-textual, meta-contextual and meta-linguistic, make experts meta-readers and writers.

The nature of expertise

Expert readers and writers develop their awarenesses over time. The issue of how these abilities develop brings to mind the old joke about the musician carrying a violin case on the streets of New York. The musician stops a passer-by and asks how to get to the famous performance venue, Carnegie Hall. The passer-by responds: "Practice, practice, practice." Practice is the most obvious resource experts have to account for their awarenesses, but not the only one. Experience and knowledge from study are other resources experts rely on. The theory of meta-reading and writing rests to some degree on proposals concerning novices and experts focusing not only specifically on literacy but also on developing expertise in many other areas. While there has been a significant amount of research on this topic over the last several decades, only some of the work is specifically pertinent to reading and writing and to helping all novices regardless of their discipline. So, for example, one of the papers in a volume of articles arising from a 1989 conference on the nature of expertise at the Max Planck Institute in Germany focuses specifically on "literate expertise" (Scardamalia & Bereiter, 1991). The insights of these scholars and those of Ruth Clark in *Building Expertise* (2008) provide a useful backdrop to theory. Other research on expertise such as that presented by Fox et al. (2008) at AERA and the insights of psychologist Ronald Kellogg (2006) on the role of reading in expert professional writing is also useful in accounting for expertise.

Beginning with literate expertise, then, Scardamalia and Bereiter (1991), researchers at the Ontario Institute for Studies in Education, note that reading expertise goes beyond and is essential to developing expertise in a particular field. They explain that reading expertise is more than a "tool skill," (1991, p. 174), i.e. more than a simple means to an end, but rather, an essential, inseparable part of the growth of expertise. Their research shows that "*...being an expert reader and writer within some domain means reading and writing in ways that maximize the productive* *interaction between these activities and others going on at the growing edge of expertise*" (Scardamalia & Bereiter, 1991, p. 175, emphasis in original). So, as readers develop their knowledge in some domain, they can use it to understand specific texts, just as doctors use their general knowledge of medicine to diagnose a specific illness. Thus, reading and the development of expertise are to some degree reciprocal; each supports the other.

Nonexperts are usually thought to lack domain knowledge, but Scardamalia and Bereiter point out that they lack the ability to integrate what they learn into their broader knowledge (1991, p. 178). In reading, comprehension involves both understanding the content of the text per se, which they call the textbase. In addition, comprehension entails integrating that textbase with prior knowledge of the domain, which they call the situational model. Expert readers apply specific strategies to achieve both comprehension and integration, such as "lexical repetition, relational terms and features of text organization" (Scardamalia & Bereiter, 1991, p. 183), along with skimming, scanning and adjustments to speed. They point out that true expertise in reading, uncommon among novices, "would involve cycles of attention to textbase and situational model, modifying each in response to problems arising from the other" (1991, p. 185).

The awarenesses of meta-readers and writers capture Scardamalia and Bereiter's elements of expertise. The expert readers in my case studies illustrate these ideas. They attend to both the content of the passages and their context. Expert EAF, the first of the Experts, read the Olympics passage in just this way. He was attending not only to the historical information in the textbase of the passage, but also to the situation the text describes, drawing on his knowledge of the history of the time from his other readings and prior knowledge of that period of time in European history. Thus, meta-textual and meta-contextual awareness work together in these concepts of textbase and situational model; moreover, this kind of response occurs whether the text is digital or printed.

A broader view of literate expertise comes from the work of University of Maryland educational psychologist Patricia Alexander, who has published extensively on reading and academic development. She makes this point in her discussion of a "Model of Domain Learning" (2003, p. 47). Alexander's studies examine reading development in such fields as physics, special education, and immunology (2003, p. 54), noting that readers develop over time through stages of acclimation to competence to expertise (2003, p. 55-57) as their knowledge of discipline or subject area and their reading ability in that area grows.

Some further insights from educational research in developing expertise beyond literacy offer additional background and support for the theory proposed here. Educational psychologist Ruth Clark's 2008 book, *Building Expertise*, for example, offers seven principles about experts and expertise that tie directly to the theory. Clark's broad discussion of research in teaching and learning shows that expertise arises from extended, deliberate practice within the domain or area that is of interest to the learner (2008, p. 9-12). Experts rely heavily on prior knowledge and can and do sometimes get stuck on a problem (2008, p. 12-14). When stuck, experts draw on both their routine expertise that arises from experience and what she calls "adaptive expertise" (2008, p.13) or the ability to apply prior knowledge and experience to a new situation. Finally, research shows that expert teamwork is most effective for solving challenging problems.

In order to provide good support to novices trying to develop expertise, teachers, librarians and community educators can look usefully at the research that has been done on experts. This research shows that experts have the several kinds of awarenesses described in this chapter. They perceive and can use text structures in various ways, when reading or writing. They draw on broader knowledge as well as prior experience to put texts they read or write into a larger context. And they rely on their knowledge of the language itself, in terms of sounds, words, sentences and meanings as they engage in meta-reading and writing. The theory relies on principles drawn from studies of literate expertise and discipline-based expertise in arguing for practice, application of prior knowledge and some collaborative work; recent developments of social media and other kinds of information sharing captured by Web 2.0 may be expanding the opportunities to share expertise in these ways. Using this understanding of meta-reading and writing, teachers can help novices move toward expanded expertise.

Schemata and expertise

Skill in literacy as well as in any particular area of activity arises from a second set of abilities cognitive psychologists describe with schema theory. Schema theory proposes that "knowledge is organized and stored in memory symbolically as generic structures" (Reznitskaya et al., 2008, p. 197). The often-cited examples are for such activities as eating out: we have a schema for menus, ordering, eating and paying. The schema for a child's birthday party might entail cake, ice cream, hats, gifts and pin-the-tail-on- the-donkey. Schemata enable readers to make predictions, a crucial aspect of the mental processing abilities to be discussed in chapter 3. Experts have schemata for aspects of the knowledge they have in their domain; literacy expertise entails schemata for how written language works.

Reznitskaya et al. (2008) propose that students may have or develop argument schemata that help them think, read and write effectively. While these writers claim that knowledge of argument schemata arise from discussion and interaction with others, most successful writers point to the influence of reading; surely some knowledge of argument arises from reading. This process occurs through the mechanism of implicit learning, discussed in detail in the next part of this chapter. Reznitskaya et al. (2008) say that argument schema theory

> ...postulates that dialogic discussions share important structural elements, such as formulating a claim, providing relevant reasons, questioning assumptions, and offering counterarguments. We project that by engaging in arguments during group discussions, students are provided with multiple instances from which the principles of argumentation can be abstracted. In other words, students generate mental representations of argument tactics, strategies, and principles, or argument schemas. (p. 198)

These cognitive psychologists summarize four studies done with elementary school students supporting their claims. They note that much of the knowledge of argument schemata may develop unconsciously, a key feature of implicit learning. And while they did not look at students' writing, their studies show students' ability to transfer their knowledge of sound argumentation to other situations (Reznitskaya, et al., 2008, p. 209).

Schema theory is one aspect of a meta-cognitive view of literacy. Examining reading research, literacy scholar Stephen Kucer has built a series of chapters around the 2004 reports of the Commission on Reading of NCTE (Kucer, 2008). Contextualizing the meta-cognitive view, Kucer summarizes the dimensions of literacy as including the cognitive, linguistic, social and developmental; he argues that every literacy event entails the interaction of these dimensions (2008, p. 29-30). This broad view captures what other scholars (Dole, et al., 1991) have described as a "bottom-up" view of reading as understanding sounds, letters, words and sentences to get meaning from print. It also captures what other scholars (Goodman, 1996; Smith, 2004) have described as a "top-down" view of reading, as understanding the whole meaning of a text in the context of other texts and the situation in which the text appears, in order to get meaning from print. Kucer's notion of dimensions captures what might be described as this meta-cognitive view of reading (Kucer, 2008, p. 39) in which readers understand and are able to exercise such abilities as evaluating, predicting, drawing inferences and conclusions consciously as they get meaning from print. Oklahoma education and reading theorists Mokhtari and Reichard (2002) have developed an instrument to measure novices' meta-cognitive awareness of reading strategies; the instrument captures the awarenesses of expert readers and can give teachers a good sense of the extent to which novices have developed them.

The meta-reading and writing theory sketched here fits into this meta-cognitive view. It proposes that meta-textual, meta-contextual and meta-linguistic awarenesses are aspects of the expertise meta-readers have. This expertise arises from general expertise with respect to literacy as well as a specific domain. It also arises from knowledge of the schemata pertinent to the specific area of expertise as well as knowledge of the argument schemata appropriate to texts in that area.

Implicit learning

In addition to using expertise in both literacy and some domain and in addition to using expertise that arises from the application of schema theory, experts achieve their status as a by-product of what cognitive psychologists call implicit learning. Implicit learning helps explain how experts acquire the schemata relevant to their field. Moreover, the phenomenon of implicit learning offers a specific reason why reading is good for novices. In a way, it's kind of like nutrition experts encouraging everyone to eat more vegetables. We know we should eat more carrots and broccoli; they are good for people who want to maintain good health. However, careful study of nutrition shows why this claim warrants attention: vegetables have important specific nutrients needed for health. In the same way, teachers can tell students to read: reading is good for you! But as with nutrition, careful study of implicit learning shows why this claim warrants attention.

The phrase "implicit learning" was coined by Reber, a cognitive psychologist (1967); its relevance for reading and writing was presented in an important paper at the Writing Research Across Borders conference in Washington, DC in 2011 by Russian writing and rhetoric scholar Tseptsov. While neither Reber nor Tseptsov provides a rigorous and explicit definition, other publications provide several angles on the process. For example, Berry (1997) writes in a collection of articles on implicit learning:

> The term 'implicit learning' is typically used to characterize those situations where a person learns about the structure of a fairly complex

> stimulus environment, without necessarily intending to do so, and in such a way that the resulting knowledge is difficult to express. (1997, p. 1)

Writing about second language learners, Ellis (2011) notes that the results of implicit learning are "abstract, unconscious and rule-like representations" (p. 36). Dornyei (2009), another second language scholar, comments on the process, pointing out that

> Implicit language learning can be seen as the consolidation, integration, and fine-tuning of linguistic information in the system, for example through...detecting other underlying patterns. ...[M]ost scholars believe that this process can only take off if the linguistic stimulus has been explicitly registered as a language representation. (2009, p. 171)

It is interesting to note that most of the work with implicit learning has been done with language learning of one kind or another, though the concept can apply to any kind of ability. It is related, also, to Polanyi's idea of "tacit knowledge," which captures the idea that people know more than they can say explicitly (1966).

Reading provides the base on which the process of implicit learning operates. It provides a complex, linguistic stimulus. Readers learn about written language through the process of implicit learning; this learning is unintentional and difficult to describe explicitly. Implicit learning, then, provides two key elements in the theory of meta-reading and writing: it explains the process by which reading contributes to experts' skill as readers and writers and it explains why reading is not only good for novices but essential to their progress toward expertise.

Academic voice

What does reading provide through the process of implicit learning beyond knowledge in the students' discipline and perhaps argument schema if Reznitskaya et al. are correct? If novices are working toward expertise in an academic environment (that is, if they are college students intending to complete a degree in some field), it can provide essential exposure to academic voice. Academic voice shares with implicit learning a difficulty with definition and measurement. Perhaps the most comprehensive set of definitions comes from a set of articles compiled by writing and rhetoric scholar Peter Elbow (1994). Elbow offers five meanings for the concept of voice in writing: first, audible voice or intonation in writing (p. xxiv)—"hearing a text is the norm" (p. xxiv). Informal writing by kids and people learning conventions often have underlining, exclamation marks, and similar features that are meant to signal sound. Kids' writing is often too close to speech. Writing is changing toward oral and audible, especially as conventions change via email. A second kind of voice is dramatic voice in writing (p. xxviii). Texts that reveal an author's or character's voice have dramatic voice—a sense of the person behind the voice.

The third kind of voice identified by Elbow is recognizable or distinctive voice in writing (1994, p. xxx). This kind of voice constitutes style, an aspect that is distinctively characteristic of a particular writer. Fourth is voice with authority—"having a voice" (p. xxxii). In this meaning, voice is about "having the authority to speak or wield influence or to vote in a group" (p. xxxii). An example is transforming a dissertation into an article, using the more authoritative voice of a scholar rather than the deferential voice of a student. Finally, there is resonant voice or presence (p. xxxiii). This aspect of voice is difficult to define and explain. Elbow gives many literary examples. With resonant voice, authors convey presence by revealing what is in both their conscious and unconscious minds. Scholars and critics disagree about this aspect of voice, but not on the other four.

Elbow's descriptions of these various aspects of voice help to clarify the set of defining features of voice but do not explain how it develops. For insight into how reading helps writers develop voice, the insights of two other writing and rhetoric scholars, Susan MacDonald (1994) and Johanna Hartelius (2011) are useful. Writing about novices and experts, MacDonald says:

> If we conceive of degrees from novice to expert practice on a continuum, there may be at least four points along the continuum that novices move through in gaining access to academic discourse:
>
> 1. Nonacademic writing
> 2. Generalized academic writing concerned with stating claims, offering evidence, respecting other's opinions, and learning how to write with authority
> 3. Novice approximations of particular disciplinary ways of making knowledge
> 4. Expert, insider prose (1994, p. 187)

Reading is good for novices because it sets the stage for implicit learning of academic voice and allows novices to move through these stages toward expertise.

Other aspects of expertise and voice

In *The Rhetoric of Expertise*, Northern Illinois University rhetorician Johanna Hartelius (2011) includes six rhetorical "congruities" that she derives through a study of writing in the areas of political science, history, medicine, and encyclopedia entries in Wikipedia. These congruities go across all these disciplines and reveal what experts know and are able to do. Though Hartelius doesn't make explicit mention of the ways these congruities are shared in the digital environment, Web 2.0 makes the sharing of expertise as easy or easier than it is on paper. It is clear that these all arise in one way or another from reading, contribute especially to meta-textual and meta-contextual awareness, and can be summarized as follows: 1) Experts connect or disconnect themselves to other experts in the field. That is, they offer references and show how their ideas fit with or argue against the ideas of others. 2) Experts show that they have an "epistemology and a methodology, a *techne*" (p. 165). That is, they make explicit use of knowledge, procedures, and systematic practices and make clear what is acceptable and not acceptable within their area of expertise. 3) Experts use their writing to explain information and ideas to the public by teaching, or by indicating that what they know cannot be taught, but must be learned through firsthand experience. That is, they know something most people don't and will share it or make clear why they cannot. 4) Experts teach others how to work in their fields, what rules to follow and what strategies to avoid. That is, they expect the public to engage in their field and provide guidance on how to become involved, rather than saying "leave it to me; I am the expert." 5) Experts make clear the exigency for their writing, sometimes by putting down what others have written. That is, they may write in response to others' writing failures or inadequacies as they perceive them. 6) Experts make a clear connection between their area of expertise and day-to-day life and issues. That is, they convey information or steps to action that people can make part of their lives on a regular basis in part through expert voice (Hartelius, 2011, pp. 164-66).

Even with Hartelius' description of voice, it is difficult to define or explain; reading allows students to develop a sense of voice. Reading provides precisely the situation of implicit learning of academic voice; students learn about academic writing, formal writing, proper voice and so on without specific attention to these features and without being able to describe what they have learned. The "stuff" of what is learned in this way through reading comprises a key benefit of it, which is that through implicit learning, students can develop an appropriate sense of formal written language and academic voice both generally and within their specific discipline or field. This sense opens the door to effective writing in college courses and beyond them in the professional world of work after graduation.

The proposals here, then, concern the awarenesses expert readers and writers have. The theory of meta-reading and writing suggests that these awarenesses are built on four bases. Experts use knowledge and skill in literacy as well as in a particular discipline, apply some aspects of schema theory, have access to implicit learning as a by-product of reading, and are exposed to academic voice through reading. The interaction of reading and writing leads experts to have meta-textual, meta-contextual and meta-linguistic awareness as they work with written texts on paper or on a screen. Those who teach at colleges and universities as well as in community settings should have as their goal helping novices move toward these awarenesses through understanding and practicing these abilities that we see in experts.

Note

1. A version of this chapter appeared in the online journal *ATD: Across the Disciplines* (2011). Used by permission.

CHAPTER SIX

SKILLS OF EXPERTS

Introduction

The case studies presented in Chapter 2 provide good support for my claim that expert readers are meta-readers who make use of meta-textual, meta-contextual and meta-linguistic awareness when they read extended non-fiction prose. The case studies also offer some, albeit limited, support for the claim that experts have reading skills that novices lack in part or entirely. In particular, expert meta-readers have an array of essential skills that make it possible for them to read extended non-fiction prose efficiently and effectively. These skills consist of those that contribute directly to the elements of expert literacy as I have defined it, that is, skills in analysis, synthesis, evaluation and application. These skills are well known as appearing at the top of Bloom's Taxonomy of Educational Objectives (the Taxonomy was updated and revised by Krathwohl, 2002).

In the case studies of experts and novices, the background questions and reading tasks elicited responses that led me to develop the idea of the awarenesses discussed earlier, but the tasks in the study do not provide much explicit support for the skills of experts. This chapter explores the nature of the skills expert meta-readers have, and illustrates them with an example of a novice reader transitioning toward expert status through an outside reading assignment I use in every course I teach. This novice read two books outside of class on topics related to course issues and wrote about them in response to a book review writing assignment. (The book review assignment for this particular class and the student's two reviews, used with her written consent, are presented in full in the Appendix to this chapter.) The course in this case is an Introduction to Sociolinguistics, designed for both majors and non-majors in Linguistics. The course covers basic background in language study and examines issues of race, class, gender, ethnicity and so on as they bear on language use.

This case study provides more direct evidence for the skills of expert readers, even though this student is not yet an expert. By examining the changes in both tone and content, the development of this novice's reading skills toward those of experts will be clear. This novice is on her way to developing expert skills in analysis, synthesis, evaluation and application, though she is clearly not an expert yet. Her book reviews also provide a good example of the kind of extended non-fiction prose novices need to learn to read and write about; as it happens, the student chose two books on literacy-related topics. My phrase "extended non-fiction prose" refers to books as well as full-length scholarly journal articles, featured cover story articles in the *New York Times Magazine* and other similar texts. These share key features: they are non-fiction, discuss complex ideas in detail, use sources, either academic sources with citation or interviews of authorities on the topic, and offer an argument or a line of thinking. It is this kind of reading that meta-readers do routinely and expertly and for which novices need to develop the skills in analysis, synthesis, evaluation and application to be discussed in detail in this chapter.

Skills in Analysis

Analytical skills include speed and flexibility, since one of the key findings of reading research is that readers who read too slowly lose track of the developing ideas of the text. According to psycholinguist Frank Smith, successful reading must be fast, selective and fully integrated with everything the reader brings to the text, i.e., nonvisual information about language and content (Smith, 2004, p. 86-89). Experts can move through the text quickly in order to sort main ideas from details. Novice readers often complain that they do not know how to highlight or mark a text because everything seems important. Meta-readers are able to persist, staying with longer texts because they can move through them at a reasonable pace. They are also flexible: skimming, scanning, and/or reading closely as the need arises based on what they are getting from the text and from their awarenesses of structure, context/purpose and language.

Analysis hinges to some degree on skills with the specialized vocabulary of a text. New vocabulary is often what makes an introductory textbook in any field difficult reading for novice readers because they are learning the vocabulary of the discipline. Experts have enough high level vocabulary to understand complex texts and get meaning. Beyond meaning, though, experts understand the specific, disciplinary implications of some words. For example, words like 'significant' or 'correlation' have particular implications in an article presenting statistical data that they do not have when used more generally. Vocabulary is one of the first challenges novices have to deal with as they take an introductory course in any discipline. In my use of self-designed reading guides in any introductory course I teach, I often provide a list of terms for students to define from the text, to build their disciplinary vocabulary. In addition, meta-readers know the forms and genres of the discipline. Bazerman's physicists, discussed further below, know how to read research reports, and they read quickly and selectively based on this analytical skill.

Experts do not surf the text "like a guy on a Jet Ski," as Nicholas Carr suggests in "Is Google Making Us Stupid?" (2008), as a result of the loss of the ability to sustain attention and focus on longer passages of text. Instead, meta-readers can and do stay with a text from the inside to get the larger points that may not be clear till the end of the reading. The skills experts have may entail skimming or scanning the whole text to get the overall gist as Bazerman's physicists do, or having enough knowledge in the discipline and its genres so that only certain parts of an article or research report are needed to get the overall point (Bazerman, 1988, p. 243). These skills allow meta-readers to carry out the analytical aspects of expert literacy.

Bazerman's interview study of physicists warrants discussion here because these experts practice the kind of meta-reading that supports my theory. Though published in 1985 in *Written Communication* as a separate article, "Physicists Reading Physics: Schema-Laden Purposes and Purpose-Laden Schema" appeared a few years later in Bazerman's *Shaping Written Knowledge* (1988). There, it serves as a detailed report of how practicing scientists work with published research articles in the context of his larger exploration of the nature of expert reading and writing in several different disciplines. He points out in the opening section of the book and repeatedly elsewhere in his work (as well as in personal communication May 25, 2009) the importance of context in how experts and others go about reading.

"Physicists Reading Physics" (hereafter PRP) is especially important to the meta-reader theory because it is one of a very few close studies of expert readers actually reading text. Bazerman conducted seven interviews with research scientists in various areas of physics. He points out that there are two key ideas from reading research that help to account for the ways in which expert readers work with text: the reader's purpose drives approach, strategy, and use of the material being read, and this purpose is shaped by the reader's prior knowledge or background. Prior knowledge leads readers to create a schema, a kind of outline or set of expectations about text content and form.

Bazerman summarizes his findings toward the end of the report. He notes that reading entails many different kinds of activities: reading bits and pieces for information, adding that information to prior knowledge, reading for particular purposes, evaluating materials while reading, and varying reading depending on prior knowledge, experience and purpose (meta-contextual awareness). In addition to all this complex and variable activity, reading is influenced by social and psychological factors such as the relevance of the reading material for an expert's own research or work situation. Bazerman's ideas are captured in my proposal that readers bring meta-textual, meta-contextual and meta-linguistic awareness to reading. The experts he worked with in the PRP study did not mark the texts they read during the study in any particular way that Bazerman commented on; he did not set a task like the one I asked of the participants in my case studies in Chapter 2. However, it is clear that these experts have the awareness and skill to analyze, synthesize, evaluate and apply material they read in extended non-fiction prose texts.

In my own teaching, I work to help students develop their analytical skills by requiring all of them to read two books outside of class, in addition to all the regular assigned reading in the course textbook and so forth. They must also write about these books in a review assignment, demonstrating that they have actually done the reading and integrating book content with course topics and issues. The book review task I set for students calls specifically for focused analysis: they must present five key ideas from the text, partly to insure that they have done the reading (see Appendix for assignment). The case studies presented in Chapter 2 show that all the experts and some of the novices (especially the students in the Honors College program) are reasonably good at getting the main ideas of a passage. The novices who were in developmental reading had difficulty getting main ideas from the texts. The case study presented here offers an example of a student novice moving toward expertise. While the first review, of *Lives on the Boundary* by Mike Rose (1989) picks up five key ideas, they are not presented as clearly as are the five main ideas in the Eckert text (*Jocks and Burnouts* (1989)) the student read for her second review. Analytical skill (as well as the other skills and awarenesses) grows with experience in reading, as Bazerman's experts show.

Skills in Synthesis

Experts can put together the text they are reading with other texts or sources of information to synthesize ideas. Research on expert readers presented at the American Educational Research Association meeting suggests that they go into reading with "multi-layered goals" and these help them use their reading to further develop subject matter expertise (Fox et al., 2008). Other research on expertise mentioned earlier includes work on reading/writing connections. Psychologist Ronald Kellogg (2006) points out that expert professional writers are typically extensive or compulsive readers (2006, p. 397-98) and use their reading to develop knowledge about their fields and about the genres used in them. Expert readers know how to draw inferences and conclusions from a text. The writer's point may or may not be explicitly stated, but is there to be drawn by an expert reader.

This skill relates to the 'beyond' or 'after' aspect of what makes experts meta-readers. They can move beyond the array on the page to see the larger concepts several writers have presented. They can also follow the lines of an argument, particularly in extended texts, comparing, contrasting and drawing together various sources to form a more complete picture or to support an argument. The extended texts I have in mind here, as I have said, include longer magazine or journal articles, monographs or books, where a complex argument is fully articulated and defended. Expert readers can see the key points of more than one text, and will mark those, omitting details, examples, comparisons and other developmental techniques. In the task I set in the case studies presented in Chapter 2, there is no need for synthesis of this kind, so those case studies do not provide any direct support for this proposal.

By looking at the ACT performance of participants in the case studies, we can get some indirect evidence of their abilities with synthesis. Some of the ACT Reading exam questions call for synthesis or closely related skills, such as this one that calls for readers to draw on ideas presented at different points in the passage:

> The passage indicates that religion, support groups and soap operas are alike in that they all: A) are circulated by a commercial culture. B) provide a way to combat loneliness. C) appear intimate but are remote. D) enable people to participate vicariously. (ACT Reading sample test, 2005)

While this question and others like it do not call for the reader to combine, compare, contrast or otherwise bring together different ideas about a topic, it does ask for the reader to see a relationship among points made that is not stated explicitly in the passage. Thus, ACT performance provides some indirect evidence of this kind of ability, and as noted in Chapter 2, all of the experts scored very well on this instrument. Neither the ACT nor the task I set in the cases provides strong evidence for synthesis abilities, but the ACT gives suggestive data. The skill is one that is essential for research writing and for many kinds of work-related tasks.

For some better support for the proposal that synthesis is a skill that expert meta-readers have and novices can and should develop, the book review assignment I require in all my classes provides somewhat better data. In the book review task (see Appendix for the assignment sheet), I require students to work on synthesis in two ways. First, they must connect each main idea from the book they have read to issues we have discussed in class or that appear in other readings they have done. In addition, when they write the second review, they can connect the second book to the first, synthesizing the information from these two sources. In the student response that is also included in the Appendix to this chapter, it is clear that the student is able to synthesize ideas from the two books. In the second review, she writes:

> After reading another book centered around education, *Jocks and Burnouts* is quite different from Rose's *Lives on the Boundary*, yet the books have a few similarities. Rose focuses on education more as a whole and the issues in that system. While Eckert looks at the education system, her primary focus is on two individual categories inside of the system. Eckert spends more time dissecting the individual relationships between students and then those relationships with the hierarchy. However, there is one main similarity between the two books. Primarily, the books discuss the structure of education which leads to segregation in individual schools therefore, leaving students segregated and disadvantaged. The authors present their information very differently, one through and autobiographical approach the other through ethnographic research, yet find very similar conclusions.

This novice reader/writer is moving toward expertise as she presents a clear connection between the two books she has read. She grasps the whole of each argument and sees the similarity in the conclusions drawn. In follow-up conversation, the student said she found the book review work challenging but extremely valuable. She hopes to become a teacher and so learned from not only the content but also the kind of thinking required by the task as assigned. This case, then, provides stronger support for the relevance of synthesis as a skill of expert meta-readers and writers.

Skills in Evaluation

Expert readers build on analysis and synthesis in order to conduct critical evaluations and apply what they glean from their reading. Their skills in evaluation entail reading for authority, currency, relevancy, accuracy, objectivity/bias and appropriateness (Lombardo, 2001; based on Association, 2008). These skills are often taught to novices in the context of library research in first-year writing courses. They are teachable and learnable skills that expert readers have and use in all kinds of reading situations, but especially when reading extended non-fiction prose. Novices, by contrast, lack these skills.

Expert readers ask questions about who the author of a passage is, how current it is, and how relevant it is for the reading purpose they have in dealing with a particular passage. They may also draw on prior knowledge to assess accuracy and objectivity, so they can see if the passage is consistent with other information they have and if it has a clear bias in one direction or another. They can also assess whether or not the material is suitable for whatever purpose they have in mind, such as use in their own writing for publication.

In terms of skill in evaluation, once again, the task I set in the case studies presented in Chapter 2 does not ask for evaluation of any kind. However, one of the experts did provide an extensive evaluation, particularly of the passage on the Michigan state capitol. Expert EDT entitled her summary of this passage "The Boring Story of the Michigan State Capitol." In the course of her reading and text marking, she commented repeatedly on the writer's use of details that she found completely irrelevant to the point of the passage. This expert was reading with a keen eye toward the summary she knew she would be asked to write at the end of her reading time, and was evaluating the information for its usefulness in the summary task. While other readers did not provide evaluative comments, this case reveals the evaluative skill expert meta-readers possess.

The importance of evaluation is readily apparent to librarians; two information literacy experts at Empire State College in New York discuss it a recent article in *College and Research Libraries* on information literacy (Mackey & Jacobson, 2011). These scholars suggest that evaluation of information found on the Web is an aspect of metaliteracy (their term) and is crucial in light of Web 2.0 social media forms:

> Metaliteracy promotes critical thinking and collaboration in a digital age, providing a comprehensive framework to effectively participate in social media and online communities. It is a unified construct that supports the acquisition, production, and sharing of knowledge in collaborative online communities. Metaliteracy expands upon the traditional skills-based approach to understanding information as somehow disconnected from emerging technologies and related literacy types. Standard definitions of information literacy are insufficient for the revolutionary social technologies currently prevalent online. (Mackey &Jacobson, 2011)

They explore a number of different aspects of literacy but ultimately note that no matter what social media venue might be used, critical reading and thinking continue to be essential for meta-readers and writers.

Naturally, I agree with this view of the need for critical evaluation on pages and screens and work with students to develop their skills in this area. In the course in which the book review assignment is given, students do get library instruction from a colleague on the library faculty, and this instruction includes exercises in evaluating websites and all reading material on the issues above. The book review task explicitly asks these novices to evaluate the books they read, and the novice whose reviews are presented here provides a much stronger evaluation in her second review than in the first. She learned not only key concepts but stronger reading and writing skills in evaluation that appear in the last paragraph of her second book review:

> *Jocks and Burnouts* was helpful in understanding how detailed research needs to be, to be conclusive. Wanting to be an educator myself to read of how categories are formed and the life long impact those categories may have was quite personal and moving. This struck a similar nature in *Lives on the Boundary*. Most American are aware of the importance education has in shaping young people yet most probably do not realize the impact that the categories and the decisions made can make in shaping those children into adults. Children are shaped through their speech communities, their relationships amongst each other, their language, their norms, and their personal or categorical goals. Despite the benefits and disadvantages each category may have, Eckert and Rose both make a very strong argument for the fact that it is better for an individual to belong to a category than be lost in the middle or the boundaries. If education and long term goals is of interest, this book is a must read.

This evaluation is noteworthy both because it provides some further synthesis of the two books this student read, and because it offers a more focused evaluation that the ending of the review of the Rose book:

> *Lives on the Boundary* illustrates the multitude of reasons why schools and college institutions struggle to make this happen for each and every student. As we have spoken numerous times in class simple words of a spoken language to conversations allow for the listener or participants to draw numerous conclusions. Rose clearly shows that factors other than language also influence education individuals receive. Yet language and ability to communicate play a huge role. We saw a similar story to Rose's ideas in the Detroit and New York research study. The study confirms that language differs based on region, race, and sex. All this being said children, students, and individuals are entitled to the same educational

> rights despite their labels or differences. This problem is endemically rooted in society yet as a future educator, I hope to break down the barriers in our educational system. Mike Rose has clearly done that through his experiences and teaching style. Although not every individual he has taught has succeeded to cross the boundary he shows that the successful stories have made the journey worth it!

I am not claiming that this novice has been transformed into an expert by virtue of reading two books and writing about them. However, her growth as a reader and writer is clear in her ability to evaluate the arguments presented in extended non-fiction prose texts.

Skills in Application

Finally, expert readers have skills in application—knowing where and how to use information from reading. They can take whole ideas or arguments or lines of reasoning and use them in their own work. They can incorporate specific facts or findings from research reports into their discussions. They know how to integrate information gained from reading and apply it to other situations, to broader questions, or to larger issues. They might use what they have read to answer a question or solve a problem, or they might integrate their reading of the work of others into their own writing. The point is that meta-readers can not only get ideas from extended non-fiction prose texts, synthesize different readings on the same issue or topic, and evaluate the material, but they can also make use of it for their own purposes.

In the task I set for the case study participants presented in Chapter 2, I did ask for a kind of use of the material, by setting up the task as one of using the passages for a school report. However, the task did not actually require the participants to write that report, only to provide a summary of the passage that could be used in this way. Here again, the case study data does not provide particular support for my theoretical claim. Other studies with expert writers, such as Bazerman's physicists (1988) and Hillesund's online and traditional readers (2010), all show their expectation that they will use the material they have read for some purpose of their own. The ACT Reading test data is not helpful on the application skill, since the test does not entail use of the passages beyond answering the questions that follow.

However, in my book review task presented here, I ask students to comment at the end of the review on the relevance of the book for their personal or professional lives. Here, I am encouraging them to think about what they have read and how it might be of use to them in other parts of the course, as well as outside my class, whether in other courses or in other areas of their lives. The application of the readings appears in the closing paragraph of both reviews quoted just previously; the student comments on the relevance of her reading, mentioning her goal of becoming a teacher and the use of these books and ideas in her future work. So, while this participant is certainly not an expert, her reading and writing show that she is en route to expertise as her skills in not only application but also in analysis, synthesis and evaluation appear in her reviews.

Summary

My case studies presented in Chapter 2 do not provide explicit support for my claim that expert meta-readers and writers have the skills of analysis, synthesis, evaluation and application as defined and discussed here. However, they do provide indirect support; the cases are consistent with other reports on expert readers' abilities (Bazerman, 1988; Hillesund, 2010). The additional case presented here, of a student moving toward expertise offers more evidence of developing skills. She is not a particularly strong writer; there are numerous weaknesses in these papers. However, she was able to analyze each of the books she read for Sociolinguistics and present key ideas in each case. In this way, she began the course with some expertise in the skill of analysis. Her ability to synthesize the ideas of the two books shows up more markedly when she comments on the similarity of the conclusions drawn by the two writers at the end of her second review. She also develops some skill in evaluation and application, noting the use of these books in her future role as a teacher. Taken together, then, this additional case and the admittedly indirect evidence from the experts and novices presented earlier in the book show that expert meta-readers have key skills in analysis, synthesis, evaluation, and application that novices lack and must develop to become critically literate students and citizens. These skills are crucial elements of critical literacy whether the extended non-fiction prose being read appears on a page or a screen. The next two chapters examine this last point in much more detail, comparing and contrasting traditional and digital reading and writing.

Appendix: Book Review assignment and student response

Book Review Assignment

During the semester, you will be required to read two books from the following list (or others you bring in for specific approval) and write brief reviews. There are two main purposes for this assignment. The first is to provide you with the opportunity to explore a range of sociolinguistic issues in greater depth. A second purpose is to provide you with the opportunity to develop and practice your skills in critical reading, essential in both your personal and professional lives. I hope you will find the books you choose interesting and enjoyable as well as challenging.

To write each of your two reviews (see due dates on the course outline), you should prepare a brief paper (approximately 500 words, or two typed pages, double spaced). Your review must include the following four elements:

1. Your review should summarize five (5) main ideas discussed in the book you are reviewing and for each major idea you summarize, you must connect it clearly and specifically to issues we have discussed in class or that appear in other readings.

2. You should look up some information about the author online or in the library and print out or make a copy of the biographical information that you find. Summarize and integrate some of this information somewhere in your review. Attach the author information to your review, and be sure to provide a proper citation to your source and documentation for this and any other sources at the end of your review.

3. Choose at least one of the following additional features to include in your review: a)Explain what the book has to do with the course and why you think I chose it as one of the readings, b)Discuss the practical implications of the book for your personal and/or professional life, c)Relate your personal experience(s) to two concepts in the text, OR d) (for second review only) Compare and contrast the two books you have read for the course.

4. Provide an evaluation of the book, positive, negative or in between.

Following is a list of approved books from which you can choose your reading. Many of these will be readily available in the OU library or your local public library; there should also be copies available online, both new and used.

Kevin Boyle. *Arc of Justice*. Henry Holt paperback, $15.
Deborah Brandt. *Literacy in American Lives*.
Diarmait Mac Giolla Chriost. *Language and the City* (on order for the course reserve list—check catalog for call number
David Crystal. *English as a Global Language*.
Diane Davies. *Varieties of Modern English*. (I can loan this one out.)
J.L. Dillard. *Black English* (on reserve, see syllabus)
Penelope Eckert. *Jocks and Burnouts: Social Categories and Identity in the High School* (on reserve and an ebook, see syllabus)
Edward Hall. *The Silent Language*.
William Mitchell. *Placing Words: Symbols, Space and the City* (on reserve)
Mike Rose. *Lives on the Boundary*.
Geneva Smitherman. *Talkin' and Testifyin'*.
Deborah Tannen. *You Just Don't Understand: Women and Men in Conversation*.

NOTE: If you do not complete both book reviews, your course grade will automatically be a 0.0.

Student response (papers used with the student's specific written consent)

BR 1 Rose: *Lives on the Boundary*

American education: This phrase has so many meanings—ask an individual who is a student at Harvard law school or a nervous kindergartener beginning his or her first day of school in the rural Midwest. In his book *Lives on the Boundary*, author Mike Rose relives his experiences with American education. Rose, the son of immigrant parents, moved to Los Angeles, California, as a young boy because his parents hoped to give him a better life. He struggled finding his way and as a result nearly became lost in the school system. This was partially due to a system error. It is because of these experiences that the author proves that their are a multitude of barriers individuals face in the American education system.

Rose first illustrates failures in education system through his school years. The author found a solace and escape from his reality through reading. It was through the language and ideas he found in literature that he was able to escape into a normal world. Not only was he learning new words and grasping a better understanding of grammar, Rose was trying to shape his identity, to figure out who he was as an individual. (Rose, 28).

He quickly learned that if he did not fit into the mainstream at school he would be labeled. This was not necessarily a label he deserved but because of testing as well as teacher's expecations in the school system, he was labeled. (Rose, 54)

A second point Rose focuses on is that individuals have the ability to break down the barriers they are facing but this requires help and support from the school system. Rose was given the opportunity part of a linguistics club followed there after by writing for the newspaper. It was through his use of language and literature he realized he could draw people in to something others may not have otherwise thought they could do or knew they were capable of doing.

The recognition of the importance of literature and language leads to the third major point Rose makes. He begins volunteering for an organization called the Teacher Corps in urban Los Angeles. Almost immediately he recognizes himself in these children and their experiences. At this point in their educational history they are failing. Rose takes a different approach to igniting the students passion for learning and language. He gives them his time and belief in their abilities that the children gain confidence, which in turn allows some of them to break away from the margins of the education system. (Rose 125) Rose provides the children an opportunity at equal education by simply seeing them as individuals rather than placing labels on the individuals. (Rose, 128)

An additional point Rose makes in *Lives on the Boundary* deals more an older population of student. After his experience at the Teacher Corps he began working for the Veteran's Program. It was his work in this program which helped individuals access an education they never had or had lost. (Rose 146) He was again experiencing many different cultures and backgrounds. It was through poetry that many students developed a linguistic competence which in turn helped in building their confidence that education could work this time for them. This idea also allowed Rose an opportunity to break down some of the barriers these individual were carrying.

His final idea on barriers faced in the education system brought him back to UCLA. Rose began mentoring in the Tutorial Center. Slightly different than his previous work experiences the individuals he began working came in without labels, they did not appear to be on the margins of the educational system. After all they were students at UCLA, a reputable college. They were bilingual, high school athletes, individuals who appeared to have what was needed to be successful. Rose quickly recognized himself in each one of these students, as he did with all the other individuals he has worked with. Things were different in the sense that these students lost themselves in their school work . (Rose 174) They needed to be successful so badly yet failed to identify their passion for classes and education. Superficially these students appeared very different from those Rose encountered in his school years, the Teacher Corps, or Veteran's Program yet their struggles in the education system was very similar. Rose was determined to make an individual story for each person.

Rose does an incredible job of highlighting and analyzing the importance of sociolinguistics in the American education system. He states:

" students need more opportunities to write about what they are learning and guidance in the techniques and conventions of that writing...They need more opportunities to develop the writing strategies that are an intimate part of academic inquiry...and critical literacy." (Rose 194)

Lives on the Boundary illustrates the multitude of reasons why schools and college institutions struggle to make this happen for each and every student. As we have spoken numerous times in class simple words of a spoken language to conversations allow for the listener or participants to draw numerous conclusions. Rose clearly shows that factors other than language also influence education individuals receive. Yet language and ability to communicate play a huge role. We saw a similar story to Rose's ideas in the Detroit and New York research study. The study confirms that language differs based on region, race, and sex. All this being said children, students, and individuals are entitled to the same educational rights despite their labels or differences. This problem is endemically rooted in society yet as a future educator, I hope to break down the barriers in our educational system. Mike Rose has clearly done that through his experiences and teaching style. Although not every individual he has taught has succeeded to cross the boundary he shows that the successful stories have made the journey worth it!

BR 2 Eckert: *Jocks and Burnouts*

Most people in American society would state America is segregated. However, is the same true for American schools? Penelope Eckert looks into this issue in *Jocks and Burnouts: Social Categories and Identity*. Eckert takes an ethnographic look into schools, specifically a few public schools in a Detroit suburb. According to Eckerts' webpage she is a Linguistics and Anthropology professor at Stanford University. Her goal is to understand social meaning through language variation. Beginning in the

1980's, Eckert focused the majority of her studies on adolescence, because she believes they are at the core of linguistic change. She saw that there had been much research on adults and language variation, yet little information on adolescence. Through her research, Eckert has learned that ethnographic research is means to achieve information which would be difficult to achieve else wise. In *Jocks and Burnouts*, Eckert focuses on two distinctly different categories and groups, Jocks and Burnouts in American schools. Jocks and Burnouts discuss how the system of education lead to segregation in individual schools. As a result, the students are segregated and disadvantaged. The author approaches this conclusion by dissecting the social networks, as well as several aspects of the SPEAKING acronym. Specifically she focuses on the participants, the norms of interaction, and the ends. It is through these five linguistic attributes that Eckert proves there is deep rooted segregation in American education, leading to segregation in society at large.

One of the first major areas Eckert focuses on are the speech communities of the Jocks and Burnouts at Belten High School. Belten High School as a whole is a speech community. Yet as Eckert spends considerable time there, she focuses more on the individual speech communities. Jocks individually would be seen as a dense speech community, as would the Burnouts. The Jocks tend to communicate with classmates their own ages and in their own grade level and as a result they loosen the community. Through the ethnographic approach, Eckert observes that there is usually one individual or a small group of individuals who transfer information to and from the hierarchy of the Jocks. At the same time, it is the Jocks involvement in school and extracurricular activities which allow them the access to much of the pertinent information. However the information a hierarchy of Jocks received is not passed along to all of the Jocks, it is passed as a chain (102). Because of this lack of communication amongst all the members of the speech community, the Jocks are seen as a less dense speech community. On the contrary, the Burnouts communicate with a range of classes and age ranges. The blending of age ranges in the Burnout category is partially due to the fact that many of these students have been playing together in their neighborhoods prior to school. Burnouts continue these friendships while in school. Wardhaugh would consider the Burnouts a very dense speech community.

The SPEAKING acronym plays another important role in differentiating the two categories, specifically the participants. At first glance the concept that the participants are different seems basic - the Jocks are a completely different group of individuals than the Burnouts.

Eckert focuses much attention on the hierarchy of Belten High School. The Burnouts relate very differently to teachers and administration than do the Jocks. The Jocks communicate more effectively with the school hierarchy. They communicate more effectively because there is a sense of trust established. As one Jock points out "If I'm arguing...for something at Mr. Jones, I'll win every time. Just because I can talk to Mr. Jones....I know how to get to him" (116). Jocks are seen as the school leaders and therefore therefore have a better opportunity to communicate more efficiently.

The author also focuses on the ends of each category. Jocks and Burnouts attend school for very different reasons. Each categories goals are quite different. For instance, "Burnouts attend school because it is necessary...In contrast Jocks welcome the opportunity to merge the personal with the institutional." (102). The Jocks participate in school activities because their goal is to attend college. However, the Burnouts know that the school does not provide them the necessary tools they need to enter the working class. In turn, they are distant and spend most of their time outside of the school itself. It is these differences which lead to further segregation among the categories. The long term goals of each category help in understanding and clarifying many of the differences.

Another important factor Eckert focuses on is the norms of interaction of each group. For example, Eckert discusses the difference in norms of interaction that the Jocks and Burnouts have with strangers, "...Jocks emphasize the importance of 'saying hi' to as many people as possible...Since Burnouts have no need for a broad school constituency, they reserve their greetings for those they know and like." (148-149). The fact that these groups have very different norms of interaction hinder their ability to communicate efficiently. In fact many students of both categories state in interviews that they do not communicate with the other category at all. At the same time, the shared norms of interaction within the individual groups help in assuring the density of their speech community. Furthermore, Eckert discusses the impact of the norms of interaction on education as a whole. She discusses that schools cater to middle class norms and career needs. Schools assign vocationally oriented students on a marginal status (101). By the school catering to a particular category, this further segregates the categories and groups.

Eckert also focuses on the act sequence or difference of syntax and phonology of the *Jocks and Burnouts*. She states that the differences in pronunciation of words and phrases is in part what differentiates the two categories. Eckert discusses the impact of the Great Vowel Shift, especially in the region of Detroit. The author supports the impact of the shift by discussing how "Burnouts back this vowel with significantly greater frequency than the Jocks." (68). These differences are rooted into the individuals' languages because of the influence of their peers not their upbringing. The differences in syntax and phonology solidifies the very specific categories of Jocks and Burnouts.

After reading another book centered around education, *Jocks and Burnouts* is quite different from Roses's *Lives on the Boundary*, yet the books have a few similarities. Rose focuses on education more as a whole and the issues in that system. While Eckert looks at the education system, her primary focus is on two individual categories inside of the system. Eckert spends more time dissecting the individual relationships between students and then those relationships with the hierarchy. However, there is one main similarity between the two books. Primarily, the books discuss the structure of education which leads to segregation in individual schools therefore, leaving students segregated and disadvantaged. The authors present their information very differently, one through and autobiographical approach the other through ethnographic research, yet find very similar conclusions.

Jocks and Burnouts was helpful in understanding how detailed research needs to be, to be conclusive. Wanting to be an educator myself to read of how categories are formed and the life long impact those categories may have was quite personal and moving. This struck a similar nature in *Lives on the Boundary*. Most American are aware of the importance education has in shaping young people yet most probably do not realize the impact that the categories and the decisions made can make in shaping those children into adults. Children are shaped through their speech communities, their relationships amongst each other, their language, their norms, and their personal or categorical goals. Despite the benefits and disadvantages each category may have, Eckert and Rose both make a very strong argument for the fact that it is better for an individual to belong to a category than be lost in the middle or the boundaries. If education and long term goals is of interest, this book is a must read.

Works Cited

Eckert, P. (1989) *Jocks and Burnouts : Social Categories and Identity in High School*. Teacher's College Press.

—. Retrieved from http://www.stanford.edu/~eckert/.

Rose, M. (1989) *Lives on the Boundary: The Struggles and Achievements of America's Underprepared*. New York: The Free Press.

CHAPTER SEVEN

READING TRADITIONAL AND ELECTRONIC TEXTS

Introduction

When I presented the ideas in this book to a class in Psycholinguistics, I raised the question of whether reading Web pages and sites is a whole new experience or not. One of my students said, about reading the Web: "It's just like opening a book!" Without any particular prompting from me, he noted that books have pictures, indexes, notes, and citations that work much like links on a page that take you to another page or site with related information. I wanted to hug him, since these views were entirely his but mirror the key ideas I have been discussing in this book. His view also leads to the satirical video on YouTube of a monk learning to use a codex with the help of a medieval helpdesk technician (http://www.youtube.com/watch?v=-xmTTzCAALc). In the video, the monk is trying to learn to use the "new" technology of a codex or printed book, coming at it from the perspective of reading on a scroll. It's a satirical look at new technology.

While the forms that appear before us digitally on computer screens do require some additional mental capacities and entail a few additional distinctive features, they are essentially "just like opening a book" as my student said, that is, not really "new." The changes have come about as technology has changed and improved. Despite claims of the "new media age" theorists (Kress, 2003) that literacy is all new in its digital form, one of the key points of this book is that the psycholinguistic processes of meta-reading and writing are essentially the same, on pages and screens. The critical literacy meta-readers and writers demonstrate relies on and demands the same key abilities found in their work with conventional printed texts; experts are able to carry their abilities from page to screen as medieval monks carried theirs from scroll to codex. However, there is accumulating data suggesting that novices are less adept at critical literacy even as the amount of reading and writing they do moves increasingly to the screen. This critical literacy is more crucial now than ever because of the pervasive use of the World Wide Web.

A brief review of the discussion thus far might provide a useful backdrop to this chapter's exploration of reading on paper and on screens. Critical literacy, simply defined as the ability to analyze, synthesize and evaluate and use ideas in written language, either through perception (i.e. reading) or production (i.e. writing), hinges on basic mental capacities. These capacities, discussed in Chapter 3, consist of seven major mental capacities: a group of five general cognitive capacities, including identification or recognition, categorization, discrimination, prediction, and limited short-term memory, along with two major linguistic capacities, the use of syntax, and psycholinguistic redundancy.

All these mental capacities are used by readers and writers as they work with the distinctive features of written language to achieve critical literacy. Meta-readers and writers need only two more mental capacities (bricolage and juxtaposition) to work with four additional distinctive features (links, images, sound, and movement) that make critical literacy as possible on the screen as on the printed page. From a psycholinguistic point of view, "hyperreading" on the Web relies on the same mental capacities and distinctive features with just these few additions.

It may also be helpful to remember that readers and writers may use their critical literacy on any text, short or long, fiction or non-fiction. However, the theory of meta-readers and writers appears most clearly when these experts work with extended non-fiction prose. Books, full-length journal articles and similar materials require the awarenesses and skills proposed here. Expert meta-readers use their abilities with these texts, whether they appear in traditional printed form on paper or in the digital environment of the screen. The similarities of reading on paper and screens are the focus of this chapter, with the goals, first, of showing how the theory plays out in both venues and second, of showing that the underlying mental capacities and distinctive features used by expert meta-readers are the same in both venues.

A good example of how the mental capacities and distinctive features help readers with the written form would be a text that is visually difficult to read, such as one that is written in handwriting that is illegible, or printing that is unclear such as in a smeared page of the newspaper. If readers can make out a few distinctive features of letters and words, they can probably read the text in spite of the interference due to the lack of clarity in the visual display. Partly, of course, the ability to read depends on knowledge of the context of the particular text, prior knowledge of the language and content of the passage and other factors described as expert meta-readers' awarenesses and skills. However, I have suggested that our essential mental capacities and the distinctive features of not only the letters but also the words, sentences and discourse structures make meta-reading and writing possible, even under difficult conditions.

Literacy makes possible so much of the way we live. I sometimes ask students in a variety of courses to think about what life would be like if we did not have written language. At first, the typical response is "no more pencils, no more books," hooray! But then, when I ask students to spend a couple of days keeping track of their interactions with written language, from reading cereal boxes at breakfast, to the newspaper, to road signs, to schoolwork, checks, printed receipts for purchases and, of course, Facebook, email, and everything else on those little screens they are so addicted to, they begin to see how reading and writing is woven into the fabric of modern life. The truth of the matter is that we could not manage our lives as we know them, at least not in the developed world, without reading and writing.

In schools and beyond them, in community settings, and at work, we expect and require of novices that they achieve the most sophisticated form of literacy, critical literacy. This goal now requires making use of critical literacy on the Internet. To see how we can achieve this goal through teaching and learning, we explore the few new features of digital reading here. By comparing and contrasting digital reading with traditional reading for both experts and novices, we can consider the larger issues of the positive and negative impact of the digital on reading and on the need for critical literacy.

Reading Online: Additional Capacities

The additional mental capacities needed for online reading are captured by the terms bricolage and juxtaposition. Both of these are visual matters, because the Internet focuses attention on the visual in a way that printed text does not. As psycholinguist Paul Kolers (1967) has said, all reading is only "incidentally visual;" his research shows that readers rely on relatively little from a page of text because so much of reading hinges on prior knowledge of both language and content. The Web, by contrast, is intentionally visual. As a result, one of the additional mental capacities essential for both production and perception is an ability to put together parts, bricolage, according to digital rhetorician and University of Illinois education professor Nicholas Burbules (1998, p. 107). Burbules defines bricolage as "*assembling* texts from pieces that can be represented in multiple relations to one another" (p. 107). Thus, bricolage is particularly about drawing together an array of materials from varied sources. The parts that are put together entail a few additional distinctive features to be discussed below, but might include images, animation and sound.

The second mental capacity needed to deal with the Internet in terms of both production and perception is juxtaposition (Burbules, 1998, p. 107). In foregrounding the visual, a Web page asks readers to see images as they are arrayed, next to each other for various specific purposes. Part of the point is to notice and attend to how the various pieces of a Web page are related to each other by their position on the screen. So juxtaposition is chiefly about how the materials are presented on a screen, elements of the layout and/or design. Burbules notes that these mechanisms are supplements to those other more conventional mechanisms, adding to the list but not deleting any of the others discussed earlier (1998, p. 107). Thus, bricolage and juxtaposition are additional, essential mental capacities needed in the digital environment. However, it is important to emphasize that these capacities add to the set of those discussed previously. They supplant but do not replace them, nor are they entirely new. Psycholinguistically, meta-reading remains the same activity focused on analysis, synthesis, evaluation and application.

Reading Online: Additional Distinctive Features

These new mental capacities for online material work with the distinctive features of Web pages in various ways. The features again overlap with those for printed language, since much, though not all, of what we see on a Web page is writing. Just as there are a few additional mental capacities needed for online reading, there are also just a few additional distinctive features of online material. The additional distinctive features of Web pages are links, images, sounds, and movement. Burbules (1998) says that the key feature (i.e., a distinctive feature) of hypertext is the link, and that links can be characterized and classified (p. 104). Links all work the same way, i.e. they produce a new page on the screen. All require hyperreading or critical reading. Burbules points out that links are fundamentally rhetorical in nature; they can be categorized in terms of the arguments through which they shape readers' responses to text (1998, p. 110-117).

The hypertexts we find on the Web are like paper texts, then, in some ways, but different from them in others. Georgia Tech digital media scholar Jay David Bolter (2001) has made this observation, noting that hypertext is close to the way we think, through associations (some examples of links appear in Bolter's Storyspace program at http://www.

eastgate.com/Storyspace.html). In contrast to print reading, where the text is supposed to be transparent so readers look directly at meaning, hypertext expects readers to attend to its form: "In following hypertextual links, the reader becomes conscious of the form or medium itself and of her interaction with it" (Bolter, 2001, p. 43). The ability to hyperread relies on those fundamental mental capacities because it relies on print reading ability. As Bolter says:

> … the World Wide Web offers us the experience of moving through a visual and conceptual space different from the space of the book, although this experience still depends on our intuitive understanding of that earlier writing space. Indeed, we depend in a variety of ways on our knowledge of print in order to read and write hypertexts. (Bolter, 2001, p. 45)

Bolter's point is that while hyperreading is particularly visual in nature, and while it draws on the additional set of distinctive features, it hinges on and is related and similar to the mental capacities and features used for printed text.

Hyperreading, according to Burbules (1998) entails a different kind of relationship to text, a different kind of reading. He suggests that there may be, or already are, some new orientations to reading. One example he cites is the practice of surfing, applicable not only to the Internet, but also to TV channels via remote control, radio stations via push-button tuning, and CD sampling. This behavior has both positive and negative consequences:

> With a surfeit of stimuli competing for people's attention, they are, on the one hand, becoming more adept at screening information very quickly, making rapid judgments about whether it is desirable, and 'parallel processing' different materials simultaneously. On the other hand, their capacities for sustained attention to any single textual source are affected as a consequence (Burbules, 1998, p. 108).

The fundamental nature of reading is evolving as strategies like surfing develop and expand. However, reading, (at least as expert meta-readers carry it out) and particularly the need for critical literacy, remains consistent, regardless of the venue. Expert meta-readers can and do sustain attention when working with extended non-fiction prose. This kind of reading is the same on pages and screens; it entails the use of the same mental capacities and distinctive features with these few additions for the visual aspects of the Web.

The distinctive features of Web pages include all of those that characterize paper-based writing, insofar as there is writing on Web pages. Additional distinctive features include images, visual items of various kinds. These are often pictures, but diagrams, charts, graphs, cartoons and other visual arrays can also be found on Web pages, and these too also appear in print. The Web allows for some additional distinctive features: links, sound, and movement. So, in linguistics courses, for instance, I send students to the Web page of the American Dialect Society by using the link to the Society's Website (http://www.evolpub.com/American dialects/EngDialLnx.html) where it is possible to hear recordings of dialect samples. Sound is also available on many radio stations which now broadcast from the Web (such as public radio station WDET in Detroit, Michigan, found at http://www.wdetfm.org) and can present sound through computer speakers. Movement is yet another distinctive feature of Web pages. Electronic birthday cards often entail animation of figures or letters or other images on the screen as the message is delivered, sometimes also with sound, musical or otherwise, as for example, at http://free.bluemountain.com). Podcasts, streaming of live events and various other ways of making information available are in a constant state of flux and development. Some of these involve some reading, but some entail only listening. To the extent that they involve reading, these few new distinctive features, along with the two additional mental capacities do not change the essential psycholinguistics of reading on paper or on a screen.

Reading Online and Critical Literacy

Burbules goes on to say that reading is also increasingly driven by a consumer orientation to various types and sources of information. Critical literacy is much more challenging when TV, newspapers, Web materials and other sources are all merged together, their relative levels of authority mostly lost. Burbules writes, "[a]s a result, the processes of selection, evaluation, and interpretation that develop information into knowledge and understanding are atrophying for many readers (or are not being developed in the first place)" (Burbules, 1998, p. 109).The critical literacy skills Burbules describes must be much more thoroughly and carefully taught now than previously, as readers' and writers' responses to texts are shaped by the Internet.

Burbules' views are supported by recent research on mental processing as people live, work, and interact online. One example of this recent work appears in a volume called *The New Literacies* (Baker, 2010) which attempts to capture the various theoretical perspectives on the changes in literacy as it interacts with new technology. Writing in this volume, University of Illinois education professors Kalantzis, Cope and Cloonan point out that "[w]ritten language is becoming more closely intertwined with the other modes, and in some respects is becoming more like them" (2010, p. 69). Even so, they concede that the visual elements on a screen are connected to written language that still entails reading. Similarly, in the same volume, Michigan State University literacy and technology professor Douglas Hartman and his colleagues discuss changes in reading comprehension required in the digital environment.

Hartman makes clear the importance of metacognition in reading, particularly on the screen. Beyond the traditional aspects of metacognition needed for reading on paper, declarative, procedural and conditional (what, how and when), dealing with electronic texts requires identity knowledge, locational knowledge, and goal knowledge (who, where, and why). These kinds of knowledge are exactly the ones that information literacy scholars also identify in their standards for critical literacy on the Web. Being able to evaluate for authority, accuracy, currency, relevancy and bias entail these kinds of knowledge. Broken down, then, they refer to precisely the skills I propose are part of critical literacy in both print and digital environments: the ability to analyze, synthesize, evaluate and apply. Thus, even scholars focused on the "new" digital environment see that the latter three types of knowledge "do not supplant earlier forms of declarative, procedural, and conditional knowledge. Rather, they extend and enrich them in startling ways" (Hartman, Morsink & Zheng, 2010, p. 146-49).

Another example of the impact of the Internet on reading, writing and thinking appears in the work of culture and technology journalist Nicholas Carr in *The Shallows: What the Internet is Doing to Our Brains* (2010). Carr writes that there are clear brain differences between those who spend a lot of time online compared to those who don't. Reporting on a study done at UCLA's Memory and Aging Center, Carr says that researchers found important differences between reading done online and reading done on paper:

> When people search the Net they exhibit a very different pattern of brain activity than they do when they read book-like text. Book readers have a lot of activity in regions associated with language, memory, and visual processing, but they don't display much activity in the prefrontal regions associated with decision making and problem solving. Experienced Net users, by contrast, display extensive activity across all those brain regions when they scan and search Web pages. …But the extensive activity in the brains of surfers also points to why deep reading and other acts of sustained concentration become so difficult online. The need to evaluate links and make related navigational choices, while also processing a multiplicity of fleeting sensory stimuli, requires constant mental

> coordination and decision making, distracting the brain from the work of interpreting text or other information. (Carr, 2010, p. 121-22)

The result is that shallow reading and shallow thinking are becoming increasingly common as people spend more time online. If we consider those who do a lot of surfing "novices," Carr's discussion reveals a good deal about the nature of novice reading online.

The problem, Carr explains, has to do with the mechanics of information processing and storage in the brain. As described earlier in Chapter 3, the mental capacities people have that are essential to literacy hinge on the ability to identify/recognize, categorize, discriminate and predict. But these capacities along with the language-related capacities for using syntax and redundancy are limited by short-term memory, well established at seven plus or minus two items (Miller, 1956). To learn, readers must move information from short-term to long-term memory. Doing so entails managing the incoming information, "cognitive load" in Carr's words (2010, p. 125). If there's too much coming in, and if the cognitive load is too great, "it becomes harder to distinguish relevant from irrelevant information, signal from noise. We become mindless consumers of data" (Carr, 2010, p. 125). This situation is the challenge facing all readers online, but especially novices.

Carr goes on to report a number of studies showing the resulting impact on learning in schools. While schools K through college have embraced computers and online instruction, the quality of the outcomes that result from the increasing use of technology has been flat or has actually declined. The brain mechanisms needed for the information processing work that student/novices must do in order to learn through reading are negatively impacted by technology:

> Evaluating links and navigating a path through them, it turned out, involves mentally demanding problem-solving tasks that are extraneous to the act of reading itself. Deciphering hypertext substantially increases readers' cognitive load and hence weakens their ability to comprehend and retain what they're reading. (Carr, 2010, p. 126)

While there's nothing wrong with skimming or scanning as a way to find information, it's not the kind of deep reading that leads to analysis, synthesis, evaluation and application. But skimming is becoming, according to Carr, the "dominant mode of reading" (p. 126). Carr suggests that this development is hardly desirable, as his metaphor makes clear: "We are evolving from being cultivators of personal knowledge to being hunters and gatherers in the electronic data forest" (p. 126).

Eyetracking Reveals Reading Patterns

Further evidence supporting Carr's concerns arises from the work of Dr. Jakob Nielsen, a Danish engineer who has studied web usability at IBM, Sun Microsystems and most currently at the Nielsen Norman Group, a computer usability consulting firm. Nielsen may be best known for his eyetracking studies that reveal how people actually read online. The studies use eye cameras and web cams to watch people as they read on the screen. Tracking eye fixations and movements, Nielsen has shown that readers look at the screen in a fairly consistent pattern that follows the shape of the letter F. Thus, they look at the top left and top right segments of the screen, read all the way across the top, and then read down the screen, looking to the right less and less as they move down (Nielsen & Pernice, 2010).

Because Nielsen and Pernice's findings are quite pertinent to how people look at Web sites and read on the screen, they warrant more thorough discussion, particularly since I did not use eyetracking of any kind in the case studies reported in Chapter 2. In their book, *Eyetracking and Web Usability* (2010), these scholars report on careful studies of how people look at websites for business purposes. They collected data from 300 participants, asking them to do both very specific as well as more open-ended tasks; the research produced 1.5 million fixations on various websites. This research, then, taps the familiar saccades and fixations of eye movements discussed previously in Chapter 3. The participants ranged in age from 18 to 64, and were balanced for gender, ethnicity, and other factors. The group included mostly full-time workers (81%), those of higher socio-economic status (65% with incomes of $50,000 or more) and college graduates (69%). This array of participants was chosen because of the business focus of the study, so the participants were selected to represent the clients of those Nielsen and Pernice serve (2010, p. 22-23). The methodology is presented at their website (www.useit.com/eyetracking/methodology).

Using eyetracking results, Nielsen and Pernice have constructed heat maps that reveal how the majority of users read a Web page when doing different kinds of reading tasks. In the quantitative tasks, they asked readers, among other things, to read a specific article and answer a question based on it (2010, p. 27). In the more open-ended tasks, readers were given a question, like "How does a windmill generate power?" (p. 29) and allowed to search as they liked to find an answer, or they were sent to a specific site to find information. In addition to tracking where participants looked, Nielsen and Pernice measured four key elements:

"task time, success score, errors, and users' subjective satisfaction" (2010, p. 30). The results of this particular study are presented against the background of the work of the Nielsen Norman Group, which has "tested more than 1,250 Web sites with more than 3,600 users in 16 nations on 4 continents" (2010, p. 38). Thus, they have a wealth of experience in this field.

Their findings show very clearly how people read a Web page, following the F shape as mentioned previously (2010, p. 115). Users do look at images, especially if they are clear and attractive (2010, p. 238) and at simulated movement (2010, p. 240). Animation can be used to get attention, show a process, display a variety of items on a single screen, entertain or communicate. The findings show that people do watch movement (called animations) carefully, especially if the purpose is instruction and the animation moves slowly and can be controlled by the user (2010, p. 302-03). The nature of links and their design is a key issue in Web usability. Nielsen and Pernice say the development of links is "one of the most difficult and time-consuming challenges for Web designers" (2010, p. 113) since users want navigation to be easy and straightforward. Thus, this research on readers looking at Web sites shows that they use the additional distinctive features of links, images, sound, and movement and pay attention to bricolage and juxtaposition.

Reading and Hyperreading: A Look at Expert Readers

A different kind of close look at experts reading online comes from Terje Hillesund, a Norwegian communications and media theorist. Hillesund reports on the ways that reading has changed because of what he calls the "material conditions" of reading (2010), by which he means the features of hyperreading discussed by Carr, Nielsen and Pernice. Hillesund did a qualitative study of ten university faculty members in various disciplines of the humanities and social sciences. Hillesund points out that they have considerable "tacit knowledge" that qualifies them as experts (2010). He completed 14 interviews with these participants, asking about where and how they read extended non-fiction prose texts of various kinds. All of the participants were experts in their fields of study, which range from history to literature to journalism to sociology. The participants included seven men and three women, ranging in age from 38 to 65. Interviews were done in the participants' offices and recorded on a digital voice recorder, usually for one to two hours. In a few cases, the conversation was continued at a later time for an additional hour. Hillesund also relied on his own experience as a scholar and expert reader (2010).

The results of these interviews are quite revealing of the nature of experts' reading and interaction with texts online and on paper. Hillesund makes an important distinction between continuous and discontinuous reading, with the former being the traditional way of reading a novel, while the latter is the reading of discontinuous texts on a variety of topics often done on the Web. Hillesund describes this kind of reading as "fragmented" while the more continuous approach typical of reading novels he calls "sustained reading" (2010). Looking at his experts, Hillesund finds that "[s]ustained discontinuous reading seems to be characteristic of scholarly expert reading" (2010). This finding applies to both books and articles. Experts commonly report that while they do read articles and books continuously, and novels always in this fashion, often this reading is "complementary," that is, related to the focal point of the scholar's work. Though online reading may be increasing, most of these experts report that "online scholarly reading is definitely discontinuous and often fragmented in character" (2010). Experts use the Web in a sustained but discontinuous way to find and download information, statistics and other material on authors or topics.

Expert readers' interviews reveal their engagement with texts in a different kind of reading that Hillesund calls "immersive reading" (2010). Prior to this kind of reading, experts report that they engage in "shallow" or discontinuous reading to browse or look through articles or other materials, in order to choose which ones they wish to examine more closely. But then, having done this discontinuous reading to find and sort out relevant items, experts use immersive reading to engage more deeply with texts. Novels are typically read at an immersive level, but nonfiction can also be read this way if readers are engaged with the ideas and lines of reasoning being presented. Hillesund says that printed materials are well suited to being read either discontinuously or immersively.

The experts in this study do engage in some online reading, especially of novels. And while they find both ebooks and electronic paper (Kindle and the like) acceptable for reading novels, the participants were not satisfied with any e-reading device for the more detailed kind of reading they do when examining articles in their research. Book marking and annotation are simply too difficult to make the reading experience acceptable. Web browsers are "the least suited for immersive reading" (2010). For immersive reading and engagement to occur, the technology really needs to be transparent, i.e., it cannot get in between the reader and the text: "hypertext, multimodality and the multifunctionality of the Web are incompatible with sustained reflective and imaginary reading" (2010).

Hillesund's experts also find reading online difficult for a different reason, having to do with the way a text is presented on the Web. Most texts, such as newspaper stories, are presented with ads and links to other related content. To really read something, at least one of the experts in the study prefers to use an iPhone, where he can scroll down so that the ads and links are off the screen and he can focus on the text and content of the article. Computers not only offer constant opportunities to click and find other materials or items of interest, but are also constant reminders of other work that needs to be done. Thus, they "make it extremely hard to maintain an act of digital reading for a substantial period of time" (Hillesund, 2010).

In terms of their physical relationship with the text, the experts in Hillesund's study try to remove themselves from their computers if they mean to engage in immersive reading. Either they sit in a different place in their offices or do this more extended reading at home and on paper. They prefer to interact with the text in some specific way like highlighting or underlining passages and/or making notes in the margins. All the participants report that any kind of computer reading is more superficial than reading on paper. Digital reading leads to more skimming and fewer annotations. Computers are good for and are used by experts for these activities: "browsing, searching, accessing, downloading and skimming text" but not for scholarly immersive reading (Hillesund, 2010).

Most participants read and write online, but favor printing out their writing and reviewing, correcting, and editing on paper before making changes on the screen. Will this approach change as the technology of electronic paper improves so that it is easier to highlight, take notes and work with text in the ways experts prefer? Will younger readers be more willing to adapt their strategies to electronic platforms? Will playing video games that entail intensive reading and writing in a shared, collaborative environment, as suggested by Arizona State literacy scholar James Paul Gee (2010, p. 165-93), allow novices the kinds of reading experiences that lead to the development of expert critical literacy? Answers will come only with increasing experience and improving technology. However, it appears that when experts are working with extended nonfiction prose and doing immersive reading, they almost always take it offline and into some more traditional printed form.

Taken together, Hillesund's findings show that expert scholars use both digital and printed texts for both reading and writing. All extant text technologies are used: the computer for finding and exploring material, but printed out paper forms or traditional books for immersive reading, and both paper for revising and editing and digital modes for "text production, …storing, disseminating, accessing, skimming and downloading of text" (2010). Computers, paper and handwriting are all used by the experts Hillesund studied. For the purposes of critical literacy in general, experts routinely and consistently go to paper. Experts make conscious choices about what they read and how they read it. Novices approach digital reading quite differently, and the contrasts point clearly to the need for careful instruction for novices to move toward expertise in both traditional and digital reading.

Measuring Novices' Reading Online

Given the explosion in the use of technology among young people, it is easy to think that surely their skills are actually quite good. College students these days certainly seem attached to their phones, tablets and other devices, using them for reading and writing/texting with an addiction-like intensity, but their abilities turn out to be as shallow as Carr claims. As mentioned in Chapter 1, a very focused definition of information literacy has been developed by the Association of College and Research Libraries, the major professional organization of research librarians and a sub-group of the American Library Association (Association, 2008). Their Information Literacy Competency Standards for Higher Education (found in the Appendix to this book and also at http://www.ala.org/acrl/standards/informationliteracycompetency) have been used as the basis of two exams which provide direct measures of novices' online reading abilities. The first of these, called iSkills was created by the Educational Testing Service, and the second, called Project SAILS, by a group of faculty and librarians working collaboratively at Kent State University in Ohio. The ACRL standards, which serve as the basis for both measures, describe activities essential to setting up a clear research goal and then finding, evaluating and using materials online. Two other measures, case studies by a librarian and a large data set examining students' use of sources in research writing reveal students' weaknesses in reading online.

The first direct test is the Educational Testing Service test of ICT [information and communication technology] skills, called the iSkills test. ETS is the purveyor of the SAT, Advanced Placement and many other standardized tests; the organization has extensive test design and administration experience with large-scale tests of various kinds. Irwin Katz, one of the lead researchers on the iSkills instrument, reports in two papers the results of studies done in 2006 on information literacy skills of college students. The iSkills test is a one-hour instrument in which students are given scenarios that measure their abilities to define, access, evaluate, manage, integrate, create, and communicate using ICT tools (http://www.ets.org/iskills/about/content/). The test is designed to measure the skills articulated by ACRL and described in its standards (the entire set of standards is at the link mentioned just above). The data are not representative of any particular group. The findings from administrations of the instrument to a random group of about 6400 high school, community college and four-year college and university students show that only 50% of the students who participated have the skills that ACRL deems essential for appropriate use of ICT tools (Katz, 2007a, 2007b).

The second measure provides further data on technologically-based reading. It comes from a different instrument designed collaboratively by librarians and faculty at Kent State University in Ohio, where they have developed the SAILS (Standardized Assessment of Information Literacy Skills) test. This instrument measures students' abilities to develop a search strategy, find, evaluate, and document their sources (Project SAILS, 2009). Like the iSkills findings, the SAILS results also show that only half of the students have the skills described by the ACRL Standards. These results along with more recent studies using similar instruments clearly indicate that student/novices' critical literacy is as shallow as Carr claims, according to Florida State University Library and Information Studies scholars Melissa Gross and Don Latham (2011).

A second way of looking at readers' abilities comes from a more individualized, case study kind of perspective. Writing in *I Found It on the Internet: Coming of Age Online* (2011), school and reference librarian Frances Jacobson Harris discusses the role of librarians in developing the literacy abilities of patrons young and old, but especially young, i.e. novices. While Harris generally supports the role and use of computers in the library and especially among teens, she cites several examples of the challenges faced by young people trying to get information online. Here's one example:

> A student of ours once ordered a book about the shipping tycoon Aristotle Onassis through interlibrary loan. I did not think this book was really what he wanted, because his history class was studying ancient Greece. When he came to pick it up, I asked him what his topic was. "Oh," he said, "it's Socrates," which he pronounced "So-crats." Restraining myself from smiling, I checked the cataloging-in-publication data on the back of the title page to see how a search on "Socrates" retrieved a book about Aristotle Onassis. It turns out that "Socrates" was Onassis's middle name.... The combination of my student's lack of background knowledge and his propensity to use keyword searching was his undoing. (Harris, 2011, p. 19).

In the first edition of this book, Harris gives an even better example of the problems novice readers have with online research and online sources:

> When one of my students conducted a search on women in the military, she found an article titled "Women at Arms" (http://www.policy review.org/aug00/Bockhorn.html). As far as she was concerned, this page was a source she found on the Internet, undifferentiated from other web-based sources. She did not recognize it as a piece from the online counterpart of a scholarly print journal, *Policy Review*. To some degree, the website's designers are responsible for her misconception. Though the *Policy Review* masthead is unmistakable, the links on the page lead to the journal's current issue, not to the August 2000 issue in which the article originally appeared. The original issue can only be accessed by deleting Bockhorn.html from the URL, not a very intuitive navigational method. My student cited this source as a web page, not as an article in a journal. While she documented some of the important information—the title of the piece, the author's name, and the URL that would lead other readers to her source—she missed important contextual information that would have helped her interpret its value.
>
> The next problem in deciphering this source is that it is not, after all, really an article about women in the military. Instead, it is an extended editorial review of two books on the topic. A bibliography generation tool like NoodleBib, with its detailed prompts, or timely input from a teacher or librarian, might have pushed my student to make this discovery. And, still, she would not have been finished with her detective work. From the online table-of-contents page of the issue, there is a link to the publisher of *Policy Review*, the Hoover Institution at Stanford University (in a short-lived collaboration with the Heritage Foundation, a conservative think tank). A little digging uncovers the Hoover Institution's mission, one which is likely to shape (i.e., bias) the content of its publications. To be thorough, my student would have had to parse out the meaning of that mission and the degree to which it affected her planned used of the source. She would also have needed to weigh the usefulness of a book review for her needs. In the end, she could regard the article as a "bread crumb" source, one she could not use outright but which would lead her to other sources she could use, such as the books being reviewed. To get that far, she would have had to read an article she would not get "credit" for and then search again, this time for the two books.
>
> Not many students would persist through all the steps just described. (Harris, 2005, p. 135-37)

I quote these examples at length because they offer case studies of the kinds of skills novices need to read well online and do not have.

A third kind of data comes from an on-going large research study of college students' use of source materials in research writing, called The

Citation Project (Jamieson, 2011). This research project entails a review of almost 2000 references that appear in 174 first-year students' research papers from 16 colleges and universities across the United States. Their findings show that only 6% of the students offer a full summary of their source material. Moreover, 46% of the references come from the first page of a source, and 70% come from the first two pages of the material the student consulted, whether paper or digital. Finally, a majority of sources presented by students were used only once in the paper (Howard, Rodrigue & Serviss, 2010; Jamieson & Howard, 2011). These findings suggest rather strongly that students are engaged in "quote mining" (Howard, Rodrigue & Serviss, 2010, p. 186), just finding a suitable piece from a source to insert. These scholars point out that using sources in this way does not prove students failed to read and understand the complete text, but the overall pattern suggests that students are reading shallowly, not using any level of awareness or skill. Similarly, in my case studies, when novices mark a sentence and say "that's important," it's the same shallow reading, on paper and online.

Digital reading calls for an awareness of bricolage and juxtaposition, as well as the ability to deal with links, images, sound, and movement. But it also calls on the same awarenesses and skills as print reading, skills experts have and novices need to develop for the purposes of critical literacy. The numerical data from the iSkills and SAILS tests of novice readers' online ability to analyze, synthesize, evaluate and apply, the more qualitative analysis offered by Harris, and the analysis of students' use of sources from The Citation Project all suggest that novices lack the necessary skills of critical literacy online just as they do on paper.

Media Use and School Performance

The amount of time young people spend with media of all kinds does not guarantee that they have or are developing the awarenesses and skills they need. Further evidence for the negative impact of media on novices' reading comes from a different kind of study done by the non-profit, nonpartisan Kaiser Family Foundation and released in 2010 (Kaiser, 2010). The California-based Kaiser Foundation focuses on health research, but also does studies related to communication and other issues, according to its website (http://www.kff.org/about/index2.cfm). The Kaiser study reports on a survey completed in 2008-09 of about 2,000 students in grades 3-12, drawn from schools and students selected at random from a sample designed to reflect students in the nation. The students completed a 40-minute written survey in class, and then about 700 volunteers kept a media diary at home for a week. The media use being tracked included watching TV and movies, listening to music, playing video games, and reading books, newspapers and magazines. Texting and talking on the phone were not included in the definition of media use. Students were asked only about recreational media use. The amounts of time spent with more than one form of media, i.e multitasking, are specifically noted.

The report shows that young people's media use has increased dramatically over time, since the Kaiser Foundation has run this study three times at five-year intervals. And while time spent reading has dropped, the decline is not statistically significant and book reading has actually increased, while magazine and newspaper reading has decreased. As cell phones have become capable of providing more access, the amount of multi-tasking has increased. Heavier media users, whose use is defined as 16 hours per day or more, who account for about 20% of the population report lower grades and less personal satisfaction. African-American or Hispanic students, 11-14, are more likely to be heavy media users. As the report notes, with respect to reading and school performance:

> Children who are heavy media users are more likely to report getting fair or poor grades (mostly C's or lower) than other children. Indeed, nearly half (47%) of all heavy media users say they usually get fair or poor grades, compared to 23% of light media users. Moreover, the relationship between media exposure and grades withstands controls for other possibly relevant factors such as age, gender, race, parent education, personal contentedness, and single vs. two-parent households. The pattern varies only for print; those with lower grades spend less time reading for pleasure than other children do. (Kaiser, 2010, p. 13)

While the report states specifically that there is not necessarily a cause-and-effect relationship here, the finding suggests a possible connection between these factors. These are novice readers, and reading less goes hand-in-hand with lower school performance.

These various studies of novice readers all point in the same general direction and show a clear contrast between experts and novices. Experts do read online but make clear distinctions between discontinuous and immersive reading. They use a different set of strategies and approaches when looking for information in connection with their research or other uses. Once they have found what they need, they engage in immersive reading of continuous nonfiction prose, almost always offline. When they read immersively, they are using their awarenesses and skills. Novices, by contrast, are "hunter-gatherers in the electronic data forest" as Carr suggests. For at least half of the students studied by various means, discontinuous and shallow reading is the norm; more time with media leads to poor school performance, not improved expertise in reading.

Summary

Critical literacy in the 21st century will continue to draw on critical literacy as we have known it from centuries past. It will continue to draw on the basic mental capacities that make the feat of literacy possible at all. These mechanisms include both essential mental capacities like identification and categorization, processes we use for literacy as well as other kinds of intellectual tasks. The additional mental capacities with language that people have, abilities to use syntax and redundancy, will also continue to be important. These capacities allow us to work with the distinctive features of letters, words, sentences, and texts to get meaning from print in reading and put meaning into print in writing. The distinctive features make critical literacy possible. The abilities to analyze, synthesize, evaluate and apply are increasingly important in dealing with the Internet. There, the additional mechanisms of bricolage and juxtaposition and the additional features of link, image, sound, and movement challenge human literate capacity. Meta-readers' and writers' abilities in print or electronic venues draw on the slightly expanded set of mental capacities and the slightly expanded set of distinctive features that make critical literacy possible.

Perhaps as technology continues to develop, more specialized uses will also develop for the various platforms, as they are called. This suggestion has been offered by Dwight Garner, a book critic for the *New York Times* in a recent evaluation of the use of various forms of technology for reading (2012). Discussing smart phones, e-readers and the iPad, Garner writes that he uses all these devices, but each one seems best for a different kind of reading. The smart phone is useful for journalism and audio books; the Kindle and other e-readers for both short and long fiction, and the iPad for big nonfiction books, including especially those with electronic footnotes that take readers directly to the source (Garner, 2012, p. 6). But each, he notes, has its downside and in any case, "it's the mental furniture that matters" (p. 6), a point consistent with the discussion in this book.

The need for the "mental furniture" of critical literacy is most urgent and clear when we look at the reading side of literate activity, chiefly because of the incredible explosion of information and text availability on the Internet. In the evolving era of digital information, whole huge libraries of material are becoming available on our desktops, our laptops, our tablets, our smart phones. Our use of meta-textual, meta-contextual and meta-linguistic awarenesses and the skills to analyze, synthesize, evaluate and apply will be increasingly essential as we are swamped by the information resources available. Everyone's skills will need to be faster, more efficient, and more effective to get what we need to interact with one another, to get work done, to exchange ideas freely in democratic societies. A key goal must be to insure that every person attains the high level of critical literacy typical of meta-readers and writers. The next chapter focuses on the writing side of meta-reading and writing. Here the same claim of essential consistency of mental capacities and distinctive features applies so that writing online is only a little different from writing on paper.

CHAPTER EIGHT

WRITING TRADITIONAL AND ELECTRONIC TEXTS

Introduction

Every time I started a chapter in this book, I wanted to use this title: "It's NOT New; It's NOT Different: Literacy on the Web." This title came to mind because my argument in this chapter and throughout this book is that the fundamental features of meta-reading and writing do not change as a result of shifting from page to screen. These claims are, I realize, quite different from those of the "new media age" scholars who argue that electronic literacy IS different from print literacy. However, the earlier chapters of this book have argued the basic mental capacities and features that are essential to human literacy as well as the awarenesses and skills that describe expert critical literacy are the same on pages and screens. For expert meta-readers and writers, my argument is that literacy is literacy, regardless of the environment. The preceding chapter on reading and this one on writing on the web address specifically the digital context of literacy.

This exploration of digital writing shows that it calls on these same essential features of human literacy as does writing on paper. There is no question that there are a few more "bells and whistles" involved in creating a web page or site, but the underlying processes are the same. For example, writers are making increasing use of the PDF format for documents, a format that makes digital documents look like printed text, and makes them unalterable, like print publications. Perhaps the print and digital forms of texts are coming together in this way to a greater degree than many people realize.

This chapter examines the ways that the few added mental capacities discussed in Chapter 7, bricolage and juxtaposition, and the few additional distinctive features (images, sounds, movement and links) shape writing on the Web. This chapter starts with a brief review of all the underlying abilities that make critical literacy possible. A number of scholars see the connection of older and newer forms of writing; their work is presented to support my claim. A guide for writers preparing materials for the web offers further support for the argument that digital writing and print-based writing do not differ significantly. Then, I describe my own beginning effort to create a website, to illustrate how the essential character of human literacy operates in the digital environment of the Internet. Examples of the website, with its various pages and links will show how the mental capacities and distinctive feature elements are used in writing on the web. Writing on the web, then, is NOT new or different for two reasons. First, it builds on the same mental capacities and distinctive features (with a few small additions) as traditional writing. Second, it relies on the same essential meta-reading and writing awarenesses and skills as does writing on paper.

Some New Terminology

Before examining digital writing, readers may need a bit of terminology. In a number of ways, the terminology that writers use to discuss new media provides inherent support for my argument. For example, the terms hypertext and hypermedia work in this way. Computer researcher David Levy, writing about the nature of documents in a digital environment, explains these terms by citing those who developed them. Levy writes:

> It was Ted Nelson who first coined the word "hypertext." Nelson and Douglas Englebart are considered to be the fathers of *computer-based* hypertext, the ability to link fragments of text together via computer, allowing the reader to follow a link from one piece of text to another. (The more recent term "hypermedia" is a further generalization of hypertext, in which not only text but other media types such as static graphics, animation, and sound are linked together. (Levy, 2001, p. 149)

Though these scholars coined the term, Levy goes on to point out that the idea of texts linked through the computer belongs to Vannevar Bush in his classic article "As We May Think," published in 1945, much before computers became the commonplace items they are today.

As I have suggested, the newer forms are simply combinations of old and new, and not really qualitatively different from them. Moreover, the texts, visuals, links, and so on that are connected through hypertext or hypermedia are read with the same mental capacities and entail the same distinctive features as traditional printed texts, with a few small additions. Finally, expert meta-readers and writers read and write both print and digital texts with the awarenesses and skills that define critical literacy.

NOT New, NOT Different?

The impact on literacy of the move to digital formats for texts of all kinds can fairly be described as a matter of some controversy. Some scholars suggest that digital writing is distinctively different from traditional writing, while others see a continuum between old and new venues for writing. Still others see that experts have the ability to work with different media in different situations, and know how to use their mental capacities and the distinctive features for their own purposes. There is, thus, a wide range of views on this issue.

To begin with a scholar who sees the digital as really different from traditional print, for example, Australian education scholar Ilana Snyder argues in *Silicon Literacies* (2002), that the rise of information and communication technologies is not simply a newer and more efficient way to exchange information, but is fundamentally different. In her introduction, she notes that the essays in the collection have some common points including that they "move away from psychological and cognitive models to concentrate on cultural and social aspects of language use, [and] the essays share common ground with the New Literacy Studies" (Snyder, 2002, p. 11). However, it may be useful to note that functional linguists and those working in social semiotics have been arguing for the importance of linguistic, cultural and social context for many years (cf. Halliday and Hasan (1976) and others). The implications of such thinking for the development of literacy skills have been made explicit in the work of some of the most highly respected psycholinguists and literacy scholars including Goodman (1996), Smith (2004) and Graff (1987).

Some researchers recognize the connection and continuity between the old and new kinds of literacy, such as UCLA educational philosopher Douglas Kellner, whose work Snyder includes in her collection. He notes the importance of traditional literacy because of the sheer volume of information. A commonplace expression that captures this idea is the notion of trying to take a sip of water from a fire hose. The more reading and writing people do online, the more important it is to be clear, precise, and focused in order to communicate effectively and not add to information overload (Kellner, 2002, p. 158). In Kellner's view, both reading and writing in the contemporary literacy landscape must make use of the same classic abilities people have had all along, abilities that carry over from dealing with printed books as well as glowing screens. This view is shared by Snyder in her more recent book, *The Literacy Wars*, where she suggests that for instructional purposes "a literacy classroom for the future must involve the effective integration of print literacy and digital literacy… to give attention to both" (2008, p. 167).

Kellner goes on to argue for true computer literacy, and it is worth noticing how his argument incorporates all the forms of print literacy I have been discussing in this book:

> Genuine computer literacy involves not just technical knowledge and skills, but refined reading, writing, research, and communicating ability. *It involves heightened capacities for critically accessing, analyzing, interpreting, processing and storing both print-based and multimedia material.* …Computer literacy thus also involves the ability to discover and access information and intensified abilities to read, to scan texts and computer databases and websites, and to access information and images in a variety of forms, ranging from graphics, to visual images, to audio and video materials, to good old print media. The creation of new multimedia websites, databases, and texts requires accessing downloading and organising digitised verbal, imagistic, and audio and video material that are the new building blocks of multimedia culture. (2002, p. 162, emphasis added)

The skills Kellner enumerates as constituting digital literacy overlap with those I discussed in the opening section of this book, as the fundamental human capacities with written language that contribute to critical literacy.

Kellner is not the only one who sees the changing landscape of literacy in this way. College writing teacher and digital literacy scholar Mark Warschauer shares this view in his 1999 book, *Electronic Literacies*. This volume reports on research Warschauer conducted in four undergraduate writing classes in different institutions in Hawaii from 1995 to 1997. Warschauer examined both the influence of electronic media on the teaching and learning of literacy on Oahu and the impact of electronic media in a context of a diverse social setting linguistically, culturally, racially, and ethnically. He studied the changes in the teaching and learning of literacy in terms of both computer-mediated communication (including asynchronous email, bulletin boards, synchronous exchanges like chat rooms and so on), and hypermedia and the Web (Warschauer, 1999, p. 6-7).

Warschauer points out that computer-mediated communication is close to traditional forms of literacy, since it entails written texts of various kinds, even though these may be read and written on screens rather than on paper. However, hypermedia and the Web appear quite different from traditional forms of literacy because they entail three distinctive characteristics: they are nonlinear; they use links to connect points of information across languages, cultures and countries; and they include visual features such as video and graphics as well as sound. The transformative nature of these changes is significant, Warschauer says, but the digital form of literacy has "not yet supplanted the page, but it has already joined it as an important medium of literate activity in modern society" (1999, p. 8). This comment suggests that Warschauer sees digital literacy as an evolved and evolving form, but neither new nor different.

Ultimately, Warschauer argues for what he calls "a plurality of literacies" (1999, p. 162). In the development of literacy, then, students must

> understand how communication varies across media and how different grammars—whether the grammar of text or the grammar of visual design…combine to express meaning. They have to learn various types of electronic literacy (such as Web research and computer-mediated collaboration) in support of print literacy (such as writing essays), and they have to learn various types of print literacy (such as scanning books for information) in support of electronic literacies (such as authoring Web pages). They have to learn the types of genres and rhetorical structures that are used in particular media and they have to learn enough about cultural and dialectical differences to choose the right communication strategies for the particular audiences that they are likely to encounter in a new medium. Most important—and here there is continuity from the practice of print literacy—students need to have a clear and meaningful purpose for the reading and writing activities that they undertake. (Warschauer, 1999, p. 162-3)

In this description, it seems that Warschauer focuses on genres or modes, topic, purpose and audience, classic features of rhetoric that have been with us down the centuries since Aristotle. That is, even in an environment that includes computer-mediated communication and hypertext, a plurality of literacies will call upon the same fundamental human linguistic abilities discussed throughout this book.

Also on the other side of this discussion is University of Wisconsin literacy scholar Deborah Brandt. In her reports on a study of 60 adult professionals in a variety of jobs in research and industry, she suggests that writing is quite different now for several reasons (Brandt, forthcoming). Brandt acknowledges Carr's work in *The Shallows* (2010) but says that he has focused on reading more or less to the exclusion of writing. Writing, however, is not the mirror image of reading, for two reasons. First, writing is not just the opposite of reading because new brain research shows that writing engages entirely different areas of the brain. Moreover, Brandt says that writing is now happening to a much greater extent than reading and is a way to solidify and recall what we learn from the texts we do read. Brandt writes:

> we are just now entering an era of *deep writing*, that is a new stage of mass literacy in which writing is spreading deeply into the daily experiences of more and more people, reconfiguring individual discourse diets. *Deep writing* is a term that also captures the deeply interactive networks in which people write now, the substrata of relationships and concerns that surpass the beginnings and ends of discrete texts. Finally, *deep writing* refers to the immersive cognitive states that writing and revising often require, driven not merely by orchestration of memory, muscle, language, and task but by the effects that writing can have on the person who writes. (Brandt, forthcoming)

Brandt says that regardless of what is happening with reading as a by-product of our time online, and as discussed by Carr, writing is changing.

This era of "deep writing," Brandt says, differs from earlier times in three specific ways. First, people are writing among other writers. This difference opens up some new possibilities for learning to write and for how people interact through writing. Second, reading goes on in the service of writing. People read to an increasing degree to find material useful in their own writing, and read much less for the sake of reading in and of itself. Finally, Brandt claims that writing "is a site of intellectual, moral and civic development." Her studies with professional writers suggest the following:

> ...when people talk about the writing that they do—including mundane, workplace writing—they readily notice its moral, intellectual and aesthetic effects on them as people. ...[T]he effects on writers can be considerable. Especially because writing unleashes language into the world—where it can have consequential impact on others—it engages people's sense of responsibility, even when they are writing anonymously or under someone else's name. ...[W]riters see their words taking public shape, and the effects of these words do not stop with the reader. (Brandt, forthcoming)

These differences have not been studied by writing researchers, but Brandt says they are major changes that need careful attention. And they are, according to her, going have a big impact on both reading and writing.

From a psycholinguistic standpoint, though, these claims of big differences warrant careful scrutiny. A careful look at these claims shows that "deep writing" is not so different, whether on the page or the screen, insofar as it calls on the same awarenesses and skills that meta-readers and writers have always had and still do; these are skills novices will need for reading and writing on paper and online. A larger community of writers and readers does not change the psycholinguistic features of literacy, whether on pages or screens. That reading supports and engages writers is captured by the skills of analysis, synthesis, evaluation and application identified here as the key skills of critical literacy. The professionals Brandt studied would surely qualify as experts who use these skills in both their reading and their writing, on paper or online. And as for the intellectual and moral implications arising from this writing, expert meta-readers and writers have surely always been aware of these implications, from Aristotle to the reporters of the Arab Spring. So, while Brandt and these other scholars claim that there are major changes afoot, a closer look shows that critical literacy on the Web continues to require the awarenesses and skills that expert meta-readers and writers have and novices need to develop.

One final perspective might be most useful to address these divergent points of view. It comes from Elizabeth Baker, University of Missouri literacy studies professor and editor of *The New Literacies* (2010). In her closing essay, attempting to draw together the various views of literacy presented in her collection, Baker advocates an "autonomous agents" position (2010, p. 304). From this perspective, individuals use "a variety of means, and each individual may engage different tools, sensitivities, and strategies to arrive at the goals of communication and understanding" (p. 304). This view has important implications for working with novices, since it allows for the use of whatever aspects of both print and digital literacies work best for a particular individual. Baker suggests the following:

> If we take an autonomous agents perspective toward new literacies, ...we not only need to teach students the necessary systems to be able to read and write with digital technologies, but we also need to teach students to flexibly use these systems to adjust as needed to accomplish their goal of reading or writing. This shifts the curriculum from simply teaching the skills of the new literacies to also teaching students to *orchestrate* a range of systems to adjust as necessary to make sense of digital texts. (Baker, 2010, p. 305).

Ultimately, reading and writing are still reading and writing, regardless of venue. The ability to "orchestrate" the various systems is the ability that experts have and novices need to develop and apply, in both print and digital environments.

Not new, not different, not really.

Defining Aspects of Digital Writing

The openness of the Web seems to invite the use of terms in variable ways, so we need some further definitions for a clear understanding of digital writing. Hammerich and Harrison (2002), a professional Web developer and a writer respectively, who have prepared websites for the Canadian government among other organizations, provide a series of definitions at the outset of their discussion of *Developing Online Content*, a printed (!) book for Web writers. Naturally, they were writing their volume much before ebooks were available, so it's hardly surprising that their guide appears in a traditional form. They separate Web writing into content, visuals and navigation. Because this book is specifically focused on writing for the Web, it offers a detailed examination of effective digital writing that makes clear its similarity to print.

Hammerich and Harrison define "content" as written text and any related graphics, video or audio directly connected to the written text. "Visuals" are a second part of Web writing, referring to design, graphics, color, photographs, and animation. These visuals include more general graphic features not directly connected to the text on the page or site. Finally, Web writing involves "navigation," that is, the mechanisms that allow users to move around among the pages on a website (2002, p. 2). Writing for the Web, then, entails principally a focus on preparing content, though the material cannot be prepared in isolation from the overall presentation. Hammerich and Harrison go on to say that "although the Web *is* a new medium, it can also be viewed as a new delivery tool for the same type of content that exists in other media such as text in print…" (p. 12). Their book is intended to help writers develop good, usable content.

These writers' position provides additional support for my claim that Web writing is "NOT new; NOT different." Their work shows that Web writing is an evolving form that draws on well-established rhetorical principles in the newer digital context. These writers make the further point that content, i.e. text, has recently been demonstrated to be where Web users focus their attention. They summarize a study tracking users' behavior and eye movements which found that users look first and foremost to the content while examining websites, with visuals as a secondary focus, and that users will not stay with a page or a site that is not well-written and usable (2002, p. 8-9). These findings are confirmed by the work of Nielsen and Pernice (2010) discussed in Chapter 7.

To evaluate good, usable Web content, Hammerich and Harrison discuss four Cs of "quality web content:" credibility, clarity, conciseness and coherence (2002, p. 110-128). The first three of these markers of quality are consistent with conventional criteria. Their standards, first, for credibility, derive from research done by librarians in setting up standards for evaluating information on the Web: authority of the writers (i.e. their expertise), accuracy of the information, objectivity in terms of point of view, currency or how up-to-date a site is, and coverage/audience issues, including whether the information is provided in sufficient detail appropriate for the intended audience (2002, p. 112). These are the familiar standards developed by the ACRL (see Appendix for full text of the Information Literacy Standards). Clarity, a second marker, entails using short, tight structure, making active, specific language choices, choosing useful titles and subheadings and setting up spacing that contributes to ease of reading; these elements are bricolage and juxtaposition in action. The third marker, conciseness, means using the smallest possible amount of material to convey key points through choices of key words, brief, structured sentences, and useful transitions.

Coherence, the fourth C of Hammerich and Harrison's quality content, is more complex than the other characteristics they discuss. It rests partly on textual cohesion, which refers to creating linguistic connections among the pages or parts of a site that have appropriate information architecture, logical relationships and pages that do not have hyperlinks or hot links that connect them to other pages (2002, p. 124). In particular, Hammerich and Harrison suggest relying on cohesive ties described by Halliday and Hasan (1976) that are just as important on screen as they are in print: repetition, synonyms, collocation (related words re-occur in close proximity), reference, conjunction, ellipsis and substitution (as cited in Hammerich & Harrison, 2002, p. 125-126). Finally, they point out that coherence relies on readers' prior knowledge and ability to predict what will appear in a text or on a site, both linguistically in terms of genre, conventions and language, and in terms of their knowledge of the topic of the site.

Quality content must have features that should be familiar to readers of *Reading, Writing and Digitizing*. Credibility, clarity, conciseness and coherence are features essential to text on both pages and screens. It is interesting to keep in mind that Hammerich and Harrison's book is intended for people who write for the Web, but it draws extensively on the mental capacities and distinctive features of users of written language that I have described. From this discussion of e-rhetoric they move on to an exploration of visual rhetoric and its practical implications for creating websites. Before examining their insights on visual rhetoric, though, we turn to additional views of scholars who explore the similarities between hypertext and hypermedia or digital writing and printed text. While digital writing entails different tools than traditional writing, the psycholinguistic processes used to generate the text, and the nature of the text itself (i.e., its distinctive features) are the same whether the text appears on a screen or printed page.

More Similarities: Print and Digital

A number of other scholars share Hammerich and Harrison's view that writing has similar requirements in print and digital environments. For example, content on the Web must meet criteria of usability, defined by five questions or areas of concern, according to Stuart Selber, a professor of English and Science, Technology and Society at Penn State University, who has published extensively on the relationship of rhetoric and literacy, including *Multiliteracies for a Digital Age* (2004) and an edited collection, *Rhetorics and Technologies* (2010). In *Multiliteracies*, Selber asks these kinds of general questions: How can users use what is on the site? How can users describe the site? What procedures do users need to use the site? How do users make sense of the site? Finally, how can users move from place to place within a site (2004, p. 71)? These categories (goals, description, procedure, interpretation and navigation) must be addressed in Web writing, but they are mostly not different from categories that must be addressed in print writing; Web writing needs audience, topic and purpose and a few other things.

A somewhat different perspective on writing from clay tablets to digital ones arrives at the same view of writing as same regardless of the change of venue. This is the position of Jay David Bolter, a professor at the Georgia Institute of Technology in *Writing Space* (2001). Bolter discusses the "space" in which writing occurs as a metaphor for the ways that writing has changed as a result of the use of computers. He points out that electronic texts are much more changeable and can shift easily because of technology. Ultimately, in Bolter's view, writers come to see "the mind itself as a writing space" (Bolter, 2001, p. 13), and so, from writers' perspectives, the place where the writing appears is moot. The range of options Bolter considers is particularly interesting since he cites possibilities across the whole history of writing. It appears, then, that Bolter thinks that writing is writing is writing, whether it is on a clay tablet or a digital one, supporting my overall point. So while there are content issues and usability issues, ultimately, digital writing is at its core the same process as any other kind of writing. It draws on the same underlying psycholinguistic principles that support the awarenesses and skills of expert meta-readers and writers.

There is also work in the psychology of perception that supports the claim that writing in a digital environment is not substantially different from writing on paper. Hammerich and Harrison (2002), add a summary of the work of psychologist Rudolf Arnheim, who separated seeing and perceiving. Hammerich and Harrison (2002, p. 154-55) note that from Arnheim's perspective, a few key principles of psychology and perception influence how people look at and process visual displays. Thus, for example, motion and change attract the eye, but need to be somewhat predictable, i.e. appearing in a predictable place on the screen, and should not be repetitive. Web design needs to strike a balance between enough information and too much clutter. Focusing reflects a reader's interest, so the objects on which the user focuses are very important. Finally, the work of Arnheim and others suggests that shape is also important; objects should be simple, consistently used and familiar. Consistency is essential. Perception is heavily based on prior knowledge and context (as cited in Hammerich & Harrison, 2002, p. 154). All of these principles draw on the basic mental capacities discussed earlier in this book and apply equally to screens and to pages.

The mental capacities I have described, in combination with the perceptual principles described by Arnheim, come into play in writing for the Web. Whether writers are preparing what Hammerich and Harrison (2002) call "online content" or designing a page or site or planning the use of various visual features, the basic mental capacities come into play. Moreover, writing for the Web also draws on the distinctive features discussed in the opening section of this book because there is written language involved. Both the cognitive/linguistic mental capacities and the distinctive features of language *per se* are involved in writing for the Web because writing entails the same operations regardless of venue.

The Rhetoric of Paper and Screen: Visual Issues

At a number of points, I have mentioned the importance of the visual in thinking about the small number of factors that are a little different on the screen than on the page. Visual rhetoric, the ways in which the visual display works persuasively, is one of those factors. In *Developing Online Content* (2002), Hammerich and Harrison devote a chapter to "The Art of Visual Rhetoric" (2002, p. 137-69). They point out at the beginning of the chapter that it is just as essential that the visual aspects of a website be clear and effective as it is that the text use proper grammar and spelling. Thus, if the goal is persuasion, all parts of what is displayed on the page or screen must work together. Their claims, then, fit well with those being presented here, suggesting that visual rhetoric and text-based rhetoric draw on the same basic principles.

The points of similarity are easy to see through a review of scholars' definitions of the phrase "visual rhetoric" and through its features or elements. A number of different scholars have attempted to define the phrase "visual rhetoric," including whole books devoted to the topic such as Hill and Helmers' 2004 volume *Defining Visual Rhetorics*. Like these editors, Hocks and Hendrick (2003, p. 5), Gee (2003, p. 14) and Faigley et al. (2004, p. 398) all agree that the concept of visual rhetoric is a highly cross-disciplinary one, drawing on "art theory, anthropology, rhetoric, cultural studies, psychology, and media studies" (Helmers & Hill, 2004, p. 19). To this list, I would add linguistics, psycholinguistics, philosophy, film studies and photography, among others. While visual rhetoric may be a relatively new term, the idea of an area of investigation crossing traditional disciplinary lines in the study of literacy is not at all new, as much of my discussion has shown. In all of my research that has focused on literacy, I find myself repeatedly venturing into a wide range of areas in the library, captured by all the Library of Congress call letters that are familiar territory for me: BF (psychology), LB (reading), LC (literacy), P (language), PE (rhetoric and composition studies), R (medical), T (technology) and Z (libraries and information). The Library of Congress doesn't know where to put this multi-disciplinary inquiry either, since it entails all of these areas of study!

The scholars named above, not surprisingly, have an array of different definitions of visual rhetoric. The most detailed and helpful for the purposes of the present discussion is presented by University of Colorado Communication scholar Sonja Foss in the final chapter of the Hill and Helmers collection (2004). Foss argues that visual rhetoric refers both to the images and other items users see on the screen and to a way of examining visual texts (p. 304). She uses these two points to present a full definition of visual rhetoric that incorporates both of them. Thus, visual rhetoric is

> the actual image or object rhetors generate when they use visual symbols for the purpose of communicating. It is the tangible evidence or product of the creative act… *Visual rhetoric* as artifact, then, is the purposive production or arrangement of colors, forms, and other elements to communicate with an audience. (Foss, 2004, p. 304)

In addition, though, visual rhetoric is

> a perspective scholars take on visual imagery or visual data. In this meaning of the term, *visual rhetoric* constitutes a theoretical perspective that involves the analysis of the symbolic or communicative aspects of visual artifacts. (Foss, 2004, p. 305-06)

Visual rhetoric, then, focuses on both visual items meant to communicate with viewers, that is, the forms of language or visual information and a way that people analyze those items. The strategies that are used to analyze visual rhetoric are essentially the same as those used to analyze verbal rhetoric; both the forms and the ways that people use these forms entail highly sophisticated linguistic and literate abilities.

Helping novices develop these abilities is the work of the authors of college writing textbooks among others. One example of this kind of work appears in the work of Lester Faigley, professor of English at the University of Texas and lead author of *Picturing Texts* (2004), a rhetoric textbook for college students. To evaluate arguments that entail visual rhetoric, Faigley and his co-authors offer a useful if lengthy list of questions helpful in analyzing both artifacts and perspectives:

> What is the basic argument? What is the claim, the position, or the point of view proposed in the text you are examining? What seems to be the purpose of this argument? Is it asking you to do something? To think differently about something? Who is the target audience? How do you know? What genre of visual is it—a poster? a cartoon? a public service ad? a commercial ad? a photograph? a billboard? Where does (or will) this argument appear? Is there anything in the image or words that surprises you, makes you laugh, makes you think differently? What visual elements help you read the argument? Is there juxtapositioning? visual metaphors? visual evidence? What else do you know about this visual? Does it remind you of something else? Is it a common logo or symbol? Are there any words? Are they used to state the main argument or to support the argument made by the visual? (Faigley et al., 2004, p. 398).

The definition of visual rhetoric can help writers understand what they are doing when they construct a website, and these questions provide a way of evaluating sites in terms of their visual and verbal rhetoric. But the key point is that the same group of questions applies to both the verbal and visual parts of the text.

This array of definitions of visual rhetoric can perhaps be summarized by turning to the all-purpose resource for writers on paper or screen, the Purdue University Online Writing Lab, or OWL. The definition of visual rhetoric there puts it into the context of the concept of visual literacy, which includes visual rhetoric, visual learning and visual thinking ("Visual

Rhetoric Overview," 2012). The key definition is as follows: "'Visual rhetoric' has been used to mean anything from the use of images as argument, to the arrangement of elements on a page for rhetorical effect, to the use of typography (fonts), and more" ("Visual Rhetoric," n.d.). The issues involved in visual rhetoric draw, then, on meta-readers' and writers' additional mental capacities with bricolage and juxtaposition, and the additional features of images, sounds, animation and links.

Visual Features

Going back to the task of writing for the Web, then, Hammerich and Harrison (2002) sort images into three categories, essentially another set of distinctive features, based on the work of philosopher and early scholar in semiotics, Charles S. Peirce, written in 1894. Hammerich and Harrison say these categories include, first, images that work as icons. These are images that resemble the things they show. For example, on a website there may be an icon of a house that allows a user to return to the site's home page. A second category of image includes indexes, which are images that provide a recognizable connection to some concept. Thus, a weathervane is an index for wind. Hammerich and Harrison note that some indexes require text for their meaning to be clear (2002, p. 141). Finally, images may be symbols, where the image makes a conventional connection to an idea. On the Web, now, underlining is the conventional symbol for a Web link.

Icons, indexes and symbols can appear, of course, in both print and digital forms. Peirce's (1894) definitions help to clarify how this can be so, even though he was writing long before the digital era:

> There are three kinds of signs. Firstly, there are *likenesses,* or icons; which serve to convey ideas of the things they represent simply by imitating them. Secondly, there are *indications,* or indices; which show something about things, on account of their being physically connected with them. Such is a guidepost, which points down the road to be taken, or a relative pronoun, which is placed just after the name of the thing intended to be denoted, or a vocative exclamation, as "Hi! there," which acts upon the nerves of the person addressed and forces his attention. Thirdly, there are *symbols,* or general signs, which have become associated with their meanings by usage. Such are most words, and phrases, and speeches, and books, and libraries. (Peirce, 1894)

As examples of signs, Peirce mentions photographs and representational art, such as drawings or paintings, which are exact likenesses of the things they depict. Indications give an idea about something, so a clock provides an indication of time or a weathervane gives an indication of wind direction. Symbols are usually words, but perhaps also larger units of text that allow us to call things to mind or to the imagination but do not show them in and of themselves, so the word apple is a symbol for the fruit itself.

Both print and digital texts use icons, indexes and symbols. Both have pictures. Both make use of indications, such as perhaps a diagram or even a clock. Both make use of words. Visual rhetoric and verbal rhetoric come together, then, in print as well as on websites; all the processing mechanisms and distinctive features reviewed here work in concert to send messages to a reader/viewer. Preparing websites effectively and efficiently requires not only an awareness of these factors, but also an awareness that they are not different on the screen than they are on the page.

Designing and Writing for the Web

Understanding these psychological mechanisms helps account for how readers or users of a website perceive and process a visual array and then use this background, Hammerich and Harrison make a number of suggestions for formatting websites. Their principles apply equally to paper texts. They begin with a discussion of perception, which entails these four elements: visual stimuli; gut-level reactions, including a search for familiar patterns; reactions based on current needs, such as context or plans or goals; building mental templates based on past experiences. These last are very powerful, drawing on prior knowledge and both direct and vicarious experiences. The point of their discussion is to make writers aware that people will "see" things differently (whether reading or viewing) based on their respective perceptions (2002, p. 143-4). The principles of perception overlap to a great extent with the mental capacities discussed earlier in this book.

A second set of psychological mechanisms discussed by Hammerich and Harrison are those described by Gestalt theory. These principles play an important role in Web design, as they are aspects of bricolage and juxtaposition. They say: "Gestalt is a general psychological theory, developed in the late 1890s and early 1900s, that described the whole of anything as greater than its parts. This theory evolved in reaction to other psychological movements…" (Hammerich & Harrison, 2002, p. 145) that analyze behavior and human responses above and beyond context. Gestalt theory is important to perception and to explaining visual reactions.

The five key principles of Gestalt that bear on Web writing can be summarized as follows: 1) Figure-ground segregation: we perceive objects against a background (such as the Rubin vase image that can be seen as two faces in profile; see http://en.wikipedia.org/wiki/Rubin_vase), and usually perceive the smaller of two items as the figure and the larger as the background. 2) Proximity: we see things close together as a group. So the smiley emoticon :-) is three symbols we perceive as a face. 3) Similarity: we perceive as a group objects that share form, size, color and so on (see examples at http://www.usask.ca/education/coursework/skaalid/theory/gestalt/similar.htm. 4) Continuity: we perceive visual objects that are part of a continuing pattern as a group. Thus, four thick lines coming together at a single point are seen as an X rather than four thick lines meeting together. 5) Closure: we prefer completed or closed figures. A pair of parentheses, (), will be perceived as a circle rather than a left and right parenthesis (Hammerich & Harrison, 2002, p. 147-49). These principles help to explain how Web users react to a site and need to be kept in mind for site design. But the ideas of Gestalt theory are more general than just the perception of visual items on a screen. The principles described here apply to thinking processes and thus to dealing with printed texts that may include visual aids just as much as they apply to websites, where the mental capacities with bricolage and juxtaposition are added to the others discussed earlier in this book.

Hammerich and Harrison include in their discussion of visual rhetoric the more general issue of how people make meaning, especially through language and image, the discipline known as semiotics (2002, p. 46, 62). Social semiotics, more specifically, is the discipline which examines "how people make meaning out of the language, actions and objects in their lives" (2002, p. 156). Visual semiotics looks at the relationships of images and print in various contexts, including on the web as well as in print. Images may *demand* if they are asking the view to take a specific action (as is the case in the U.S. government draft poster found at http://www.loc.gov/exhibits/treasures/trm015.html) if they show people looking directly at the viewer, or they may *offer*, if they show people looking elsewhere, giving a viewer the option to partake or not as a choice (see, for example, an offer for recreation at http://www.recreation.gov/marketing.do?goto=acm/Explore_And_More/exploreArticles/BearCreekLake.htm).

Proxemics also figures in here, adding the analysis of distance between people or between people and objects.

Perspective within an image also reflects the designer's or artist's or photographer's point of view. Emphasis results from the point of view taken by the presenter of the image. Horizontal angles also have an impact—"frontal views create involvement" (Hammerich & Harrison, 2002, p. 162) while the "oblique view creates detachment" (2002, p. 162).

Vertical angles give messages about power within the image and between the viewer and those in the image—does the viewer look up at or down on or straight at the people or objects in the image? These issues and questions apply just as much to pictures that go with a text as they do to people's direct experiences in the world or to vicarious experiences on paper or screen. In preparing for Web writing, then, all these factors must be taken into account. But these issues with respect to images apply to photos inserted into any traditional written document just as much as they do to Web sites.

Preparing to Write for the Web

Finally, Hammerich and Harrison translate all their research into specific guidelines for writing for the Web. Their design tips come from writers who work in Web design. A few of the key points can be summarized here:

> Fonts—use Arial, 12-14 point, not all caps, limit bold and italics and limit typeface variation.
>
> Words, lines and spacing: no hyphens, flush left, ragged right, text lines 40-60 characters, extra space between type lines, space between paragraphs, consistent spaces between words, limit center justified text.
>
> Color: use for emphasis, don't overuse, use color consistently, be careful about brightness and colors next to one another, use high contrast.
>
> Color and eye effect: strong colors are tiring; blue is better as background. Think about color-blindness.
>
> Backgrounds: avoid patterns that distract; limit watermarks; white and light blue are good for background; watch that background doesn't interfere with color for links.
>
> Images: Not too big for screen overall; icons should be simple and distinct; common style for all icons; don't mix metaphors in image; add text labels to images if needed to clarify. (Hammerich & Harrison, 2002, p. 165-66)

In the next section, I will illustrate how these principles might be put to use in the creation of a personal website.

A more recent book on writing for the Web draws on many of the same points made by Hammerich and Harrison. In *Writing for the Web*, professional Web writer and instructor Lynda Felder (2012) skips much of the theory that Hammerich and Harrison present to provide a slim set of guidelines and exercises for those learning to write for the Web. The book reads like a first-year composition textbook for a college writing course, since it covers the same essential points that most textbooks offer to those learning academic writing. Felder (2012) covers a very condensed version of Aristotle's *Rhetoric*, the importance of revision, grammar and style, along with advice about images, sound, animation and links. That is, the key issues in Web writing are the key issues in traditional writing, with a few additions. Not new, not different, not really!

Case Study of Web Site Development: Alice Makes a Website

When I began work on this book, it was much more difficult to create a personal website than it is now as I prepare a final draft of this manuscript. Some of the ease of creation comes with the development of systems such as online course management software, widely used now in higher education, such as Blackboard, Moodle and others. In addition, Google has set up a basic system for web design, Google Sites. It is this very basic tool that I used to create my site. I needed just a few simple lessons from our information technology office to be able to create my own site, and to be able to access and maintain it easily. It was surprising to me how much easier the process had become, but not surprising that I considered the same kinds of issues in creating my site that I have considered in writing this book, or that I consider as a journal editor or writing teacher. Finally, I thought that an exercise in writing for the Web would provide an important data source for this chapter, especially since, in the case studies presented earlier, I did not ask my participants to write online at all. It may be important to keep in mind that my site is just a static website; while it does include a link to a blog, but it does not have a wiki, or any other features of Web 2.0 social media.

Once I understood the basic mechanisms for editing the site, which are quite similar to Word or any word processing program, it became quite easy to put items on my page. I constructed the site with an eye toward presenting examples of the two additional kinds of mental capacities (bricolage and juxtaposition) needed to work online, and the four additional distinctive features (image, sound, movement and links) that make digital writing a bit different from traditional writing. The site can be found at https://sites.google.com/site/alicehorningliteracy/ and the various elements will be quite obvious. I have included a photo, a text (my curriculum vitae), and links to some of my online publications. One of the links is to the Youtube video on the medieval helpdesk, and it entails animation. The additional distinctive features all play a role on the site.

A few notes from site construction provide some insights into what it takes to write for the Web. I did have to think about how to get the picture on to the site, and here, instruction was certainly helpful. The IT fellow who showed me how to work with the Google Sites program showed me how to copy a picture from my department's website and paste it into my personal site. This action makes use of bricolage, taking pieces and putting them together in a certain way. When I looked at the site, I had to think about layout, i.e. juxtaposition, to decide where to put the picture. Once I had the picture, moving it to the center of the site was easy using the layout button on the editing screen in Googlesites.

Putting the picture on the site is one way of using an image. There are plenty of others. I also put on the site the Youtube video (the "Medieval Helpdesk" spoof), another kind of image that also provides an example of animation. That video is accessed through a link, another distinctive feature, and it offers sound, as does the link to my podcast conversation about literacy with the folks at Xavier University of New Orleans. Naturally, all of the material on my site is quite basic, but once I understood the techniques, it was simple to put it together in an hour or two. And that, really, is my point: writing for the Web is a bit different than traditional writing on paper, but not *much* different. Bricolage and juxtaposition play a role, as do the additional distinctive features. But none of these is much beyond traditional writing on paper, though the importance of the visual may be greater on a website. Even creating links that take the reader or viewer to other sites is a very simple process. I needed all the same mental capacities and distinctive features I use to write on paper, especially when creating text for the site, like the "About me" section. And I did think a bit more carefully about audience and voice for this latter piece, as it is distinct from the links and other materials I placed on the site. I am hardly an expert, but I have created a basic site and it did not call for extraordinary abilities. Not new, not different, not really.

It's NOT New; It's NOT Different: Digital Literacy

I set about to write this chapter with the question "what does it mean to write for the Web?" In the course of trying to answer this question, I traveled a complex, winding road with many side paths. A quick review of the additional mental capacities of bricolage and juxtaposition shows that these small additions address the visual character of digital literacy. The Web also entails a small set of distinctive features beyond those of print: images, sounds, animation and links; Hammerich and Harrison's guidelines point to some aspects of layout and design that can make a difference to how effective a site is, but again these are not much different from the considerations of traditional printed texts. Scholars whose work addresses the contact points between print and digital literacy seem to agree that the differences are not significant. Moreover, even those who might disagree with me, such as Deborah Brandt (forthcoming), will see that their claims that digital writing is all new and different are open to question.

To really understand writing for the Web, this chapter has examined manuals and other advice offered specifically for Web design and writing. Even those who write design books, like Hammerich and Harrison (2002), discuss the consistent features of good writing across print and digital landscapes. From the perspective of rhetoricians like Selber (2004), Bolter (2001) and Faigley (2004), as well as those working on visual rhetoric like Hill and Helmers (2004), the key issues are very much the same whether the "text" being created will appear on a printed page or a screen. Moreover, the theoretical underpinnings, drawing, for instance, on Gestalt theory, are also essentially the same.

Ultimately, I decided that the only way to really understand writing for the Web was to do it myself. Over the time I have been working on this project, the programs for Web design and production have been improving steadily. When I first wanted to learn to make my own website, information technology instructors at my university told me I would have to first learn HTML, and then buy and learn to use a complex software package. I am guessing I was not the only person who wanted to develop such skills, since at least basic site creation is now widely available through Google's Google Sites program. In addition, it's easy to see that course management software used in education, such as Blackboard or Moodle, is essentially a website creation mechanism. Once I learned the basic mechanisms for site creation, it was surprisingly easy to make a simple site of my very own. It's certainly true that access to straightforward programs has made Web writing easy, but is also true that writing in a digital environment is not fundamentally different from writing in a traditional environment for the printed page.

Using the core principles of literacy established in the opening section of this book, then, makes clear that writing for the Web is neither new nor different. Instead, as I have been arguing, it draws on the same mental capacities needed for print literacy and uses the same distinctive features of print as well as a few others. Most of the scholars whose work bears on writing for the Web seem to share my view, one way or another, that print literacy is relevant to and essential for Web literacy and that expertise in traditional literacy carries over and applies to digital literacy. The simple website I created as an exercise for this chapter illustrates that writing for the Web is comparable to writing for paper in most ways.

CHAPTER NINE

WHAT TO DO ON MONDAY: SUGGESTIONS FOR TEACHING

Introduction

Everyone knows we are supposed to eat more fruits and vegetables. This directive comes from everywhere, including not only your personal physician but also the United States Department of Agriculture plate found at its website (http://www.google.com/imgres ?imgurl=http://chalkcenter.org/2011/06/02/myplate_green%2520USDA% 2520Plate%2520Planner%25202011.jpg&imgrefurl=http://chalkcenter.org /2011/06/&h=336&w=370&sz=63&tbnid=LnaN5J6YJdUZ3M:&tbnh=90 &tbnw=99&zoom=1&docid=TJP522tlBvPZ3M&sa=X&ei=gEehT7uIJ5H 06AGyo5SUCQ&ved=0CFIQ9QEwBA&dur=3917), showing half of a healthy plate of food consisting of fruits and vegetables. Reading is good for you the same way that fruits and vegetables are good for you: both provide the essential nutrition (intellectual or physical) for a healthy life. There is ample evidence already discussed that too many novice readers and writers are functioning in *The Shallows* (Carr, 2010). The shallows are a sort of "junk food" approach to intellectual nutrition.

Various scholars whose work has been discussed in these pages advocate "deep" reading and writing of the kind experts already do; reading and writing extended nonfiction prose is essential to developing expertise. This chapter further explores the idea that literacy is "good for you," offering a review of the overall goal of critical literacy to define exactly what it is about literacy that makes it "good for you." The contrast of experts to novices brings into sharp relief the awarenesses and skills that experts have and novices need to develop. Three specific sets of recommendations: for teachers, for educational enterprises of all kinds, and for classroom teaching make clear how novices can develop their expertise and move toward becoming meta-readers and writers.

Literacy is Like Fruits and Vegetables

Literacy provides intellectual nutrition, but it does so in very particular ways. If novice readers and writers are skimming the surface of texts, as Carr claims in *The Shallows* (2010), they are not getting the intellectual nutrition that literacy can provide. Literacy offers several specific sources of intellectual sustenance that are essential to healthy participation in a democratic society. But just as eating peas, broccoli or apples does not necessarily appeal to kids because parents or the government say so, literacy doesn't appeal to kids necessarily either. To achieve widespread academic critical literacy as defined here, novices must be invited[1] into it by expert teachers who understand the mental abilities involved, the distinctive features of language, the awarenesses and the skills of meta-readers and writers and who can attract novices to the rewards of literacy. The appeal can be based on the notion that literacy is a challenge, or fun, or a good basis for interacting with others (an attraction many young people certainly already see in all the social media of Web 2.0). Teachers know literacy is good for novices, and they can parlay this knowledge to make it appealing for them. The appeals teachers can use rely on these key features that expertise in literacy has to offer: implicit learning of academic voice, pleasure, connections that lead to empathy, efficiency, and career development through audience awareness.

Appeal 1: Developing voice through implicit learning

A first way to invite novices into the process of becoming meta-readers and writers is to help them see that they can learn to write effectively through reading. As discussed in Chapter 5, reading sets the stage for the process called "implicit learning," whereby novices might learn appropriate writing without conscious effort and without being able to say how they learned it, as described by cognitive psychologist Reber (1967). What is learned through reading, at least among college students and other novices, is academic voice. Appropriate academic voice is hard to define and harder to convey, but a sense of it comes from the work of Bowden (1999), Elbow (1994) and Yancey (1994). It is important to understand this admittedly abstract concept because appropriate voice is an essential element of expert meta-writing that can really only be developed through reading. Stonybrook University rhetorician Peter Elbow has written about it in detail.

Voice of the kind that experts have and novices can develop is best captured by Elbow when he discusses voice with authority, or "having a voice" (1994, p. xxxii). In this meaning, voice is about "having the authority to speak or wield influence or to vote in a group" (1994, p. xxxii). An example is transforming a dissertation into an article—getting the more authoritative voice of a scholar, i.e. an expert, rather than the deferential voice of a student, i.e., a novice. Elbow discusses resonant voice or presence (1994, p. xxxiii). This aspect of voice is also difficult to define and explain. Elbow gives many literary examples. With resonant voice, authors convey their presence by revealing what is in both their conscious and unconscious minds. Elbow concedes that scholars and critics disagree about this aspect of voice. A better explanation of voice in the context of experts and novices appears in *The Rhetoric of Expertise* (2011), as also discussed in Chapter 5. According to Northern Illinois University rhetorician Johanna Hartelius, expert voice entails six rhetorical "congruities" that she comes to through a study of writing in the areas of political science, history, medicine, and encyclopedia entries (Wikipedia). These congruities go across all these disciplines and others (Hartelius, 2011, pp. 164-66).

These characteristics of expert voice give a sense of it; reading allows students to develop a sense of voice. Having voice in this way is an issue of power. An example of this kind of development appeared in the student book reviews presented in Chapter 6; that novice was moving toward expertise and her voice was stronger in the second review that in the first. Reading provides precisely the situation of implicit learning of this expert, academic voice; students learn about academic writing, formal writing, proper voice and so on without specific attention to these features and without being able to describe what they have learned. The "stuff" of what is learned in this way through reading comprises a key benefit of it, which is that through implicit learning, novices can develop an appropriate sense of formal written language and academic voice. This sense opens the door to effective writing in school and out. So, reading is good for novices in this first sense that it invites them to engage in implicit learning of voice which can be used in writing.

Appeal 2: Pleasure

A second way in which reading is good for novices is revealed in new research on what happens in the brain during reading. Science writer Annie Murphy Paul (2012) discusses studies showing that reading fiction stimulates not only the language portions of the brain but also many other areas. The results of brain scans help to account for why, as she says, "the experience of reading can feel so alive" (2012, p. 6). The vicarious experiences readers get through books do stimulate the same regions of the brain as would be active in real experiences of similar type. In addition, reading offers an opportunity to see the world the way another person sees it, and this experience can change the way people interact with one another. Reading helps us solve complex problems just the way a computer simulation can teach complex skills like flying or surgery. Though the research reported by Paul focused on the reading of fiction, surely there is carryover to non-fiction reading as well. According to this research, then, reading offers novices a wide range of brain stimulation and opportunities to learn to deal with complex ideas and emotions.

Appeal 3: Connection/empathy

The positive impact of reading in the form of brain stimulation leads to the third reason why it is beneficial. Experiences that help people understand others turn out to have a much larger impact than just better course grades, academic performance or job outcomes. Experiences that help people understand others, according to Harvard cognitive scientist Steven Pinker, lead to lower rates of violence in society at large (2011). Pinker shows that over time, violence has declined in society generally, a development he ascribes to six different processes, one of which is what he calls "The Humanitarian Revolution" (p. 129-88). In this revolution, a key element is the growth of literacy. Pinker cites statistics showing an increase in literacy reflected in book production rates (p. 172) and in literacy rates among both men and women (p. 174). He claims that "[r]eading is a technology for perspective-taking" (p. 175), leading to greater empathy as readers share the thoughts and feelings of another. Greater empathy leads to less violence, as he says:

> technological advances in publishing, the mass production of books, the expansion of literacy, and the popularity of the novel all preceded the major humanitarian reforms of the 18th century. ...[T]he explosion of reading may have contributed to the Humanitarian Revolution by getting people into the habit of straying from their parochial vantage points. (Pinker, 2011, p. 177)

The shift in perspective that comes from reading can arise, according to Pinker, from both fiction and non-fiction (p. 175). So, finally literacy is not only good for novices, but it also contributes to a more humanitarian and less violent society at large. Novices can be invited to become expert meta-readers through which they will develop this important kind of empathy.

Appeal 4: Efficiency

Yet another basis for the appeal of expertise in literacy has to do with efficiency. I often use this attractive idea when I work with students in developmental reading. I ask how many of them enjoy reading textbooks and don't mind when they have to read a chapter two or three times to get all the ideas and information they know they should understand. Most novices and all college students I work with like to get school work done as quickly as possible, but they also like to get good grades. While developing appropriate strategies for reading with expert skills in analysis, synthesis, evaluation, and application takes work, the struggle is worth it. In my developmental course, we set a goal of getting all class members to a level of ability where they can read a textbook chapter once and get everything they should get. This invitation is one most novices respond to very positively. The strategies discussed below can help them move toward expertise.

Appeal 5: Career development

A final way that novices can be invited to work toward literacy expertise lies in the uses of reading as a means of career exploration and development. In reading within a discipline, students can use the experience to find out more about that discipline and the kinds of texts and work the discipline requires. Again in the case study in Chapter 6, the student was reading as a developing professional in education, and her reviews reflect her growing sense of herself as a practicing teacher. Expert meta-readers and writers already have this sense; novices can be invited to use their reading experiences to begin developing it.

Reading, then, is good for people and especially for novices hoping to develop expertise not only in reading, but also in whatever discipline or career area or activity they wish to pursue; it is also essential to full participation in a democratic society. Novices can be invited into meta-reading and writing based on a variety of appealing characteristics. Reading is especially important to novices trying to also develop writing ability because reading sets the stage for the implicit learning of academic voice that is essential to success in school and beyond. Reading is also good for novices along with experts because it stimulates the brain in the same ways that actual experience does, providing for a wide range of learning opportunities. Finally, reading is good because among the things people learn from reading is an understanding of and an appreciation for the perspectives of others. The resulting broadened view may have contributed to the decline of violence over time, and certainly opens the way to a more thoughtful and well-informed population, a point made by Pinker and a number of other scholars including Deborah Brandt (2001).

Critical Literacy as the Goal

The theory proposed here is that critical literacy as defined is a set of awarenesses and skills that experts have and novices are developing. This critical literacy is usually thought of in the context of teaching and learning in schools; I think of it in terms of students/novices in higher education as that is my profession, but this critical literacy bears also on the situation of adult learners in programs such as adult basic education as well. In these situations, then, the following definition has been the basis for the discussion here:

> Academic critical literacy is best defined as the psycholinguistic processes of getting meaning from or putting meaning into print and/or sound, images, and movement, on a page or screen, used for the purposes of analysis, synthesis, evaluation and application; these processes develop through formal schooling and beyond it, at home and at work, in childhood and across the lifespan and are essential to human functioning in a democratic society.

Expert meta-readers and writers have this critical literacy by virtue of their meta-textual, meta-contextual and meta-linguistic awarenesses and by their use of the skills of analysis, synthesis, evaluation and application. It is the goal to which teachers and learners in any setting aspire.

A lot of people are concerned about literacy, from world organizations like the United Nations, to individual countries whose literacy rates are not where they need to be by any measure, to American college teachers who see the vast majority of their students as lacking in literacy skills. This widespread concern is appropriate, since in order for people to function well and participate fully in contemporary society, critical literacy is essential. The concern is also appropriate in the face of literacy as an evolving phenomenon: neither the forms of literacy, printed as well as digital, nor the skills of people are standing still. The social media phenomenon developed over the years this book was being written, for example; my first book was typed on a WANG word processor, barely a super typewriter. Thus, if the goal is for all people to attain critical literacy, that goal is focused on a fast-moving, ever-changing target. To reach the goal of universal critical literacy, it will be essential for scholars, teachers, parents, students, government officials, school administrators, college presidents and ordinary citizens to understand the essential but evolving features of critical literacy as I have defined them. Helping novices move toward expert meta-reading and writing can best be achieved through three specific approaches: providing professional development for teachers in every discipline, enhancing teachers' understanding of the implications of meta-reading and writing for every field, and equipping teachers with specific intensive and extensive strategies for the classroom.

Helping Novices, Part 1: Professional Development for Teachers in Every Discipline[2]

Professional development on literacy for teachers should have two key goals. Teachers in every discipline need to know more, especially about reading, to support novices' development of critical literacy abilities. Teachers need to have background on and understanding of the nature of the reading process. Recent research has shed much light on the nature of reading as a by-product of increasingly sophisticated technology, such as CT scans, MRIs and other ways of seeing what the brain does when people read. The research sheds light on expert reading and on reading problems, such as dyslexia. In this way, understanding the new insights on the psycholinguistic processes of reading are a first area where some professional development for teachers can be useful.

With respect to this first goal, there are many ways to help teachers learn more about reading. Many colleges and universities now offer the opportunity to join a Faculty Learning Community on a particular topic, and several institutions I've worked with (Xavier University of New Orleans and Long Island University in New York among others) have given teachers this kind of opportunity to focus on reading and literacy. Typically, an FLC meets as an informal seminar, sharing common readings, discussions and insights from various disciplines about a topic. As a consultant to these groups, I have suggested reading such current books as *Reading in the Brain* (Dehaene, 2009) and such articles as Hillesund's (2010) "Digital Reading Spaces: How Expert Readers Handle Books, the Web and Electronic Paper." These research reports will give teachers a full understanding of current findings on expert meta-readers. Understanding the nature of the reading process will allow teachers to see ways to improve students' reading activity. Professional development of this kind is one of the approaches mentioned in the NCTE Policy Research Brief (2011), as well as an approach favored by Seattle University English professor and writing across the curriculum scholar John Bean (Bean & Weimer, 2011).

If a Faculty Learning Community is not an option, information drawn from these kinds of sources can be presented at regular staff meetings, single occasion faculty seminars or perhaps through webinars or podcasts teachers can access online at their convenience. Such discussions might well ask teachers to focus on what reading instruction is available to them in textbooks they may already be using. Debrah Huffman's (2010) study of common composition textbooks' approaches to reading yields strong consensus on six types of reading useful to students in college and beyond (attentive, expressive, interpretive, evaluative, comparative and projective) that might serve as a heuristic for evaluating book choices if an instructor is adopting a more reading-focused approach to teaching, in any discipline.

Another option for faculty development is the adoption of a common book for professional reading, a kind of faculty book group. As director of the writing program at my institution for a few years, I set up a committee of faculty to choose a book for us to read during the summer, when most people were not teaching. At staff meetings in the fall, we used the book as a springboard for discussion and sharing of teaching techniques consistent with what we learned from the reading. The afore-mentioned Dehaene book (2009) or another current book on reading like *Proust and the Squid: The Story and Science of the Reading Brain* by Maryanne Wolf (2007) would work well for this purpose. If there is financial support available, sending faculty members from various disciplines to conferences at the local, state, regional or national level is obviously also a useful strategy to help them learn about expert literacy.

From these kinds of experiences, faculty can develop strategies for working with students in class. In addition, there are ways for professional development to meet the goal of providing teachers with useful ways to approach reading in class, in the context of work they are already assigning; intensive strategies to provide this kind of help are discussed below. For example, if a campus uses a common book, an increasingly important and useful program, the reading of that book provides a perfect opportunity to help students develop faster and more effective reading strategies. Sometimes, the common book can be the basis for a link between college students and local high school students. This kind of connection might be facilitated through a National Writing Project site or through an intermediate school district or other umbrella group such as a local literacy organization. Cross-institutional conversations among faculty or among student/novice groups could be a particularly helpful motivational tool. Faculty development is one way to help them help novices move toward expertise in critical literacy.

Helping Novices, Part 2: Focus on Reading across Curriculum

A second way for teachers who are expert meta-readers and writers to help novices develop their abilities is with discipline-focused approaches to reading and writing. In general, teachers know the types of texts common in their disciplines and can show students the genres and shared features of these kinds of writing, both on paper and in digital form. The standard report of an experiment in science or social science (with sections like Review of Literature, Methodology, Results, Discussion), or the conventions of literary criticism, or the nature of linguistic argumentation are all forms that are familiar to experts but are not so obvious to novices. I have discussed the need to help novices in these ways previously in two pieces that discuss reading across the curriculum in *ATD: Across the Disciplines*. This publication is an online journal specifically devoted to cross-disciplinary teaching and learning (see "Reading across the curriculum as the key to student success" at http://wac.colostate.edu/atd/articles/horning2007.cfm and "Where to place the manicules: A theory of expert reading" at http://wac.colostate.edu/atd/articles/horning2011/index.cfm).

Yet another approach is for both experts (teachers) and novices (students) to work on what Mark Bauerlein, author of *The Dumbest Generation* (2008) and Nicholas Carr, in *The Shadows* (2010) call "slow reading." Any sort of program that encourages students to spend at least an hour a day focusing on the extended, uninterrupted reading of challenging non-fiction prose material will help to deepen and extend their reading experience and move them toward meta-reading. Teachers can build on this experience by teaching students to analyze, synthesize, evaluate and apply the information and ideas they learn from their reading to their other work or other areas of their lives. Requiring extended independent reading and writing can also give students more opportunities to practice these skills; this strategy is discussed in more detail below.

Helping Novices, Part 3: Classroom Strategies for Intensive and Extensive Reading and Writing in Writing Classes and Beyond[3]

Specific teaching strategies constitute a third approach for teachers to help novices develop their expertise in critical literacy, both in writing or English classes and in all courses across the curriculum in post-secondary school settings, in adult basic education and in various kinds of professional development classes, seminars and workshops in career settings as well. The goal of helping novices move toward expertise so they can read and write with the awarenesses and skills of experts in both print and digital contexts can be achieved through specific strategies that can make faster, better reading possible for everyone. These strategies can be roughly divided into intensive work with specific types of texts that may be assigned as part of regular course work and extensive work with a variety of different kinds of materials on paper and in electronic forms. This division makes it easier to present the strategies in an organized fashion; in practice, some or all of them may be useful in a variety of settings.

Intensive Strategy 1: Understanding reading

As a first strategy, novice readers, like teachers, need to understand the nature of reading in both print and digital contexts; teachers can share what they might have learned through their own professional development. Effective reading is fast, not precise and not strictly or even mostly a visual activity. These characteristics of reading are quite interesting and easily demonstrated with a few simple psycholinguistic exercises. Kenneth Goodman's work contains many examples of the right kinds of exercises (1996), as does the work of Frank Smith (2004) and Steven Pinker (1994), such as this one from *The Language Instinct*, constructed long before text messaging became common. The example illustrates something of how redundancy works in language: "Thanks to the redundancy of language, yxx cxn xndxrstxnd whxt x xm wrxtxng xvxn xf x rxplxcx xll thx vxwxls wxth xn "x" (t gts lttl hrdr f y dn't vn kn whr th vwls r)" (Pinker, 1994, p. 181). Goodman's exercises show how readers rely on letter-sound relationships, sentence structures and context to get meaning from print, rarely reading every word on the printed page. These psycholinguists can help both teachers and students understand the nature of the reading process in ways that will allow them to read faster and better. Knowing a bit about the processes involved in expert meta-reading and writing contributes to the awarenesses novices need to develop in a general way and so can improve their sense of themselves as moving toward expertise.

Intensive Strategy 2: Overt teaching of critical reading skills

Novices can be taught specifically and overtly how to do critical reading so that they can develop the key skills of critical literacy in all the reading that they do. They must be able to analyze, including summary of key points, main ideas and the point of view of a writer. They must be able to synthesize, that is, draw ideas together from several sources to support their own views and ideas. Readers should in addition be able to evaluate what they are reading, judging authority, accuracy, relevance, timeliness, and bias. Finally, when readers can do all these things, they should then be able to apply information and ideas from reading to their own writing or other purposes. There are a number of good guides to classroom activities that lead readers in this direction, including Bean and Weimer's *Engaging Ideas* (2011, p. 161-82), and Nilson's *Teaching at Its Best* (2010), along with Keene and Zimmermann's *Mosaic of Thought* (1997). Although the latter book is addressed to K-12 teachers, the strategies and approaches described, such as a reader's workshop that includes silent reading, a mini lesson, some workshop time for students to exchange responses and whole-class exchange, can easily be used at the college level. Keene and Zimmermann advocate the focused teaching of reading comprehension strategies, which can help move readers to the critical literacy essential to successful reading in college and beyond. This approach can and should be expanded to include critical evaluation skills, speed, search capabilities, web page design, video conferencing skills and other strategies, which will be essential for high levels of literacy in a digital age according to Leu et al. (2004, p. 1589).

Intensive Strategy 3: Modeling by reading aloud

It's clear to most faculty that students do not read the way teachers think they should and the way teachers themselves read. One way to help students understand the kind of reading that is expected of them is to model it by reading aloud and showing students what they can and should be doing. This approach has been shown to be useful by University of Rhode Island education scholar Julie Coiro (2011), working with online materials. In reading aloud, teachers can illustrate how to analyze, synthesize, evaluate and apply ideas in both print and digital venues. They can also help students learn to deal with an array of "online cueing systems" (such as highlighted texts, hot links and other cues) that are now commonly used when texts are drawn from the Internet. These skills are crucial to careful reading of both print and Web-based sources; novices definitely don't have them and definitely do need them.

Intensive Strategy 4: Intensive reading through the use of reading guides

Teachers can also provide focused practice in reading in every assignment that they give, building readers' skills over the course of every term through the use of a carefully constructed set of reading guides. The guides are a way for teachers to achieve their own course goals by helping the students do assigned work more effectively and efficiently. Some examples are provided in Syracuse University education professor Harold Herber's *Teaching Reading in the Content Areas* (1978), an old but thoughtful approach to moving students from reading the lines of a text to reading between and beyond those lines (1978, p. 56). Herber's procedures would fit well with standard assessment techniques currently in widespread use: determining learning outcomes and creating reading guides that help students achieve those outcomes.

Herber advocates reading guides that at first help students get literal meaning, to develop basic comprehension and vocabulary, suitable perhaps for the introductory chapters of a textbook. This first level helps students with analysis of the text. Then, he suggests reading guides that move students to an interpretive level, where they must read to create, support or respond to generalizations made by their texts. In this work, the kind of think-aloud approach suggested by Haswell et al. (1999) might be helpful, especially in combination with discussion in class or online that encourages critical evaluation of the material. Finally, Herber recommends reading guides that help students synthesize and apply concepts from the reading to the broader issues and problems under discussion in the course, using both material from the reading and other knowledge readers may have, from class discussion, now from Internet sources, and other materials. In my own experience using reading guides of this kind, I have found that students do become stronger readers over time, and in addition, the reading guides serve as a basis of lively classroom discussion, small group work, and a source of peer pressure to make sure students actually do the reading. The reading guides are a key approach to helping novices develop all the skills of expert meta-readers.

Intensive Strategy 5: Discourse synthesis

The work of Carnegie Mellon reading scholar Nancy Spivey (1997) suggests additional types of reading and writing tasks that can support students' development as active readers and writers. Her studies of what she calls discourse synthesis offer opportunities for novices to develop expert reading and writing abilities. Spivey defines discourse synthesis as "the process in which writers are engaged when they read multiple texts and produce their own related texts" particularly for the purpose of the writing task and in which they use the texts they have read in some direct way (1997, p. 146). Spivey conducted four studies of the discourse synthesis process, three of which involved undergraduates as participants and one of which examined developing skills among younger students.

These studies entailed having participants generate their own texts based on materials they were given to read. The participants were given a variety of rhetorical situations and audiences, such as preparing a research proposal or an informative article about a local event for newcomers to the area. The findings show that writers shape their meanings with organizational patterns, make selections on the basis of given criteria of relevance, and generate inferences that integrate material that might seem inconsistent or even contradictory (Spivey, 1997, p. 191). Discourse synthesis, a kind of task common not only in college composition but also in disciplinary writing assignments, offers clear opportunities for students to practice reading more actively within their respective disciplines. This kind of task fits well with the NCTE Policy Research Brief (2011), which advocates the use of low stakes writing assignments to help students engage more fully with reading, as well as the use of a variety of texts at a variety of levels of difficulty (2011, p. 16-17). The work Spivey recommends will help novices to focus on meta-textual and meta-linguistic awareness as well.

These first five strategies will work especially well for novices as they work with course materials they are required to read and write about as part of regular assignments. Teachers can use all of them to accomplish multiple goals with a specific set of tasks. These strategies not only enable teachers to focus on the learning goals of the particular course they are teaching, but also allow them to build novices' awarenesses and skills as they move toward expert meta-reading and writing.

Extensive Strategy 6: Scaffolding with text material

Most faculty don't aim to help students become experts, at least not in introductory or general education courses. Instead, to achieve ordinary instructional goals, most faculty want students to DO the reading and write about concepts and content from reading and class discussion that connect their learning in the course. Helping novices move toward the awarenesses and skills of experts can be done through the process education scholars call scaffolding, described by a number of scholars in the field (Kucer, 2008, p. 51; Manzo, et al., 2009, p. 46; Bransford, et al., 2000, p. 213-16; Yancey, 2009, p. 262-66). Like the scaffolding outside a building, put up temporarily while workers do construction or painting or similar work, scaffolding for learning provides temporary support to students while they develop the awarenesses and skills needed to be effective and efficient readers and learners.

A more formal definition of scaffolding grows out of the work of Russian psychologist and educator Lev Vygotsky, in connection with his idea of the Zone of Proximal Development (1978, p. 86-87). The ZPD accounts for what a student might be able to do with help, i.e. scaffolding. Although Vygotsky was writing about children, the concept of providing support through scaffolding can be useful for older students as well. Educational researchers describe the scaffolding processes in reading instruction as including "cuing, prompting, analogies, metaphors, questioning, elaborations and remodeling," according to reading researcher Janice Dole and her colleagues (1991, p. 255). Effective instruction of the kind suggested here leads students to develop increasing skill in reading, leading to a "gradual release of responsibility" (1991, p. 255), by teachers and increasing assumption of that responsibility by students. This latter process of moving students to take on more of the work of reading and learning by themselves as teachers step back and remove the scaffolding is captured by the concept of "fading" as discussed by Vermont education scholar Anthony Manzo and his colleagues (2009, p. 46). Scaffolding is essential when students are working in their Zone of Proximal Development.

Textbook writers and publishers spend fortunes of money on providing supporting materials to help students read their texts efficiently and effectively. These materials are increasingly available online, as are a growing number of the texts themselves, thanks to the company called CourseSmart, a consortium of many of the major textbook publishers (including Pearson, Cengage, McGraw-Hill, John Wiley and Macmillan) (http://www.coursesmart.com/overview). While not all of these materials are useful and effective, some of them are. They can change the reading experience in significant ways as two *New York Times* writers found in exploring these systems (Eisenberg, 2011; Olsen, 2011). The use of them can provide students with a kind of scaffolding, supporting stronger reading until students are able to read quickly and critically on their own.

Teachers can review these materials and encourage or require students to use them if they are appropriate and helpful to the overall goal of improving reading. In a chapter of *Engaging Ideas* (2011) focused on reading issues called "Helping Students Read Difficult Texts," Bean and Weimer support this kind of approach, recommending an array of low stakes writing tasks in conjunction with reading that can move students toward faster and more effective reading, such as having students take notes that include writing "What It Says" and "What It Does" statements for each paragraph of an article (2011, p. 170), summary-response notebooks (2011, p. 178), interviews with the author (2011, p. 179) and translations of complicated passages into ordinary language (2011, p. 179-80). In any course or setting, this kind of work builds both the awarenesses and the skills of meta-reading and writing.

Extensive Strategy 7: Scaffolding with graphic organizers

Research in second language learning suggests that students can improve their reading and learn about discourse structures useful to writing at the same time through the use of graphic organizers. Jiang and Grabe (2007), writing about teaching reading to ESL learners, discuss the usefulness of having students read to find text elements to put into visual diagrams that make clear their understanding of text structure, building meta-textual and meta-linguistic awareness. A series of boxes with arrows for a process text, or a t-shaped diagram for pros and cons of an argument are two obvious examples. Graphic organizers allow students to see the organizational structure of a text as they work through the content being presented. Bean and Weimer (2011, p. 179) also point out the usefulness of this approach. For some students, a visual representation is more helpful than a traditional outline. In addition, having seen the visual layout of a particular discourse structure, students can then use that same structure in their own writing.

Extensive Strategy 8: Extensive reading for practice

Adults in the United States population at large, both students and others, are reading extended nonfiction prose less and less, as discussed in the studies presented in the Introduction to this book, so there is a clear need for more reading and more practice with focused critical reading. In my own teaching, I have been moving to create more reading practice, integrated with a writing task in my outside reading assignment, illustrated in the case study in Chapter 6. My assignment requires that students read two books outside of class from a short list of choices of current books on topics related to those discussed in the course. They must also write about these books in reviews that not only summarize key ideas but also tie them to concepts in the course, making cheating difficult. The assignment calls for analysis, synthesis, evaluation and application.

I grade these reviews and they count in students' course grades for Nilson's (2010) recommended 20% of the course grade, so that they must do this work; the incentive is very important in getting students to comply. The most interesting thing is that although I do not usually discuss the reading task in class beyond casual questions about what they are reading and their reactions to the books, this work has changed students' behavior, responsiveness and level of engagement in every one of my classes, from developmental reading to graduate-level courses in psycholinguistics and sociolinguistics. I believe this response arises because not only are these novices building the awarenesses of meta-readers and writers, but also they are especially building the meta-contextual awareness that experts have and rely on in their reading and writing. I am convinced that novices can move toward expertise in critical literacy only through extensive reading that works this way in every course or learning experience in school settings and elsewhere.

Extensive Strategy 9: Learning to read in specific disciplines

To be an expert reader in a particular subject area, students need to come to understand the genres and conventions of that discipline. Thus, in the natural and social sciences, for instance, understanding research reports that use the typical APA form (Statement of Problem, Review of the Literature, Methodology, Results, Discussion, Conclusion) is one way to facilitate reading in these areas. More detailed understanding of where an article fits in a body of work on a topic may also be helpful to students and other novice readers. While teachers in any discipline will already have an intuitive understanding of the discourse conventions of their discipline, several studies of reading practices within subject areas can provide helpful background for discussion.

Literacy scholar Charles Bazerman's study of physicists reading (1988), for example, reports the reading approaches of seven practicing physicists in several different research fields within that science. In this study, Bazerman, who chairs the Department of Education at the University of California Santa Barbara, conducted detailed interviews with these scientists about their reading and then observed them actually searching for and reading materials in their fields. Bazerman found a number of distinctive features of these scientists' reading: they have a clear purpose for their reading and rely on a schema, defined by Bazerman as "structured background knowledge" (1988, p. 236). Bazerman's study offers evidence of meta-textual and meta-contextual awareness among these science experts.

There is also useful research on the nature of communication patterns in different disciplines that can be helpful to those teaching reading across the curriculum. Bean and Weimer take up this point in their approach to helping students read difficult material, pointing out that students often lack an understanding of both the cultural and rhetorical contexts for a text (2011, p. 172-73). Similarly, Sussex University professor Tony Becher's investigation of twelve different academic disciplines examines the nature of both written and oral exchange of ideas in the pure sciences, applied sciences, social sciences, humanities and several other areas that don't fit into one of these recognized academic categories, including law, geography and mathematics (1989, p. 2). Across the disciplines, teachers can help novices learn to recognize the discourse conventions of the kinds of texts produced in that field, and also learn to write them once they understand the conventions and expectations. In doing so, novices build the meta-textual, meta-contextual and meta-linguistic awarenesses of experts.

Extensive Strategy 10: Learning to read critically on screens

Because of the ever-expanding array of digital texts, novices must be invited to develop their awarenesses and skills both on paper and online. One kind of text that addresses students' need to deal with digital/visual as well as printed texts is rhetoricians Odell and Katz's *Writing in a Visual Age* (2004), a text and reader for college writing courses. In their presentation, Odell and Katz discuss the reading and analysis of these web page elements: layout, including columns and spaces; page design, including tension and alignment; pictorial graphics including photos and drawings; representational graphics such as pie charts and bar graphs, and other features like color and font (2004, p. 23). Their text provides multiple opportunities for students to read for writing using both print and digital materials. This work calls on novices to use the additional mental abilities of bricolage and juxtaposition and the additional distinctive features of digital material: images, sound, movement and links.

Similarly, Florida State University rhetoric scholar, Kathleen Blake Yancey, a leader in college composition, pointed out in her Chair's address to the national convention of writing teachers in the United States in 2004 that students are increasingly working with texts of various kinds outside of school settings, and increasingly online. A full discussion of these implications of present and coming search strategies and other aspects of multi-modal online reading and writing appears in the work of John Battelle (2005) and in Thomas Friedman's *The World is Flat* (2006). These writers' views are consistent with those of the Association of College and Research Librarians, whose Information Literacy Standards describe the essential skills in evaluation novices need; these Standards appear in the Appendix to this book. Novices working to develop their meta-reading and writing as defined here must develop their ability to analyze, synthesize, and especially to evaluate material on both pages and screens.

Summary

I have made three key points throughout this book: First, critical literacy entails meta-reading and writing which relies on our basic human mental abilities and the inherent features of language; these abilities and features, and the awarenesses and skills experts have are the same in both print and digital environments. Second, because the fundamental features of reading and writing remain the same, the digital venue is not the all-new, all-different phenomenon some scholars have suggested. Finally, if we can reach a common understanding about what critical literacy is and how novices can develop the expertise of meta-readers and writers, there is great potential for reaching the goal of universal critical literacy, a goal essential to the informed citizenry required by any democratic society.

At the outset, I set up a specific definition of critical literacy, chiefly because one of the problems in all literacy studies is the lack of a fully explicated definition of what it is. This definition states that

> Academic critical literacy is best defined as the psycholinguistic processes of getting meaning from or putting meaning into print and/or sound, images, and movement, on a page or screen, used for the purposes of analysis, synthesis, evaluation, and application; these processes develop through formal schooling and beyond it, at home and at work, in childhood and across the lifespan and are essential to human functioning in a democratic society.

The definition is meant to show the common features of literacy in both print and electronic settings and to show that critical literacy specifically entails going beyond simply putting meaning into or getting meaning out of print to require the critical skills of analysis, synthesis, evaluation, and application. By this definition, many people are novices because this definition requires much more complex skills beyond getting main ideas in both reading and writing.

Chapter 1 discussed this issue of definition. Literacy is a term with many definitions and implications. It is used to refer both specifically to ability with written text, and more generally to refer to a level of skill or knowledge in any field, such as "computer literacy" or "music literacy." Because of the negative implications of the term "illiteracy," I have avoided using that word anywhere in this discussion. Individuals who have not yet developed the abilities in the definition presented above are considered novices in this discussion. They are not uneducated, but may not yet have the academic critical literacy of meta-readers and writers.

To clarify the differences between experts and novices, Chapter 2 offers a series of case studies. Taken together, the five experts all show meta-textual, meta-contextual and meta-linguistic awareness to some degree. They understand and offer examples of their ability to see the structure of a text, and how the text fits into a larger universe of texts and ideas. Moreover, they notice and can describe the language of the text per se, meta-linguistic awareness. The novices, by contrast, have little to no awareness of text in these ways, whether they read on paper or online. The case studies also show that experts have an array of skills in analysis, synthesis, evaluation and application. The novices can apply these skills to a much more limited degree, chiefly focusing on analysis of content. They lack some or all of the skills of experts at taking a text apart to understand it at a literal level. While some students, especially those in the Honors College program at my university, are more skilled at analysis, relatively few students have strong skills in synthesis of different texts on the same topic, or evaluation, or application of materials to other tasks, like writing. The case studies make the contrast between experts and novices clear.

When I reflected on the data in the case studies, one thing that stood out to me was that the underlying psycholinguistic abilities readers and writers have are consistent across the experts and the novices. Everyone in my studies had the basic mental abilities essential to reading and writing. All could identify or recognize, categorize, discriminate, predict and use short-term memory, albeit limited to seven plus or minus two items. Linguistically, we are able to use psycholinguistic redundancy and syntax to put meaning into print and get meaning from print, wherever and however it comes before our eyes. These basic mental abilities were explored and illustrated in Chapter 3.

Meta-readers and writers use these abilities to work with texts that have distinctive features of language at four levels, rudimentary, basic, intermediate and advanced, as presented in Chapter 4. The rudiments of critical literacy are the orthographic and graphological features. The basic elements include word structure, morphology and lexical meaning. The intermediate level offers distinctive features of sentences, discourse forms and the genres of written language. Finally, at the most advanced level, the distinctive features are the rhetorical modes and forms of argument. These distinctive features, like the mental abilities, apply to all kinds of printed and digital texts. Both experts and novices have them and use them in order to get meaning from printed and digital texts in reading and to put meaning into texts on paper or the screen in writing.

Chapters 5 and 6 explore the distinctions I saw between the experts and the novices in the case studies in Chapter 2. In Chapter 5, I described experts' awarenesses that constitute meta-reading and writing. Experts are able to go before, after, around and within texts (hence, "meta") to perceive and produce meaning. These awarenesses fall into three categories. Meta-textual awareness is an awareness of the structure and organization of texts. Meta-contextual awareness entails knowing how a text fits with other texts and materials in a field or discipline. Meta-linguistic awareness is awareness of the language of the text and whatever specialized uses of language may be needed for the ideas under discussion. These awarenesses apply equally to reading on paper and on the screen. The data in my case studies suggests that in general, novices lack these awarenesses. A few of my novices who are in the Honors College program have some awareness of these kinds, but the awarenesses are not common among the novices.

Chapter 6 takes up the skills of experts. The skills in analysis, synthesis, evaluation, and application are easy to see among the experts. The experts were on the whole more focused on the task of summarizing the passages they read. Because of this focus, and because they are expert readers, they analyzed the texts they read easily, seeing the main ideas and skipping the details. Although the summary writing task did not call for synthesis, some of them were able to bring in prior knowledge or context and put it together with the content of the passage, a kind of synthesis. None of the novices demonstrated this ability. The experts made clear their judgment of the passages, while the novices said little by way of evaluation of either content or style. And finally, on the simple criterion of summary length, it is clear that the experts were more able to use what they learned from the reading of the passages, while the novices struggled just to get the main ideas of the material. The skills of the experts appeared regardless of whether they were reading on paper or online.

As critical literacy has continued to expand in electronic forms such as websites and social media, two additional mental abilities and four additional distinctive features have developed; these additional elements are considered in Chapter 7. These changes do not lead to entirely new forms, despite arguments for such a claim from the "new media age" theorists like Gunther Kress (2003). Instead, they represent the on-going healthy evolution of critical literacy. The additional mental abilities are, first of all, bricolage, the creative process of assembling web sites or pages from pieces (links, images and so on). Juxtaposition has also been suggested as a key underlying ability; the ability to convey a message through thoughtful placement of elements in relation to one another, or to notice and make use of such juxtaposing when getting meaning, is essential to critical literacy.

Bricolage and juxtaposition work with the additional distinctive features of images, sounds, movement, and links, and these, too, are presented in Chapter 7 as part of the discussion of the similarities and differences between reading on paper and online. Kress and others suggest that links are a completely revolutionary development, but ancient texts make clear that this is not the case. Similarly, the ability to attach sound and movement to a text is new if we are talking about reading on screens, but sound, images and movement have been with us since movies and television. Even children's picture books have little sound chips available now. Thus, while the forms of critical literacy continue to change, they are not as completely new and different as some have suggested.

The material reviewed in Chapter 8, "Writing Traditional and Electronic" expands the argument that writing on the Web is not new or different from print writing. Here as in the other chapters, I show again that writing is writing regardless of the venue in which it is carried out. It relies on the same mental abilities as does writing for print, with the addition of bricolage and juxtaposition, and the same distinctive features, with the addition of links, sound, movement and images. While writing for the Web requires an awareness of visual rhetoric, that rhetoric works with the same essential principles of persuasion presented by Aristotle centuries ago. Learning to write for the Web is becoming easier as the software for websites becomes more accessible to people; my website presented in the chapter is a great example of how easy it is now to create a basic site. Even though Web writers can use images, sounds, movement, and links, they must still be able to put meaning into a site for the purposes of analysis, synthesis, evaluation, and application.

This final chapter has offered ways for teachers in a variety of settings to help novices move toward the expert meta-reading and writing that constitutes critical literacy. The key question is how to make it possible for every person to reach this goal. The claims and findings presented in this book point to a clear series of steps that lead to critical literacy for one and all. The first of these is the need for widespread agreement on a clear definition of critical literacy. Naturally, I think my definition meets this need. If we are to achieve the goal of universal critical literacy, a clear description of this phrase is an essential first step. However, it seems to me that national and global groups like the United Nations should address this matter and come to some consensus. Once consensus is reached, the definition ought to be shared and ought to be the basis for programs to reach the goal of universal critical literacy.

Finally, though, it is essential that the overall goal of critical literacy be made clear and that no lesser achievement be considered acceptable. Funding must be provided under the auspices of both global organizations like the United Nations and through national government programs to achieve critical literacy for all citizens. Realistic targets and assessment should also be part of the program along with a plan for consistent measurements to see if the goal is being achieved. Perhaps every five years a more thorough survey might be done to see global progress toward this goal. Only with more detailed information can we assess progress toward the goal of global critical literacy. More funding and better information seem obvious, but if they are based on the understanding of the nature of critical literacy perhaps these obvious goals can actually be realized. Critical literacy is crucial to full participation in contemporary society for political, economic and social purposes.

I was motivated to write this book because I know that literacy has been good for me personally and professionally. As a linguist, I have studied reading and writing as psycholinguistic processes to understand their common features. As a researcher, I have watched and listened to readers working with texts on paper and online, studying the processes by which they get meaning from print and produce meaning in texts; the distinctions between experts and novices are clear to me. As a reader of many online sources and a student of Web writing, I have seen that reading and writing online entail some additional characteristics, but they are not as entirely new and different as some scholars have suggested. Finally, as a teacher, I have worked with many literacy novices, and I am confident that my strategies for intensive and extensive work can help us achieve widespread critical literacy essential to full participation in contemporary democratic society. I hope every reader of this book will share in this important enterprise.

Notes

1. I am indebted to my colleague, Dr. Catherine Haar, for suggesting the importance of inviting novices to develop literacy as "good for you" but not like eating peas because Mom says so.

2. I am indebted to Drs. Randall McClure and Dayna Goldstein for permission to use a portion of my chapter to appear in a book they have in development for this section of the discussion.

3. I am indebted to Reference Guides in Rhetoric and Composition series editor Dr. Charles Bazerman and co-editors Dr. Anis Bawarshi and Dr. Mary Jo Reiff for permission to use a portion of my chapter from the forthcoming *Reconnecting Reading and Writing* for the discussion here.

APPENDIX

Appendix A: Information Literacy Competency Standards for Higher Education (ACRL, 2012)

These standards were reviewed by the ACRL Standards Committee and approved by the Board of Directors of the Association of College and Research Libraries (ACRL) on January 18, 2000, at the Midwinter Meeting of the American Library Association in San Antonio, Texas. These standards were also endorsed by the American Association for Higher Education (October 1999) and the Council of Independent Colleges (February 2004).

Standards, Performance Indicators, and Outcomes

Standard One

The information literate student determines the nature and extent of the information needed.

Performance Indicators:

1. The information literate student defines and articulates the need for information.

   Outcomes Include:

   a. Confers with instructors and participates in class discussions, peer workgroups, and electronic discussions to identify a research topic, or other information need
   b. Develops a thesis statement and formulates questions based on the information need
   c. Explores general information sources to increase familiarity with the topic
   d. Defines or modifies the information need to achieve a manageable focus

e. Identifies key concepts and terms that describe the information need
f. Recognizes that existing information can be combined with original thought, experimentation, and/or analysis to produce new information

2. The information literate student identifies a variety of types and formats of potential sources for information.

Outcomes Include:

a. Knows how information is formally and informally produced, organized, and disseminated
b. Recognizes that knowledge can be organized into disciplines that influence the way information is accessed
c. Identifies the value and differences of potential resources in a variety of formats (e.g., multimedia, database, website, data set, audio/visual, book)
d. Identifies the purpose and audience of potential resources (e.g., popular vs. scholarly, current vs. historical)
e. Differentiates between primary and secondary sources, recognizing how their use and importance vary with each discipline
f. Realizes that information may need to be constructed with raw data from primary sources

3. The information literate student considers the costs and benefits of acquiring the needed information.

Outcomes Include:

a. Determines the availability of needed information and makes decisions on broadening the information seeking process beyond local resources (e.g., interlibrary loan; using resources at other locations; obtaining images, videos, text, or sound)
b. Considers the feasibility of acquiring a new language or skill (e.g., foreign or discipline-based) in order to gather needed information and to understand its context
c. Defines a realistic overall plan and timeline to acquire the needed information

4. The information literate student reevaluates the nature and extent of the information need.

Outcomes Include:

d. Reviews the initial information need to clarify, revise, or refine the question
e. Describes criteria used to make information decisions and choices

Standard Two

The information literate student accesses needed information effectively and efficiently.

Performance Indicators:

1. The information literate student selects the most appropriate investigative methods or information retrieval systems for accessing the needed information.

   Outcomes Include:

   a. Identifies appropriate investigative methods (e.g., laboratory experiment, simulation, fieldwork)
   b. Investigates benefits and applicability of various investigative methods
   c. Investigates the scope, content, and organization of information retrieval systems
   d. Selects efficient and effective approaches for accessing the information needed from the investigative method or information retrieval system

2. The information literate student constructs and implements effectively-designed search strategies.

   Outcomes Include:

   a. Develops a research plan appropriate to the investigative method
   b. Identifies keywords, synonyms and related terms for the information needed
   c. Selects controlled vocabulary specific to the discipline or information retrieval source
   d. Constructs a search strategy using appropriate commands for the information retrieval system selected (e.g., Boolean operators, truncation, and proximity for search engines; internal organizers such as indexes for books)
   e. Implements the search strategy in various information retrieval systems using different user interfaces and search engines, with different command languages, protocols, and search parameters
   f. Implements the search using investigative protocols appropriate to the discipline

3. The information literate student retrieves information online or in person using a variety of methods.

Outcomes Include:

a. Uses various search systems to retrieve information in a variety of formats
b. Uses various classification schemes and other systems (e.g., call number systems or indexes) to locate information resources within the library or to identify specific sites for physical exploration
c. Uses specialized online or in person services available at the institution to retrieve information needed (e.g., interlibrary loan/document delivery, professional associations, institutional research offices, community resources, experts and practitioners)
d. Uses surveys, letters, interviews, and other forms of inquiry to retrieve primary information

4. The information literate student refines the search strategy if necessary.

Outcomes Include:

a. Assesses the quantity, quality, and relevance of the search results to determine whether alternative information retrieval systems or investigative methods should be utilized
b. Identifies gaps in the information retrieved and determines if the search strategy should be revised
c. Repeats the search using the revised strategy as necessary

5. The information literate student extracts, records, and manages the information and its sources.

Outcomes Include:

a. Selects among various technologies the most appropriate one for the task of extracting the needed information (e.g., copy/paste software functions, photocopier, scanner, audio/visual equipment, or exploratory instruments)
b. Creates a system for organizing the information
c. Differentiates between the types of sources cited and understands the elements and correct syntax of a citation for a wide range of resources
d. Records all pertinent citation information for future reference
e. Uses various technologies to manage the information selected and organized

Standard Three

The information literate student evaluates information and its sources critically and incorporates selected information into his or her knowledge base and value system.

Performance Indicators:

1. The information literate student summarizes the main ideas to be extracted from the information gathered.

   Outcomes Include:
   a. Reads the text and selects main ideas
   b. Restates textual concepts in his/her own words and selects data accurately
   c. Identifies verbatim material that can be then appropriately quoted

2. The information literate student articulates and applies initial criteria for evaluating both the information and its sources.

   Outcomes Include:
   a. Examines and compares information from various sources in order to evaluate reliability, validity, accuracy, authority, timeliness, and point of view or bias
   b. Analyzes the structure and logic of supporting arguments or methods
   c. Recognizes prejudice, deception, or manipulation
   d. Recognizes the cultural, physical, or other context within which the information was created and understands the impact of context on interpreting the information

3. The information literate student synthesizes main ideas to construct new concepts.

   Outcomes Include:
   a. Recognizes interrelationships among concepts and combines them into potentially useful primary statements with supporting evidence
   b. Extends initial synthesis, when possible, at a higher level of abstraction to construct new hypotheses that may require additional information
   c. Utilizes computer and other technologies (e.g. spreadsheets, databases, multimedia, and audio or visual equipment) for studying the interaction of ideas and other phenomena

4. The information literate student compares new knowledge with prior knowledge to determine the value added, contradictions, or other unique characteristics of the information.

Outcomes Include:

a. Determines whether information satisfies the research or other information need
b. Uses consciously selected criteria to determine whether the information contradicts or verifies information used from other sources
c. Draws conclusions based upon information gathered
d. Tests theories with discipline-appropriate techniques (e.g., simulators, experiments)
e. Determines probable accuracy by questioning the source of the data, the limitations of the information gathering tools or strategies, and the reasonableness of the conclusions
f. Integrates new information with previous information or knowledge
g. Selects information that provides evidence for the topic

5. The information literate student determines whether the new knowledge has an impact on the individual's value system and takes steps to reconcile differences.

Outcomes Include:

a. Investigates differing viewpoints encountered in the literature
b. Determines whether to incorporate or reject viewpoints encountered

6. The information literate student validates understanding and interpretation of the information through discourse with other individuals, subject-area experts, and/or practitioners.

Outcomes Include:

a. Participates in classroom and other discussions
b. Participates in class-sponsored electronic communication forums designed to encourage discourse on the topic (e.g., email, bulletin boards, chat rooms)
c. Seeks expert opinion through a variety of mechanisms (e.g., interviews, email, listservs)

7. The information literate student determines whether the initial query should be revised.

Outcomes Include:

a. Determines if original information need has been satisfied or if additional information is needed
b. Reviews search strategy and incorporates additional concepts as necessary
c. Reviews information retrieval sources used and expands to include others as needed

Standard Four

The information literate student, individually or as a member of a group, uses information effectively to accomplish a specific purpose.

Performance Indicators:

1. The information literate student applies new and prior information to the planning and creation of a particular product or performance.

Outcomes Include:

a. Organizes the content in a manner that supports the purposes and format of the product or performance (e.g. outlines, drafts, storyboards)
b. Articulates knowledge and skills transferred from prior experiences to planning and creating the product or performance
c. Integrates the new and prior information, including quotations and paraphrasings, in a manner that supports the purposes of the product or performance
d. Manipulates digital text, images, and data, as needed, transferring them from their original locations and formats to a new context

2. The information literate student revises the development process for the product or performance.

Outcomes Include:

a. Maintains a journal or log of activities related to the information seeking, evaluating, and communicating process
b. Reflects on past successes, failures, and alternative strategies

3. The information literate student communicates the product or performance effectively to others.

Outcomes Include:

a. Chooses a communication medium and format that best supports the purposes of the product or performance and the intended audience
b. Uses a range of information technology applications in creating the product or performance
c. Incorporates principles of design and communication
d. Communicates clearly and with a style that supports the purposes of the intended audience

Standard Five

The information literate student understands many of the economic, legal, and social issues surrounding the use of information and accesses and uses information ethically and legally.

Performance Indicators:

1. The information literate student understands many of the ethical, legal and socio-economic issues surrounding information and information technology.

Outcomes Include:

a. Identifies and discusses issues related to privacy and security in both the print and electronic environments
b. Identifies and discusses issues related to free vs. fee-based access to information
c. Identifies and discusses issues related to censorship and freedom of speech
d. Demonstrates an understanding of intellectual property, copyright, and fair use of copyrighted material

2. The information literate student follows laws, regulations, institutional policies, and etiquette related to the access and use of information resources.

Outcomes Include:

a. Participates in electronic discussions following accepted practices (e.g. "Netiquette")
b. Uses approved passwords and other forms of ID for access to information resources

c. Complies with institutional policies on access to information resources
d. Preserves the integrity of information resources, equipment, systems and facilities
e. Legally obtains, stores, and disseminates text, data, images, or sounds
f. Demonstrates an understanding of what constitutes plagiarism and does not represent work attributable to others as his/her own
g. Demonstrates an understanding of institutional policies related to human subjects research

3. The information literate student acknowledges the use of information sources in communicating the product or performance.

Outcomes Include:

a. Selects an appropriate documentation style and uses it consistently to cite sources
b. Posts permission granted notices, as needed, for copyrighted material

REFERENCES

Alexander, P.A. (2003). Profiling the developing reader: The interplay of knowledge, interest and strategic processing. In C.M. Fairbanks, J. Worthy, B. Maloch, J.V. Hoffman, & D.L. Schallert, (Eds.), *52nd Yearbook of the National Reading Conference* (pp. 47-65). Oak Creek, WI: National Reading Conference.

Alliance for Excellent Education. (2006). *Are they really ready to work?: Employers' perspectives on the basic knowledge and applied skills of new entrants to the 21st century U.S. workforce.* Retrieved from http://www.21stcenturyskills.org/documents/FINAL_REPORT_PDF9-29-06.pdf.

American College Testing. (2006, 1 March). *Reading between the lines: What the ACT reading test reveals about college readiness.* Retrieved from http://www.act.org/research/policymakers/reports/reading.html

—. (2010). *A first look at the Common Core and college and career readiness.* N.p.: ACT, Inc. Retrieved from http://www.act.org/commoncore/pdf/FirstLook.pdf

—. (2011). *The condition of college & career readiness.* Retrieved from http://www.act.org/research/policymakers/cccr11/pdf/ConditionofCollegeandCareerReadiness2011.pdf.

Anderson, R., Spiro, R.J., & Anderson, M.C. (1978). Schemata as scaffolding for the representation of information in connected discourse. *American Educational Research Journal 15*(3), 433-40.

Arum, R. & Roksa, J. (2011). *Academically adrift: Limited learning on college campuses.* Chicago: University of Chicago Press.

Association of College and Research Libraries. (2008). *Information literacy competency standards for higher education.* Chicago, IL: ACRL. Retrieved from http://www.ala.org/acrl/standards/informationliteracycompetency

Bain, A. (1990). Excerpts from *English composition and rhetoric.* In P. Bizzell & B. Hertzberg (Eds.), *The rhetorical tradition: Readings from classical times to the present* (pp. 875-876). Boston, MA: Bedford Books. (Reprinted from *English composition and rhetoric,* 1866)

—. (1887). *English composition and rhetoric* (Enlarged ed.). New York: D. Appleton and Company.

Baker, E.A. (2010). New literacies, new insights: An exploration of traditional and new perspectives. In E.A. Baker (Ed.), *The new literacies: Multiple perspectives on research and practice* (p. 285-311). New York: Guilford Press.

Battelle, J. (2005). *The search: How Google and its rivals rewrote the rules of business and transformed our culture*. New York: Portfolio.

Bathrobe's Chinese, Japanese and Vietnamese Writing Systems. (2012). Retrieved from http://www.cjvlang.com/Writing/writviet.html

Bazerman, C. (1988). *Shaping writing knowledge: The genre and activity of the experimental article in science*. Madison, WI: University of Wisconsin Press.

Bauerlein, M. (2008). The dumbest generation : How the digital age stupefies young Americans and jeopardizes our future (or, don't trust anyone under 30). New York: Jeremy Tarcher/Penguin.

Bean, J. & Weimer, M. (2011). *Engaging ideas: The professor's guide to integrating writing, critical thinking, and active learning in the classroom* (2nd ed.). San Francisco: Jossey-Bass.

Becher, T. (1989). *Academic tribes and territories: Intellectual enquiry and the cultures of disciplines*. Milton Keynes, England: Open University Press.

Berry, D.C. (1997). Introduction. In D.C. Berry (Ed.), *How implicit is implicit learning?* (p. 1-12). Oxford, England: Oxford University Press.

Bettinger, E.P., Evans, B.J. & Pope, D.G. (2011). *Improving college performance and retention the easy way: Unpacking the ACT exam*. Cambridge, MA: National Bureau of Economic Research. Retrieved from papers.nber.org/papers/w17119

Bishop, M.J. (2001). The systematic use of sound in multimedia instruction to enhance learning. *Dissertation Abstracts International, 61*(7-A), 2669.

Bizzell, P. & Hertzberg, B. (Eds.). (1990). *The rhetorical tradition: Readings from classical times to the present.* Boston, MA: Bedford Books.

Blake, B.E. & Blake, R.W. (2002). *Literacy and learning: A reference handbook*. Santa Barbara, CA: ABC-CLIO.

Bolter, J.D. (2001). *Writing space: Computers, hypertext and the remediation of print* (2nd ed.). Mahwah, NJ: Erlbaum.

Bowden, D. (1999). *The mythology of voice*. Portsmouth, NH: Boynton/Cook Heinemann.

Bowen, W.G., Chingos, M.M. & McPherson, M.S. (2009). *Crossing the finish line: Completing college at America's public universities.* Princeton, NJ: Princeton University Press.

Brandt, D. (2001). *Literacy in American lives.* New York: Cambridge University Press.

—. (forthcoming). Deep writing. In R.J. Spiro (Ed.), *Reading at a crossroads: Disjunctures and continuities in conceptions and practice of reading in the 21st century.* New York: Routledge.

Bransford, J.D., Brown, A.L., & Cocking, R.R. (2000). *How people learn: Brain, mind, experience, and school* (Expanded ed.). Washington, DC: National Academy Press.

Burbules, N.C. (1998). Rhetorics of the web: Hyperreading and critical literacy. In I. Snyder (Ed.), *Page to screen: Taking literacy into the electronic era* (pp. 102-122). London: Routledge.

Bush, V. (1945, July). As we may think. *The Atlantic.* Retrieved from http://www.theatlantic.com/magazine/archive/1945/07/as-we-may-think/3881/

Carr, N. (2008, July-August). Is Google making us stupid? Retrieved from http://www.theatlantic.com/magazine/archive/2008/07/is-google-making-us-stupid/6868.

Carr, N. (2010). *The shallows: What the Internet is doing to our brains.* New York: W.W. Norton.

Castro-Caldas, A. & Reis, A. (2003). The knowledge of orthography is a revolution in the brain. *Reading & Writing, 16* (1-2), 81-97.

Christou, C. & Bulthoff, H.H. (2000). Perception, representation and recognition: A holistic view of recognition. *Spatial Vision, 13*(2,3), 265-275.

Clark, R.C. (2008). *Building expertise: Cognitive methods for training and performance improvement* (3rd ed.). San Francisco, CA: John Wiley & Sons.

Coiro, J. (2011). Talking about reading as thinking: modeling the hidden complexities of online reading comprehension. *Theory into Practice, 50*(2), 107-15. doi:10.1080/00405841.2011.558435.

Council of Chief State School Officials and the National Governors Association. (2010). *Common Core State Standards Initiative.* Washington, DC: Author. Retrieved from http://www.corestandards.org/

Cuban, S. & Cuban, L. (2007). *Partners in literacy: Schools and libraries building communities through technology.* New York: Teachers College Press and Chicago: American Library Association.

Dahl, R. (1990). "Poison." *Tales of the unexpected.* New York: Vintage Books/Random House. (Original work published 1953.)

Dehaene, S. (2009). *Reading in the brain: The science and evolution of a human invention.* New York: Viking Penguin.

Demetrion, G. (2005). *Conflicting paradigms in adult literacy education: In quest of a U.S. democratic politics of literacy.* Mahwah, NJ: Erlbaum.

Dole, J.A., Duffy, G.G., Roehler, L.R. & Pearson, D.P. (1991). Moving from the old to the new: Research on reading comprehension instruction. *Review of Educational Research, 61*(2), 239-64.

Dornyei, Z. (2009). *The psychology of second language acquisition.* Oxford, England: Oxford Uuniversity Press.

Eimas, P.D., Siqueland, E.R., Jusczyk, P., & Vigorito, J. (1971). Speech perception in infants. *Science, 171*, 303-306.

Eisenberg, A. (2011, December 18). When science leaps from the page. *New York Times*, Business, p. 4.

Elbow, P. (1994). Introduction. In P. Elbow (Ed.). *Landmark essays on voice and writing* (pp. xi-xlvii). Davis, CA: Hermagoras Press.

Ellis, N.C. (2011). Implict and explicit SLA and their interface. In Sanz, C. & Leow, R.P. (Eds.) *Implicit and explicit language learning: Conditions, processes, and knowledge in SLA and bilingualism* (pp. 35-48). Washington, DC: Georgetown University Press.

Faigley, L., George, D., Palchik, A., & Selfe, C. (2004). *Picturing texts.* New York: W.W. Norton.

Felder, L. (2012). *Writing for the web: Creating compelling web content using words, pictures and sound.* Berkeley, CA: New Riders/Pearson.

Figure/Ground. (2011). Rubin face-vase. Retrieved from http://psylux.psych.tu-dresden.de/i1/kaw/diverses20Material/ www.illusionworks.com/html/figure_ground.html

Foss, S.K. Framing the study of visual rhetoric: Toward a transformation of rhetorical theory. (pp. 303-13). In Hill, C.A. & Helmers, M. (Eds.). *Defining visual rhetorics* (pp. 1-23). Mahwah, NJ: Lawrence Erlbaum Associates.

Fox, E., Maggioni, L., Dinsmore, D.L., & Alexander, P.A. (2008, March). The multi-layered reading goals of expert readers: Bridging between knowledge, interest, and strategy use. Paper presented at the American Educational Research Association conference, New York.

Friedman, T. L. (2006). *The world is flat: A brief history of the twenty-first century.* New York: Farrar, Straus and Giroux.

Fromkin, V., Rodman, R., & Hyams, N. (2011). *An introduction to language* (9th ed.). Boston: Wadsworth, Cengage Learning.

Functional illiterate. (1966). In J. Stein. (Ed.) *The Random House dictionary of the English language.* (unabridged ed., p. 574). New York: Random House.

Garner, D. (2012, March 18). The way we read now. *The New York Times*, Sunday Review, p. 6.

Gee, J.P. (2003). *What video games have to teach us about learning and literacy.* New York: Palgrave Macmillan.

—. (2010). A situated-sociocultural approach to literacy and technology. In E.A. Baker (Ed.), *The new literacies: Multiple perspectives on research and practice* (p. 165-93). New York: Guilford Press.

Gerbino, W. (1997). Solving by redundancy and misunderstanding by simplification. In V. Cantoni, V. DiGesu, A. Setti & D. Tegolo (Eds.), *Human and machine perception: Information fusion* (pp. 147-154). New York: Plenum Press.

Gleick, J. (2011). *The information: A history, a theory, a flood.* New York: Pantheon Books.

Gogate, L.J. & Bahrick, L.E. (2001). Intersensory redundancy and 7-month-old infants' memory for arbitrary syllable-object relations. *Infancy, 2*(2), 219-231.

Goodman, K.S. (1996). *On reading.* Portsmouth, NH: Heinemann.

Grabe, W. & Kaplan, R.B. (1996). *Theory and practice of writing: An applied linguistic perspective.* London: Longman.

Graff, H.J. (1987). *The legacies of literacy: Continuities and contradictions in western culture and society.* Bloomington, IN: Indiana University Press.

Gross, M. & Latham, D. (2011). What's skill got to do with it?: Information literacy skills and self-views of ability among first-year college students. *Journal of the American Society for Information Science and Technology, 63*(3), 574-83. doi:10.1002/asi.21681

Halliday, M.A.K. & Hasan, R. (1976). *Cohesion in English.* London: Longman.

Hammerich, I. & C. Harrison. (2002). *Developing online content: The principles of writing and editing for the web.* New York: John Wiley & Sons.

Harklau, L. (2003). Generation 1.5 students and college writing. Retrieved from http://www.cal.org/resources/digest/0305harklau.html

Harris, F.J. (2005). *I found it on the Internet: Coming of age online* (1st ed.). Chicago: American Library Association.

—. (2011). *I found it on the Internet: Coming of age online* (2nd ed.). Chicago: American Library Association.

Hartelius, E.J. (2011). *The rhetoric of expertise.* Lanham, MD: Lexington/Rowman & Littlefield Publishers.

Hartman, D.K., Morsink, P.M. & Zheng, J. (2010). From print to pixels: The evolution of cognitive conceptions of reading comprehension. In E.A. Baker (Ed.), *The new literacies: Multiple perspectives on research and practice* (p. 131-64). New York: Guilford Press.

Haswell, R.H., Briggs, T.L., Fay, J.A., Gillen, N.K., Harrill, R., Shupala, A.M., et al. (1999). Context and rhetorical reading strategies. *Written Communication, 16*(1): 3-27.

Haswell, R., Gunner, J., Calhoon-Dillahunt, C. & Redd, T. (2012). Reviews of *Academically adrift: Limited learning on college campuses. College Composition and Communication, 63*(3), 487-506.

Helmers, M. & Hill, C.A. (2004). Introduction. In Hill, C.A. & Helmers, M. (Eds.). *Defining visual rhetorics* (pp. 1-23). Mahwah, NJ: Lawrence Erlbaum Associates.

Herber, H.L. (1978) *Teaching reading in content areas* (2nd ed.). Englewood Cliffs, NJ: Prentice-Hall.

Hill, C.A. & Helmers, M. (Eds.). (2004). *Defining visual rhetorics.* Mahwah, NJ: Lawrence Erlbaum Associates.

Hillesund, T. (2010). Digital reading spaces: How expert readers handle books, the Web and electronic paper. *First Monday 15*(4). Retrieved from http://firstmonday.org/htbin/cgiwrap/bin/ojs/index.php/fm/article/view/2762/2504

Hocks, M.E. & Hendrick, M.R. (Eds.). (2003). *Eloquent images: Word and image in the age of new media.* Cambridge, MA: MIT Press.

Horning, A.S. (1987). *Teaching writing as a second language.* Carbondale, IL: Southern Illinois University Press.

—. (1993). *The psycholinguistics of readable writing: A multidisciplinary exploration.* Norwood, NJ: Ablex.

—. (2002). *Revision revisited.* Cresskill, NJ: Hampton Press.

—. (2007, May 14). Reading across the curriculum as the key to student success. *Across the Disciplines, 4.* Retrieved from http://wac.colostate.edu/atd/articles/horning2007.cfm

—. (2011). Where to put the manicules: A theory of expert reading. *ATD: Across the Disciplines, 8*(2). Retrieved from http://wac.colostate.edu/atd/articles/horning2011/index.cfm

Howard, R.M., Rodrigue, T.K. & Serviss, T.C. (2010). Writing from sources, writing from sentences. *Writing and Pedagogy 2*(2), 177-192. Retrieved from http://writing.byu.edu/static/documents/org/1176.pdf

Huffman, D. (2010). Towards modes of reading in composition. *Reader: Essays in reader-oriented theory, criticism, and pedagogy, 60*, 162-88.

Huot, B. (2007). Consistently inconsistent: Business and the Spellings Commission report on higher education. *College English, 69*(1), 512-25.

Hyland, K. (2000). *Disciplinary discourses: Social interactions in academic writing*. Harlow, England: Pearson Education Limited.

Hyland, K. & Tse, P. (2004). Metadiscourse in academic writing: A reappraisal. *Applied Linguistics, 25*(2), 156-77.

Illiteracy. (1966). In J. Stein. (Ed.) *The Random House dictionary of the English language*. (unabridged ed., p. 710). New York: Random House.

Jiang, X. & Grabe, W. (2007). Graphic organizers in reading instruction: Research findings and issues. *Reading in a Foreign Language, 19*(1), 34-55.

Jamieson, S. (2011). *The citation project*. Retrieved from http://site.citationproject.net/?page_id=220

Jamieson, S. & Howard, R.M. (2011). Unraveling the citation trail. *Project Information Literacy Smart Talk,* no. 8, The Citation Project, August 15, 2011. Retrieved from http://projectinfolit.org/st/howard-jamieson.asp

Jolliffe, D.J.& Harl, A. (2008). Texts of our institutional lives: Studying the reading transition: from high school to college: What are our students reading and why? *College English, 70*(6), 599-617.

Kaiser Family Foundation. (2010). *Generation M^2: Media in the lives of 8- to 18-year-olds*. Retrieved from http://www.kff.org/entmedia/upload/8010.pdf

Kalantzis, M., Cope, B. & Cloonan, A. (2010). A multiliteracies perspective on the new literacies. In E.A. Baker (Ed.), *The new literacies: Multiple perspectives on research and practice* (p. 61-87). New York: Guilford Press.

Kalyuga, S. (1999). Studies in split-attention redundancy. *Dissertation Abstracts International 59*(11-A), 4055.

Kaplan, R.B. (1966). Cultural thought patterns in intercultural education. *Language Learning, 16*, 1-20.

Katz, I.R. (2007a). ETS research finds college students fall short in demonstrating ICT literacy. *College & Research Libraries News, 68*(1), 35-7.

—. (2007b). Testing information literacy in digital environments: ETS's iSkills assessment. *Information Technology and Libraries, 26*(3), 3-12. Retrieved from http://www.nd.edu/~fboze/ital/sept2007/katz.html

Kazemek, F.E. & Rigg, P. (2002). Literacy definitions. In B.J. Guzetti (Ed.), *Literacy in America: An encyclopedia of history, theory, and practice* (p. 310-13). Santa Barbara, CA: ABC-CLIO.

Keene, E. O. & Zimmerman, S. (1997). *Mosaic of thought: Teaching comprehension in a reader's workshop*. Portsmouth, NH: Heinemann.

Kellner, D.M. (2002). Technological revolution, multiple literacies, and the restructuring of education. In I. Snyder (Ed.), *Silicon literacies: Communication, innovation and education in the electronic age* (pp. 154-169). London: Routledge.

Kellogg, R.T. (2006). Professional writing expertise. In K.A. Ericsson, N. Charness, P.J. Fletovich & R.R. Hoffman (Eds.), *The Cambridge handbook of expertise and expert performance* (pp. 389-402). New York: Cambridge University Press.

Kelly, K. (2006, May 14). Scan this book! *New York Times*. Retrieved from http://www.put-that-there.org/PORTABLEDOCUMENTFORMATS /MEDIA/ ScanThisBook.pdf

Kirsch, I.S., Jungeblut, A., Jenkins, L. & Kolstad, A. (1993). *Adult literacy in America*. Washington, DC: Government Printing Office.

Knowlton, B.J. (1998). The relationship between remembering and knowing: A cognitive neuroscience perspective. *Acta Psychologica, 98*, 253-265.

Kolers, P. (1967). Reading is only incidentally visual. In K.S. Goodman & J.T. Fleming (Eds.), *Psycholinguistics and the teaching of reading* (pp. 8-16). Newark, DE: International Reading Association.

Kolin, P.C. (2012). *Successful writing at work* (3rd concise ed.). Boston: Wadsworth Cengage.

Krashen, S.D. (1983). The din in the head, input, and the language acquisition device. In J.W. Oller, Jr. & P.A. Richard-Amato (Eds.), *Methods that work: A smorgasbord of ideas for language teachers* (pp. 295-301). Cambridge, MA: Newbury House.

Kress, G. (2003). *Literacy in the new media age*. London: Routledge.

Kucer, S.B. (2005). *Dimensions of literacy: A conceptual base for teaching reading and writing in school settings*. 2nd ed. Mahwah, NJ: Erlbaum.

—. (Ed.). (2008). *What research really says about teaching and learning to read*. Urbana, IL: National Council of Teachers of English.

Learning a living: First results of the adult literacy and life skills survey. (2005). Ottawa, Canada and Paris, France: Statistics Canada and the Organisation for Economic Co-operation and Development.

Leki, I. (2004). Meaning and development of academic literacy in a second language. In Huot, B., Stroble, B. & Bazerman, C. (Eds.), *Multiple literacies for the 21st century* (pp. 115-28). Cresskill, NJ: Hampton Press.

Leu, D. J., Kinzer, C. K., Coiro, J. L., & Cammack, D. W. (2004). Toward a theory of new literacies emerging from the internet and other information and communication technologies. In R. B. Ruddell & N. J. Unrau (Eds.), *Theoretical models and processes of reading* (5th ed.) (pp. 1570-1613). Newark, DE: International Reading Association. (Original work published 2000)

Levitin, D.J. (2006). *This is your brain on music: The science of a human obsession*. New York: Plume/Penguin Group.

Levy, D.M. (2001). *Scrolling forward: Making sense of documents in the digital age*. New York: Arcade/Time Warner Trade.

Literacy. (1966). In J. Stein. (Ed.) *The Random House dictionary of the English language*. (unabridged ed., p. 836). New York: Random House.

MacDonald, S.P. (1994). *Professional academic writing in the humanities and social sciences*. Carbondale, IL: Southern Illinois University Press.

Mackey, T.P. & Jacobson, T.E. (2011). Reframing information literacy as a metaliteracy. *College and Research Libraries, 72*(1), 62-78. Retrieved from http://crl.acrl.org.huaryu.kl.oakland.edu/content/72/1/62.short

Malabou, C. (2008). *What should we do with our brain?* New York: Fordham University Press.

Man, J. (2000). *Alpha beta: How 26 letters shaped the western world*. New York: Wiley.

Manzo, A.V., Manzo, U.C. & Thomas, M.M. (2009). *Content area literacy: A framework for reading-based instruction* (5th ed.). Hoboken, NJ: Wiley.

Mayer, R.E. (2001). *Multimedia learning*. Cambridge: Cambridge University Press.

Meta. (1966). *Random House dictionary of the English language*. Unabridged ed. New York: Random House.

Miller, G.A. (1956). The magical number seven plus or minus two: Some limits on our capacity for processing information. *Psychological Review, 63*, 81-92.

Mokhtari, K. & Reichard, C.A. (2002). Assessing students' metacognitive awareness of reading strategies. *Journal of Educational Psychology, 94*(2), 249–259. doi: 10.1037//0022-0663.94.2.249

Mulderig, G.P. (1982). Nineteenth-century psychology and the shaping of Alexander Bain's *English Composition and Rhetoric*. In J.J.

Murphy (Ed.), *The rhetorical tradition and modern writing* (pp. 95-104). New York: Modern Language Association.

Murray, T.S., Kirsch, I.S. & Jenkins, L.B. (1998). *Adult literacy in OECD countries: Technical Report on the First International Adult Literacy Survey.* Washington, DC: Government Printing Office. Retrieved from http://nces.ed.gov/pubs98/98053.pdf

Nathan, R. (2005). *My freshman year: What a professor learned by becoming a student.* Ithaca, NY: Cornell University Press.

National Council of Teachers of English. (2011). Reading and writing across the curriculum: A policy research brief. *Council Chronicle, 20*(3), 15-18.

Nielsen, J. & Pernice, K. (2010). *Eyetracking web usability.* Berkeley, CA: New Riders/Peachpit/Pearson.

Nilson, L.B. (2010). *Teaching at its best: A research-based resource for college instructors* (3rd ed.). San Francisco, CA: Jossey-Bass.

Odell, L. & Katz, S.M. (2004). *Writing in a visual age.* Boston: Bedford/St. Martin's.

Olsen, P.R. (2011, December 18). Journey of a bookworm. *New York Times*, Business, p. 9.

Paris, C.R., Thomas, M.H., Gilson, R.D. & Kincaid, J.P. (2000). Linguistic cues and memory for synthetic and natural speech. *Human Factors, 42*(3), 421-431.

Paul, A.M. (2012, March 18). Your brain on fiction. *The New York Times*, Sunday Review, p. 6.

Peirce, C.S. (1894). What is a sign? Retrieved from http://www.marxists.org/reference/subject/philosophy/works/us/peirce1.htm.

Petersson, K.M., Reis, A. & Ingvar, M. (2001). Cognitive processing in literate and illiterate subjects: A review of some recent behavioral and functional neuroimaging data. *Scandinavian Journal of Psychology, 42*(3), 251-67.

Pew Charitable Trusts. (2006). *The national survey of America's college students.* Retrieved from http://www.air.org/files/The20Literacy20of20Americas20College20Students_final20report.pdf

Pinker, S. (1994). *The language instinct.* New York: HarperPerennial.

—. (1997). *How the mind works.* New York: W.W. Norton.

—. (2011). *The better angels of our nature: Why violence has declined.* New York: Viking Penguin.

Polanyi, M. (1966). *The tacit dimension.* Garden City, NY: Doubleday.

Project SAILS. (2009). Standardized assessment of information literacy skills. Kent State University, 2000-2009. Retrieved from https://www.projectsails.org/.

Reber, A.S. (1967). Implicit learning of artificial grammars. *Journal of Verbal Learning and Verbal Behavior, 5*, 855-63.

Reeves, L.M., Hirsh-Pasek, K. & Golinkoff, R. (1998). Words and meaning: From primitives to complex organization. In J.Berko Gleason & N.B. Ratner (Eds.), *Psycholinguistics* (2nd ed.) (p. 157-226). Fort Worth, TX: Harcourt College Publishers.

Reynolds, M. (1995). *Reading for understanding* (2nd ed.). Belmont, CA: Wadsworth Publishing.

Reznitskaya, A., Anderson, R.C., Dong, T., Li, Y., Kim, I., & Kim, S. (2008). Learning to think well: application of argument schema theory to literacy instruction. In C.C. Block & S.R. Parris (Eds.). *Comprehension instruction: Research-based best practices.* (2nd ed.). (pp. 196-213). New York: Guilford Press.

Rose, M. (1989). *Lives on the boundary.* New York: Viking Penguin.

Rothblum, L., Bergman, B. & Band, O. (1987). *Hebrew: A language course: Primer* (Ivrit Alphon). New York: Behrman House.

Scardamalia, M., & Bereiter, C. (1991). Literate expertise. In K.A.Ericsson & J. Smith (Eds.), *Toward a general theory of expertise: Prospects and limits* (pp. 172-94). Cambridge, England: Cambridge University Press.

Sadoski, M. & Paivio, A. (2001). *Imagery and text: A dual coding theory of reading and writing*. Mahwah, NJ: Lawrence Erlbaum Associates.

Scardamalia, M. & Bereiter, C. (1991). Literate expertise. In K.A. Ericsson & J. Smith (Eds.), *Toward a general theory of expertise: Prospects and limits* (pp. 172-94). Cambridge, England: Cambridge University Press.

Scribner, S. & Cole, M. (1981). *The psychology of literacy.* Cambridge, MA: Harvard University Press.

Scribner, S. & Cole, M. (2007). 'Unpackaging literacy.' In B.V. Street & A. Lefstein (Eds.), *Literacy: An advanced resource book* (pp. 1008-13). London: Routledge, Taylor & Francis. (Original work published 1978)

Selber, S.A. (2004). *Multiliteracies for a digital age.* Carbondale, IL: Southern Illinois University Press.

—. (Ed.). (2010). *Rhetorics and technologies: New directions in writing and communication.* Columbia, SC: University of South Carolina Press.

Sherman, W. H. (2005). Toward a history of the manicule. In R. Myers, M. Harris & G. Mandelbrote (Eds.). *Owners, annotators and the signs of reading* (pp. 19-48). New Castle, DE: Oak Knoll Press.

Smith, F. (2004). *Understanding reading* (6th ed.). Hillsdale, NJ: Erlbaum.

Snyder, I. (Ed.). (2002). *Silicon literacies: Communication, innovation and education in the electronic age*. London: Routledge.

—. (2008). *The literacy wars: Why teaching children to read and write is a battleground in Australia*. Crows Nest, Australia: Allen & Unwin.

Spivey, N. N. (1997). *The constructivist metaphor: Reading, writing and the making of meaning*. San Diego: Academic Press.

Stainburn, S. (2010, January 3). The case of the vanishing full-time professor. *New York Times*. Retrieved from http://www.nytimes.com

Stierer, B. & Bloome, D. (2007). Reading words: A commentary on key terms in the teaching of reading. In B.V. Street & A. Lefstein (Eds.), *Literacy: An advanced resource book* (pp. 52-55). London: Routledge, Taylor & Francis. (Original work published 1994)

Street, B.V. (2011). Literacy inequalities in theory and practice: The power to name and define. *International Journal of Educational Development, 31*(6), 580-86. doi: 10.1016/jedudev.2010.09.005

Stross, R. (2006, 12 March). Anonymous source is not the same as open source. *New York Times*, Business, p. 3:5. Retrieved from http://www.nytimes.com.

Tierney, R.J. (2009). Literacy Education 2.0. In J.V. Hoffman & Y.M. Goodman (Eds.), *Changing literacies for changing times: An historical perspective on the future of reading research, public policy and classroom practices*. (pp. 282-303). New York: Routledge, Taylor and Francis.

Tinto, V. (1993). *Leaving college: Rethinking the causes and cures of student attrition*. (2nd ed.) Chicago: University of Chicago Press.

Tseptsov, V. (2011, Feb.). Transmission of implicit knowledge: Toward the expert levels of reading and writing competence. Paper presented at Writing Research Across Borders II, Washington, DC.

United Nations Development Program. (2004). *Human development report, 2004*. Retrieved from http://hdr.undp.org/2004.

United Nations. (2006). *United Nations literacy decade*. Retrieved from http://hdr.undp.org/en/media/hdr04_complete.pdf.

U.S. Department of Education. (2005). National Center for Education Statistics. *Integrated Postsecondary Education Data System*. Retrieved from http://nces.ed.gov/pubs2006/2006155.pdf.

—. (2006). *National assessment of adult literacy: A first look at the literacy of America's adults in the 21st century.* National Center for Education Statistics. Retrieved from http://nces.ed.gov/NAAL/PDF/2006470_1.PDF.

—. National Center for Education Statistics. (2007). *The condition of education 2007* (NCES 2007-064). Washington, DC: U.S. Government Printing Office. Retrieved from http://nces.ed.gov/pubs2007/2007064.pdf.

U.S. National Endowment for the Arts. (2007). *To read or not to read: A question of national consequence.* Washington, DC: National Endowment for the Arts. Retrieved from http://www.nea.gov/research/ToRead.pdf.

—. (2009). *Reading on the rise: A new chapter in American literacy.* Washington, DC: National Endowment for the Arts.

Vincent, D. (2003). Literacy literacy. *Interchange, 34*(2/3), 341-57.

Visual rhetoric: Overview. (n.d.). In Purdue Online Writing Lab. Retrieved from http://owl.english.purdue.edu/owl/resource/691/01/

Vygotsky, L.S. (1978). *Mind in society: The development of higher psychological processes.* Cambridge, MA: Harvard University Press.

Wade, N.J. & Swanston, M.T. (2001). *Visual perception: An introduction* (2nd ed.). East Sussex, England: Psychology Press Limited.

Wagner, D.A. & Kozma, R. (2005). *New technologies for literacy and adult education: A global perspective.* Paris: UNESCO.

Warschauer, M. (1999). *Electronic literacies: Language, culture, and power in online education.* Mahwah, NJ: Lawrence Erlbaum Associates.

Wiley, T.G. (1996). *Literacy and language diversity in the United States.* McHenry, IL: Center for Applied Linguistics/Delta Systems Co., Inc.

Wolf, M. (2007). *Proust and the squid: The story and science of the reading brain.* New York: Harper Collins.

World Bank. (2011). *Literacy rate, adult total (of people ages 15 and above).* Retrieved from http://data.worldbank.org/indicator/SE.ADT.LITR.ZS

Yancey, K.B. (Ed.) (1994). *Voices on voice: Perspectives, definitions, inquiry.* Urbana, IL: NCTE.

—. (2004). Made not only in words: Composition in a new key. *College Composition and Communication, 56*(2), 297-328.

—. (2009). The literacy demands of entering the university. In L. Christenbury, R. Bomer, & P. Smagorinsky (Eds.), *Handbook of adolescent literacy research* (pp. 256-70). New York: Guilford Press.

Yeni-Komshian, G.H. (1998). Speech perception. In J. Berko Gleason & N. Bernstein Ratner (Eds.), *Psycholinguistics* (2nd ed.). (pp. 107-156). Fort Worth, TX: Harcourt College Publishers.

Yeung, A.S. (1999). Cognitive load and learner expertise: Split attention and redundancy effects in reading comprehension tasks with vocabulary definitions. *Journal of Experimental Education, 67*(3), 197-217. Retrieved from http://www.jstor.org.huaryu.kl.oakland.edu/stable/view/20152596.

Zhou, S. (2000). Audio-visual redundancy and visual potency in bad news: Effects on memory and evaluations. *Dissertation Abstracts International, 61*(3-A), 809.

INDEX